Stay Up Pompey!

THE STORY OF PORTSMOUTH FC'S FIRST SEASON IN THE PREMIERSHIP

by Pat Symes

With photography by Mike Walker and Mick Young

The Parrs Wood Press
MANCHESTER

First Published 2004

THE PARRS WOOD PRESS

St Wilfrid's Enterprise Centre
Royce Road, Manchester, M15 5BJ
www.parrswoodpress.com

© **Pat Symes, Mike Walker & Mick Young 2004**

ISBN: 1 903158 56 7

Printed and bound in Slovenia

CONTENTS

ACKNOWLEDGEMENTS

Portsmouth Football Club was a mass of stories during 2003-2004, some of them ordinary enough but others so bizarre and perverse that they would have defied the imagination of a script-writer. We can only thank them for keeping us enthralled, entertained, perplexed and amused all at the same time. There is no club quite like Pompey, as its legion of supporters will testify. For creating this book we have assembled a team of our own, the same which performed so moderately in putting together last year's "Sleeping Giant Awakes", in a further search for a best-seller. I'm afraid this is not it. Consumed by his enthusiasm, Andy Searle of The Parrs Wood Press, Manchester was again the instigator, hoping, as with every book he publishes, that this will set him up for life. Peter Simm and Rob Dean have attempted to make sense of the rambling manuscript with the careful application of important things like punctuation, while Mike Walker and Mick Young reveal here the results of a winter grappling with the intricacies of digital photography on windswept touchlines. Harry Potter fan Alex Crook conjured up the player profiles but this book would not have been possible in its present shape without the forensically detailed research of Jim Baldwin. Staggering in the depth of the information he supplied, the job of all of us was made far easier. We only wish he got out more.

Pat Symes
Southsea
July, 2004

1.

The Men For All Seasons

WHEN HARRY REDKNAPP SAID, IN Pompey's champagne-soaked moment of euphoria, that staying in the Premiership would be harder than winning the first division title, many supporters thought his comments to be unnecessarily pessimistic. After all, Pompey had just won the championship by a country mile and all that staying up involved was coming 17th out of 20 at worst. But the old red fox knew what he was talking about. For ten years he had kept West Ham alive in an increasingly competitive and hostile environment and knew what it took to survive. One year he took the Hammers to fifth spot, but the majority of his decade as West Ham manager was spent with only one aim: To stay in the Premiership at all costs. With the top flight now awash with television money, it did not pay to drop out through relegation. Norwich, Ipswich, Bradford, Barnsley, Coventry, Derby, Nott-

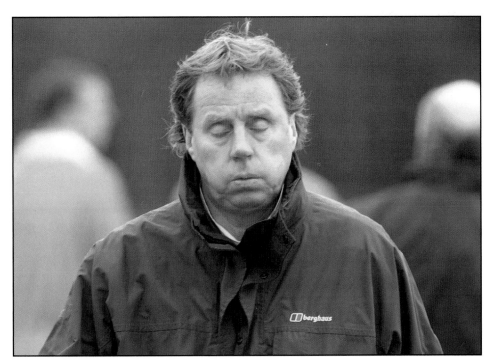

Harry Redknapp contemplates the enormity of the task ahead.

ingham Forest, some of them large, regional clubs, had allowed the Premiership's financial lifeline to slip from their grasp and had either drowned spectacularly or were in prolonged recovery. Even West Ham, without Redknapp's guile, had gone down as Pompey went up, and it is best not to even talk about what happened to Wimbledon.

Promotion from the first division was worth at least £20m to each of the three clubs coming up. Some, like West Bromwich Albion and Watford, chose to keep the money in their pocket and face the prospect of an early relegation with a clear conscience. Others chose to spend this colossal windfall on players and hope upon hope that relegation did not follow immediately because the carnage involved in getting rid of high wage earners was often a horrendous spectacle. So, while there was a huge bonanza suddenly available, it came with a heavy price and responsibility. Redknapp knew it more than anyone, except perhaps his assistant Jim Smith, whose old Derby side was in the process of being dismantled in the wake of relegation. Within days of celebrations finishing, Redknapp was preaching caution. The reasons were clear and, while Pompey were about to embark on a brave new adventure, the map ahead was laden with hazards and pitfalls. Supporters, eagerly renewing their season tickets even before the previous season had ended so triumphantly, were surprised at Redknapp's warnings of dire times ahead. "The fans are going to have to get used to losing," he said. "The difference in standards between the first division and

Jim Smith - aware of the pitfalls of promotion from his Derby days.

the Premiership is massive. Absolutely massive."

Two things worried the Pompey boss above all else. Firstly, there was the team. How many of those who had taken the club into the Premiership for the first time could now be expected to cope against world class opponents each week? They had done him and the club proud in the first division, but as a group they were not young and, for many, the challenge ahead represented uncharted waters. And then, secondly, there was Fratton Park.

The famous old stadium had witnessed championship wins 50 or more years ago, but it had seen better days and with a capacity of not much more than 20,000 - the smallest in the division - it was not going to attract high-class players used to appearing in the modern stadia springing up elsewhere across the country. The revenue from such small attendances was also not going to make much, if any, difference so that the money burden looked as if it would again fall on the willing shoulders of Milan Mandaric, the club's Serbian-born chairman, who had sunk more than he intended of a fortune made from the computer industry in his adopted America into reviving the south coast's sleeping giant. Strip away everybody else, however worthy, the club still revolved around the Redknapp-Mandaric axis. They were the only people to matter in the grand scheme of Portsmouth Football Club, and how they interacted would ultimately decide if Pompey made the best of their opportunity or went down in history as a one-season wonder.

Redknapp got busy, as only he can among contemporary managers, in bringing in players he felt would improve his squad. Between the end of May, as contracts started to run out, and the end of August when the transfer window closed, the manager brought in ten new players and two more on loan. Later, when it reopened for business in January, another five came to Fratton Park permanently with Petri Pasanen and Lomana Lua-Lua borrowed from elsewhere. It was not all one way either. Between the end of June 2003 and the end of March 2004, some 16 players traded in their blue shirts for those of other clubs, loans were too numerous to mention and in the summer of 2004 a further nine players were jettisoned in the search for a playing staff worthy of England's finest domestic competition.

As we now know, Fratton Park may have been a financial hinderance, but it proved to be a major asset in playing terms. Unlike so many of the new, antiseptic, featureless, lookalike stadia to be found elsewhere in the Premiership, Fratton Park was a throwback to the famous old grounds where fans were in the face of opponents, where every insult, every taunt,

Milan Mandaric - broad shoulders to carry the burden.

STAY UP POMPEY!

**Fratton Park - a financial hindrance,
but an asset in playing terms.**

every breath could be felt down the necks of even those with the biggest of reputations - and they didn't always like it. Fratton Park was an intimidating place to play and the club's ten Premiership wins played a prominent role in the club's eventual successful battle to stay up. Only Arsenal, Manchester United, Chelsea and Newcastle won as often or more often at home - and there were some mighty victims, United and Liverpool prominent among them.

It was playing away from home in those shining new edifices up and down the country which so nearly undermined Pompey's Premiership credentials. The away record was appalling, there was no other satisfactory way to describe it. At one stage until late into March, it looked as if Pompey might go through the whole season without an away win for the first time in more than 100 years of competitive football. Wins at Blackburn, who

had won at Fratton Park, and then at doomed Leeds prevented that happening, but it was paltry consolation for those, often as many as 3,000, who had travelled at great expense to all corners every other week with so little to show for their devotion.

Pompey's season was divided into three distinct phases: An early-season flourish, fuelled by the neat adrenaline of promotion, even took them for 24 beautiful hours to the top of the table in August. Then, as autumn's falling leaves gave way to the harsh realities of winter, came the second phase in which Pompey slid remorselessly down the table as many, including Redknapp, had predicted to a place around the relegation zone and the fear that going down was indeed the club's destiny. The third phase came at a time when the hour was at its darkest. Over the last ten matches, which included games against Arsenal and Manchester United, Pompey lost only once, at already-relegated Leicester of all places, to secure their position in the Premiership for one more fruitful year at least. Leicester dogged Pompey's footsteps as they had done the previous year in the first division. At one stage it looked that year as if they might even deprive Pompey of the championship before being forced to settle for the runners-up position and, here in the Premiership, Micky Adams' team attempted once again to keep pace. They failed, of course, going down with a Wolves side never equipped to stay up from day one, and troubled Leeds, but, if there was any minor satisfaction to be gained by Leicester, it was that they managed the double over Pompey, a feat matched only by monied Chelsea and moderate Everton.

The season's turning point, it may be an exaggeration to say, came in the home match with the old enemy

Leicester City dogged Pompey's progress throughout the season, as they had done the previous year.

STAY UP POMPEY!

It was Kevin Phillips' miss at Fratton Park in March which turned Pompey's season.

threatened a third win but, if there was a turning point within a turning point, it came in injury time as Pompey clung on to a precarious 1-0 lead. In just about Southampton's only attack of note, Kevin Phillips had Pompey hearts in mouths as he cut in from the left and beat Shaka Hislop with a fierce right foot shot which cannoned back into the goalkeeper's grateful arms from the inside of a post. A few inches the other way and Saints would have escaped with an undeserved draw, but even that would have meant little in the context of what it would have done to Pompey in terms of local prestige and damage to self-confidence. Instead, Pompey grew visibly from that result and put together a sequence of superb performances which guaranteed safety and which ultimately left them in a comfortable 13th place, one place and two points behind their great Hampshire rivals. It was a significant occasion.

Redknapp's frenetic transfer activity will be examined in greater detail elsewhere in this book, but he was never afraid to back his judgement, or that of his scouts, and his favoured agents. Some of the new signings contributed fully to the great Premiership adventure, some of them less so, and some not at all. Perhaps the best was the first, early in the summer when Pompey persuaded Maccabi Haifa

Southampton. When Saints came to Fratton Park in March, they had already beaten Pompey twice comparatively easily, while Pompey's confidence was low, as low in fact as it had been all season after a long series of poor results. Had Saints inflicted a third defeat who knows what might have happened, but the damage to morale would have been hard to sustain and it's difficult to then imagine Pompey embarking on such a distinguished late run while red and white laughter rang in blue ears yet again. Luckily for Pompey, Saints were a poor side that day and hardly ever to let Yakubu Ayegbeni move to Fratton Park for a down-payment of around half a million pounds, but which rose sharply in the event of a sell-on. Yakubu's 19 goals made him just about the Premiership's goalscoring discovery of the season. Dejan Stefanovic became the club's costliest player at £1.85m, but he gave good service in defence alongside stalwarts Arjan De Zeeuw and Linvoy Primus. Teddy Sheringham was an inspired choice to replace Paul Merson, though at 38 he was inevitably more effective at the start of the season than at the end. Sheringham's quality - and his goals - helped Pompey settle to the higher grade and, while he was not able to sustain that level of performance for long, fans should thank him for his class and his quality. Patrik Berger enjoyed scoring the winner against Liverpool early in the season but his injury problems, which had ruined his last year or two at Anfield, returned with a vengeance, while the languid Amdy Faye was at his most effective in the early months of the season when he was fresh from Auxerre and when £1.5m looked a snip. Like Yakubu, Vincent Pericard made a loan permanent but was struck down with injuries, while Dutchman Harald Wapenaar never did enough to suggest he might supplant Hislop. Boris Zivkovic, Sebastien Schemmel and Pavel Srnicek flattered to deceive. Later, in January, Redknapp brought in Eyal Berkovic to bring some zest and cunning to the midfield alongside the ever-improving loan star Alexei Smertin. Ivica Mornar from Anderlecht, Sebastian Olszar and

John Curtis were not able to hold down regular places over the second half of the season and Petri Pasanen was allowed to return to Ajax after his time ran out. Lomana Lua-Lua was the most controversial of the loan signings; some liked his unpredictability, some - like Bobby Robson - did not.

Overall, the multitude of incomers provided plenty of entertainment, a feature high on Redknapp's list of priorities, but the players who emerged with the most to give at the critical hour were those already in place. Hislop was as accomplished as any keeper, consistently, in the Premiership, Matt Taylor shrugged off horrendous, career-threatening injuries to regain his place and much of his old swagger down the left, Steve Stone exceeded perhaps even his own expectations with some vivid displays down the right, but the real heroes were Primus and De Zeeuw. For the best part of half a season, Redknapp ignored Primus in the belief that the Premiership might be a step too far. But once he had been restored, so masterful were his displays that chants of "Linvoy for England" were not without genuine merit. Player of the year, though, and deservedly, was the Dutch medical man De Zeeuw, who gave one terrific performance after another in the heart of Pompey's resistance, never once shirking a challenge, never once giving an inch to the household names he encountered week in week out. If one man personified the club's determination to succeed against the odds, it was De Zeeuw. By the time the season ended he was 34, but neither the club nor those who watched his fierce, unflinching commitment to the Pompey cause considered he warranted anything less than the new, two-year contract offered to him. Fit, powerful and proud, De Zeeuw encapsulated the spirit, the very essence of Pompey.

The one drawback, and it was a considerable one, was that the size of the wage bill rose to an unprecedented, for Pompey, £20m a year. In effect, it swallowed up the money which came the club's way from being promoted. Always at the back of the chairman's mind was the thought that if his club was relegated, the demotion would have to be accompanied by a mass clear-out of players, many of them only recently installed. The example of Leeds was a shocking daily reminder of how greed, overweening ambition and stupidity can undermine and destroy within weeks even the most powerful of clubs. Mandaric was evidently happy to go along with Redknapp's constant stream of signings, otherwise he would not have sanctioned them, but he too counselled caution; don't spend more than you can reasonably afford. What helped Redknapp throughout the first two years of his management was that the transfer market was suited to buyers. Fees changing hands between clubs became much reduced, often minimal, as clubs at all levels attempted to make sense of their wage bill. The result was that good players were being jettisoned for no other reason than that they cost too much to keep. No one was better at exploiting this advantage than Redknapp, although there were

agents to feed, signing-on fees to be negotiated and sundry other financial considerations which often made up for the lack of a transfer fee.

While Pompey are never going to be a club for whom money is no object, unless a Russian billionaire steps forward, they would have had more to spend if they had been watched by more people. It's a simple economic fact. But Fulham, in exile at Loftus Road, were the only club to engender less at the turnstiles and this led Mandaric to double his efforts to construct a new stadium capable of holding around 35,000 people. There is no doubt Pompey could attract many more than they can at the moment if a new stadium replaced Fratton Park, and the chairman did his best to hurry along the process in negotiations with landowners around the present ground and by presenting to the city council a set of plans that outlined his vision for the future. With 15,000 season-ticket holders, fans will be hoping it will not be long before a new stadium emerges amid Pompey Village, the money-making aspect to the whole project, but no one is taking anything for granted until the day the bulldozers move in. Until then, Pompey must cling on to the belief that they can stay in the Premiership on limited resources, pocketing the television and positional reward cash and not over-relying on the goodwill and the wallet of the chairman.

In terms of support Pompey can compare with anyone. If there was a league table for sheer volume of support and blind loyalty

Clockwise from top left: Yakubu - 19 goals, De Zeeuw - unflinching commitment, Primus - "Linvoy for England" was the cry, and Stefanovic - record signing and a rock in defence.

STAY UP POMPEY!

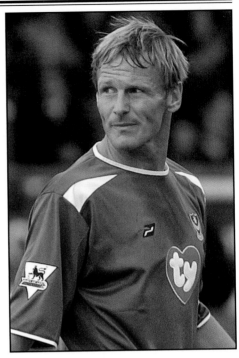

Clockwise from top left: Stone - exceeded his own expectations, Sheringham - quality and goals, Berger - winner against former club Liverpool, and Taylor - recovered from serious injury.

THE MEN FOR ALL SEASONS

Portsmouth's fans would surely have been crowned champions. Pompey have always had a large fanatical following, more vociferous even than those rival fans at clubs where a regular supply of trophies is taken for granted. Perhaps it was the novelty of the Premiership that set them off; John Westwood would tell you that Pompey fans have always been bigger and better and it made no difference if they were playing Manchester United or Carlisle. Arsene Wenger could not believe it, Thierry Henry wore a Pompey shirt in tribute and Patrick Vieira was dumbstruck by the intensity of the backing Pompey received even in overwhelming defeat in the FA Cup at Fratton Park. Millions on television saw for themselves those qualities of furi-ous endorsement which Pompey fans like to believe makes them special. The noise made by 20,000 inside Fratton Park, even for the most mundane of matches, would move the most blase of players and raise the level of performance of ordinary players beyond their true range of ability. Not that there were many mundane matches when Pompey were involved. It was a battle to stay up from before Christmas and, although safety was achieved with four matches remaining, every game seemed to be important. Perhaps the fans had something to do with that.

Underlying it all was the Redknapp/Mandaric relationship. One day they could be praising each other, sharing intimate long distance phone calls to compare red

Above and overleaf: Two views of the proposed new stadium and leisure complex.

Internal Cross Section Looking North

wines, and the next they could be at each other's throats. The massive row in the middle of May 2004 did neither of them any credit but made Pompey fans, silent for once, aware how much the club relied on them both. "We want Milan with Harry and Jim", they chanted, more out of hope than expectation of them becoming friends again. But they did, almost instantly. The truth is that they needed each other. Mandaric is in his late 60s with a succession of failures in terms of managers behind him. English football was a draining and costly business but, from nowhere, Redknapp had come along and given him something to show for his investment, namely two years of wonderful entertainment and a measure of success. Who would have thought after Graham Rix had fled Fratton Park in tears that, within two years, Pompey would be beating Liverpool (twice) and Manchester United and

drawing at Highbury. Redknapp was 57 when the season ended, not in the first flush of youth as a football manager (begging Sir Bobby Robson's pardon) and wealthy enough to have retired years ago. But he needed football and he needed a club like Pompey where any kind of success, however trivial, was greeted with tremendous appreciation. Talk of going to Spurs was wide of the mark and would have been a huge task for anyone. Pompey was the right club for him after West Ham and Mandaric was the right kind of chairman. Their infamous row blew over as fast as it blew up because they needed each other, and those Pompey fans, for whom the club is everything, should be grateful that they did.

What happens two years on is anybody's guess because things change fast in this most volatile and crazy of sports. We can only look back on the extraordinary sea-

Mandaric and Redknapp - made for each other.

son of 2003-2004 and remember the highs and lows, the ins and outs, the words and the actions. It was a season always to be cherished, a season when "Stay Up Pompey!" was a battlecry from the heart.

2.

Summer in the City

WHAT DO DARREN ANDERTON, Patrik Berger, Mark Bosnich, Michael Carrick, Neil Collins of Dumbarton (yes, that one), Nikos Dabizas, Kevin Davies, Paolo Di Canio, Colin Healy, Dario Hubner, Klas Ingesson, Martin Keown, Mark Kinsella, Saliou Lassissi, Jobi McAnuff, Andy Marshall, Jermaine Pennant, Kevin Phillips, Stipe Pletikosa, Milan Rapaic, Nigel Reo-Coker, Teddy Sheringham, Guiseppe Signori, Josef Simunic, Dario Srna, Stijn Vreven, Abel Xavier, Zlatko Zahovic and Ludo Roy of Hearts have in common? Answer: they were all targets, or were alleged to have been targets, of Harry Redknapp in the first two weeks of May 2003 as he began the monumental job of building a team capable of competing in the Premiership. It was not going to be easy and he, above all, realised the enormity of his task. For all bemused Pompey fans knew, by the daily torrent of names, at least half the players didn't exist. Zlatko Zahovic sounded like an anagram and as for Roy of Hearts, it might just have well been Roy of Melchester Rovers. Of that lot, only Sheringham and Berger actually joined Pompey, but Redknapp had scouts, contacts and agents far and wide so the

Darren Anderton - a favourite son of Fratton Park pictured here in 1992. He was one of many linked with Pompey during the summer.

long list would not have surprised those who knew him or the way he worked in the transfer market.

The litter was still being cleared from the streets of Portsmouth and Southsea Common in the wake of

Paul Merson's reign as the King of Fratton Park was effectively over when he failed to turn up for the promotion party.

Pompey's glorious championship-winning celebrations in the middle of May as Redknapp and faithful number two Jim Smith planned for the future, and it was likely to be a future without Paul Merson. One man alone could not have brought the first division title to Portsmouth but, while many contributed to what was essentially a team success, undeniably Merson was the single biggest inspiration; his knowledge, his experience and his determination to prove Aston Villa wrong were key reasons for Pompey's surge from perpetual obscurity at the wrong end of the division to champions almost overnight.

Merson and Pompey were coming to the end of a beautiful but short relationship and that much was evident on the day the rest of the squad were parading the trophy on an open-top bus through the jubilant highways and byways. Merson was not there. And don't think he was not missed. Merson was the captain, the man to whom the trophy should have been presented, because he deserved to have it presented to him. Courtney Pitt was there, Jamie Vincent never looked happier, but Merson was away, watching his son on some draughty touchline playing schools rugby on the football club's biggest civic day for a decade or more.

The trophy was handed instead to Nigel Quashie in Merson's absence but the huge crowds wanted to pay tribute to their hero captain, not to his stand-in. Milan Mandaric was fuming, especially in the light of Merson's recent admission that his gambling compulsion had again gripped him and threatened to overwhelm his life. Mandaric wanted a proper explanation and Merson was summoned later to explain himself, but the damage had been done and Merson was obviously, even in early May, not going to be part of Pompey's first season in the Premiership.

STAY UP POMPEY!

So Redknapp had to start the job of replacing him, and others, even while a whole city was still in a state of euphoria. There were no surprises in the retained list. Jason Crowe, who had contributed to the promotion with two goals at Crystal Palace, was freed, as were Carl Tiler, Luke Nightingale, Tom White and Lee Molyneux. Nightingale never lived up to his early promise, largely because injuries wiped two years from his still-young career, while Tiler, a £400,000 signing from Charlton, was best remembered for a cracking own goal against Norwich before falling out of favour once Graham Rix had been replaced by Redknapp. White headed for Bognor, Molyneux for Derry City, Nightingale followed Steve Claridge to Weymouth after a couple of months at Southend and Tiler retired to Nottingham to begin a life outside football. There was a certain sentimental attachment to Crowe, who arrived from Arsenal and suffered more than most from the frequent change in manager during the early Mandaric years. Frozen out by Tony Pulis, recalled by Claridge and Rix, he spent more time out of the side than in it once Redknapp had assumed command. Heading off to Grimsby after a trial period, Crowe spent the 2003-4 season struggling at the wrong end of the second division.

Three more players followed them out of Fratton Park at the start of what was sure to be a hectic summer of transfers. Gianluca Festa, his job done, headed home to a footballing dotage in Cagliari and will go down in Pompey history as one of the most inspired signings of the Redknapp era; a defender no longer wanted at Middlesbrough but who had one good year left in him. It was happy for Pompey that he chose to spend it at Fratton Park. Lassina Diabate grafted in midfield after arriving from Auxerre and, in an unassuming sort of way, played an important role alongside more flamboyant players in midfield, not the least of them being Merson. Redknapp feared that his lack of pace might count against him in the Premiership, so there was no offer of a new contract, while Sasa Ilic, brought back from Hungary on a temporary basis, was also told he was not required on the voyage into the unknown.

There would surely have been others to follow had they not been protected by contracts which took them on at least another year. No wonder Vincent was smiling that happy day at the Guildhall. Without having played a single match during the promotion season, there was a clause in the left-back's contract which decreed that if Pompey gained promotion he would receive a £2,000 a week pay increase. Pompey had no option but to pay it. Vincent was in good company. Pompey would listen to offers for Neil Barrett, Mark Burchill, Lewis Buxton, Mark Casey, Yoshikatsu Kawaguchi, Carl Pettefer, Courtney Pitt, Carl Robinson, Chris Tardif and, of course, Vincent. None made an impression in the first division and none were likely to make any at all in the Premiership, but it is one thing to make players available in a deflated market, it is another to expect them to drop out of the cosy nest willingly at a time of mass footballing redundancies.

Gianluca Festa, his job done, headed home to a footballing dotage in Cagliari and will go down in Pompey history as one of the most inspired signings of the Redknapp era.

STAY UP POMPEY!

Chief Executive Peter Storrie knew where the blame lay for his and Redknapp's former club's predicament, and did not want Pompey to suffer the same fate.

It was against this background Redknapp had to work. Hamstrung by a body of sub-standard performers either not wanted or unwilling to move on, the manager still had to equip the club with far better players than he possessed and arguably better than the club had ever possessed. That meant transfer fees, signing-on fees, agents' fees and a wage bill big enough to rival the national debt. Convincing the chairman to spend, spend, spend when he had already done nothing but spend, spend, spend was going to be a problem, but Redknapp had succeeded where many others had failed in bringing a smile to the old boy's face and giving him tangible reward for his colossal outlay. The failures of Alan Ball, Pulis, Claridge and Rix were long forgotten and Redknapp was in a terrific bargaining position, a position he had to exploit if Pompey were to justify their promotion. Mandaric liked and respected Redknapp and, in turn, was worshipped by the Pompey fans who realised how important was his financial clout. At least the burden would now be eased by Sky TV's money as the result of promotion but, in all other respects, the club entered the Promised Land still unable to fend for itself.

A full house at delapidated Fratton Park guaranteed only just over 20,000 paying customers; there were no hospitality boxes and revenue from commercial sources did not yet match the club's new status among the elite. At least Pompey were better off than West Ham. Stripped of their place in the Premiership, they were now a division below Pompey and forced by straitened economic circumstances to sell all their best players, those accumulated by Redknapp over ten years of careful planning. It would have been easy for Redknapp to have gloated, but he felt, publically, only sorrow for West Ham's predicament, while Peter Storrie, once chief executive at Upton Park, blamed the chairman Terry Brown and others for the famine which was about to replace what should have been a feast. Pierre van Hooijdonk, Matt Holland, Eyal Berkovic and Les Ferdinand were the latest names to be linked with Pompey as May drew to a close and, since these were less speculative, it gave fans some indication in which direction Redknapp and Pompey were intending to move. All of them were high-calibre players who would improve the squad, but none of them would come cheaply. To stay and survive in the Premiership was going to come at a high cost.

In the meantime the chairman was attempting to resolve the Merson issue. There was talk of a rift, talk of Merson being told to apologise, but there is no doubt his non-appearance at Pompey's big

day had hurt Mandaric deeply. It was seen as a snub to his team-mates, a snub to the chairman, a snub to the supporters who so wanted to pay homage and, above all, a snub to the city. Mandaric said as much. "Paul has done a tremendous job for us and we will never forget that. We had a little bit of a thing after he did not come to the parade but if, say, my daughter does something I don't understand, I want her to explain. It was the same with Paul." Redknapp had already begun to plan without Merson for the coming year and that was why the likes of Sheringham and Berkovic were being considered as alternatives and why Holland was Pompey's first serious target in what was to prove a predictably hectic close season.

Mandaric, meanwhile, in deference to his age and to his wallet, was looking for others to share the cost of the club he had grown to love so much. In committing himself for another three years, the beleaguered chairman said he was prepared to accept on to the board other people who might like to become involved but there were no takers and, while in the short term the glory was his, so too was the massive undertaking required to keep Pompey afloat.

May drifted into June and the club's supporters were getting twitchy. Where were the new signings? They need not have worried because Redknapp had been working furiously behind the scenes to find the right quality and, in Holland, the Pompey manager was dealing with a player he knew well from their days together at West

Ham. In fact, it was Redknapp who had allowed Holland to follow a familiar path to Bournemouth on a free transfer and must have thought he had made a mistake when he was later sold on to Ipswich for £800,000. Ipswich could no longer afford his wages and Holland, much against his wishes and those of his family, had come to the conclusion that he had to leave Portman Road. Holland was just the sort of player Pompey needed; hard-working, never in trouble with referees, goal-scoring from midfield and still only 29. Pompey felt they had a great chance to sign him, but Holland delayed his decision until he had played for his adopted Republic of Ireland in their Euro 2004 qualifying matches with Albania and Georgia. At £750,000, he would have been a snip and, until he went away with Ireland, Pompey were clear favourites.

Patrik Berger - needed little persuasion from Redknapp to move south.

But Holland was only one of several players interesting Pompey and as June progressed it was revealed that more than one was close to signing, in some cases people who had probably never even have heard of Portsmouth until Harry came calling. Boris Zivkovic was one such player. Croatia's captain had been an integral part of Bayer Leverkusen's rise to European fame and the same could be said for the Serbian Dejan Stefanovic, who might at least have been aware of Pompey from his days at Sheffield Wednesday. Not that it mattered who or what they knew. The important part in this mercenary-dominated world was persuading world class players they should join Portsmouth on their Premiership adventure. Patrik Berger came into the world class category. Liverpool did not appear to want him but, providing he was clear of the injuries which had ruined his final year or two at Anfield, there was

Vincent Pericard got his release at last from Juventus.

of those or what they had achieved. It was inevitable that Pompey should be linked with the mercurial Di Canio bearing in mind his close relationship with Redknapp at West Ham, but wages were going to be a bit of problem and, with others close to signing, the deal did not develop as quickly or as smoothly as his many admirers at Fratton Park had hoped. Later, after Di Canio had chosen Charlton, Redknapp regretted not making more of an effort to sign the Italian genius, but the move fell down and, in the main, over the period of the summer, Pompey did get the players they wanted. Holland sadly was another to escape their clutches. Back from his international commitments, Holland was linked briefly with Glenn Hoddle's Tottenham, but then Charlton entered the frame, a solid club with a well-considered, unostentatious manager and a capable set of players, but the deciding factor was less straightforward. From his rural home in Suffolk, Holland could commute easily to south east London. It was that which tipped the balance against Pompey and, with Di Canio heading in the same direction, they were setbacks Redknapp could

plenty of football in him. Leeds appeared to be the only rivals for Berger but, after a lightning trip south and talks with Mandaric, Storrie and Redknapp at Port Solent, the Czech Republic star agreed to sign there and then. Unlike Merson, Berger was prepared to move his family south, settling for a spot not a million miles from Redknapp's own luxurious base near Sandbanks.

The other serious targets at this juncture, early in June, were Sheringham, Di Canio and Berkovic and no one could deny the quality

Eyal Berkovic even went on Israeli TV expressing his desire to move to Pompey but this transfer took some months to complete.

have done without at this juncture of the summer.

Luckily other deals were nearer completion. Berger soon put pen to paper and the gangling Vincent Pericard at last got his release from Juventus to become a permanent Pompey player. Pericard's year on loan had gone better than expected. Nine goals in 32 appearances had contributed greatly to Pompey's promotion and, although there were inevitable fears about his ability to repeat that at a higher level, at £200,000 it was hardly a risk. Sheringham was just about the oldest outfield player in the Premiership, but the former Manchester United and England star had never relied on pace, had not gained weight or lost interest and felt that his ejection from White Hart Lane was a touch premature. In truth, Tottenham could not afford him and, with tales of £25,000 a week wages, it was something of a shock to find Pompey pursuing him so hard. There was a hint that Sheringham might add his vast experience to the coaching staff but Redknapp could see no room for him there and if the player was ever going to leave the capital, it would have to be as a player, purely and simply.

Berkovic, meanwhile, went on television at home in Israel to indicate that he would be prepared to join Pompey if he could not find a solution to an apparent problem with Kevin Keegan. Manchester City started quoting figures of £4m for Berkovic and, when it became clear Pompey were not going to pay that for him, a truce broke out between Keegan and his highly-skilled but volatile and moody midfielder. As it happened, and to Pompey's benefit, that truce was only temporary. Berger was keen to make the public aware that Redknapp had played a crucial part in persuading him to sign above Leeds and ahead, it later emerged, of Liverpool's arch-rivals Everton: "Harry was a big influence on me. I was at Liverpool for seven years and had a great time, but moving is part of the game. My daughter was born there and I would have loved to have stayed at Liverpool but now I am looking forward to the new challenge." Redknapp was not slow to reciprocate. "It is a major coup. We did well to get him but once the deal was underway, it happened very quickly."

Yet more speculation, some of it informed, some of it not. The latest batch of names included David May of Manchester United and the talented Haydn Mullins at Crystal Palace, available at £750,000. There was more talk also of Chris Powell, Charlton's left back, and the Serbian goalkeeper Dragoslav Jeuric, but none of those were developing as fast as those concerning Zivkovic and Stefanovic. Chairman Mandaric held meetings in Monaco with the representatives of both players. Zivkovic was at least a free agent but Vitesse Arnhem made it clear they wanted the best part of £2m for their man. Pompey's resolve was tested when it became known that Rangers were showing more than a passing interest in Stefanovic so that a fee of £1.85m, a club record, was quickly agreed and the player just as rapidly joined Pompey. Who would have

Boris Zivkovic, Croatia's captain, was a free agent after helping Bayer Leverkusen establish themselves as a European power.

thought it? Pompey beating a club of Rangers' size to sign a player, or of Leeds' prominence within the game, to nick another. This was all fairytale stuff for the average Pompey fan, who was used to his club grovelling around for cut-price bargains and usually being disappointed.

Back on the south coast, officials were attempting to turn Fratton Park into a Premiership stadium, but it was going to take more than a lick of paint while overworked box office staff struggled as best they could to cope with the huge demand for tickets. There was still plenty going on in terms of player news. Dundee had given up their attempts to lure Mark Burchill back across the border but there were disconcerting rumours about Matt Taylor, the bustling left-back Merson had once likened to Roberto Carlos. That may have been a little flattering and overwhelming for a first division player but Taylor had been only behind Merson and Linvoy Primus in terms of what he achieved in Pompey's promotion season and the grapevine suggested the former Luton player would not start the season. A routine ankle injury that forced him to miss the run-in to promotion had not been a success. Indeed, Redknapp later admitted that there were fears at that stage of the summer that Taylor might never play again. Only after he had been sent to a specialist in war wounds did Taylor begin his long haul back to full fitness, and it was beyond Christmas that he began to approach known form.

The Merson saga showed no signs of coming to an end. Another Pompey legend, Steve Claridge, offered sympathy to Merson after recounting his own difficulties in shaking off a gambling addiction. Claridge said he had lost £750,000 in two years of failed betting but had now overcome it and his bank account was now in the black for the first time. "It's the biggest thing I have ever done inside or outside football and if I can manage it, so can Merson. But it is down to him. He has got to want it and to do it for himself." Another long-running

story concerned the Wimbledon youngsters Reo-Coker and McAnuff. It had rumbled on since Christmas and showed no signs of being resolved. Wimbledon were in administration and were close to moving 70 miles to Milton Keynes, but at last it looked as if Redknapp would win the day when a combined fee was agreed. Reo-Coker had even agreed personal terms and McAnuff had made it clear he would be happy to join Pompey. Within a week, and just when it seemed the deal was in Pompey's grasp, it all collapsed. The administrator was not keen to sell off key assets cheaply and, although Pompey threatened to sue, it all petered out unsatisfactorily and it cannot have pleased the Pompey hierarchy when the players concerned later joined West Ham. Mandaric said: "We had agreed a price and shaken hands on it. In my book the rest were formalities."

Steven Reid of Millwall preferred Blackburn, Jody Morris went to Leeds, but Stefanovic was regarded as another coup for Pompey once his move had been signed and sealed. Delighted Redknapp said: "He's a terrific passer of the ball, he passes like a quality midfield player and he is fantastic in the air." The signing of Zivkovic was taking longer to formalise. There was interest from Germany and Pompey's task was made all the harder because an army of advisors were slowing down the deal at a time when Pompey wanted to get it over and done with. One of the men who helped decide it in Pompey's favour was Robert Prosinecki, whose single glorious year at

Fratton Park still made fans misty-eyed with nostalgia, advised his compatriot to get himself down to Pompey sharpish.

Once it became obvious Berkovic would not, for the time being, be joining Pompey, all efforts were concentrated in persuading Sheringham to extend an already distinguished career at the top by one more year. Pompey were not going to break the bank for him. His wages, while huge by normal standards, were nowhere near the reported £20,000 a week and he would not get a coaching job. Take it or leave it. Sheri took it. No fee changed hands but it was still a big outlay by Pompey for whom such prestigious signings were still a novelty. At the signing ceremony, Sheringham said all the right things about taking his new club on to "better things", taking a swipe at Hoddle for letting him go, while Redknapp reckoned Sheringham and Merson could play in the same team without any bother.

It promised to be a tremendous season already. Most of Redknapp's Premiership managerial contemporaries spent May and June on Caribbean beaches or resting bruised egos after long and, in most cases, unrewarding seasons. But the Pompey boss knew he dared not do the same. His team was hopelessly inadequate in quality and numbers and he needed to replenish it as quickly and as cheaply as

Sheringham signs on the dotted line.

Shaka Hislop - along with Redknapp mourned the loss of former West Ham colleague Marc-Vivien Foe.

aged to cut himself on the dog's bowl. Dripping with blood, Harry needed six stitches. But that dog, a bull terrier called Rosie, was to play a key role in yet another Pompey signing, as we shall see.

There was sadness also. Harry and Shaka Hislop mourned the death of their former West Ham colleague, Marc-Vivien Foe, who collapsed and died playing for Cameroon at a ridiculously early age. Hislop said: "The thing I remembered about him is that he would always have a smile on his face." Redknapp confessed that he had only recently made an inquiry about Foe's availability and agreed that his death put everything in perspective.

he could. By the end of June, Redknapp had either signed or was close to signing Stefanovic, Berger, Zivkovic, Sheringham and Pericard and others were in the pipeline. In many respects it had so far been a productive summer for him, but not everything had gone his way. Self-confessed domestically inept, Redknapp had been entrusted by wife Sandra with feeding the dog. But this simple task proved not as straightforward as it should have been and Redknapp somehow man-

3.

Ready, Teddy, Go

NOT OFTEN IN THE RECENT HIS-tory of Portsmouth Football Club has a fixture list caused quite so much excitement and anticipation around Fratton Park as did that for 2003-04. When it was announced there was a discernible buzz beyond the ancient stadium. "Only when I see it will I actually believe we are in the Premiership," said one fan, and it was a sentiment endorsed by all Pompey supporters at home and abroad. No more ramshackle Millmoor, no more draughty Priestfield. Delete Walsall and Crewe, insert Old Trafford and Highbury, and, of course, two matches with the dreaded Southampton to decide the unofficial championship of Hampshire.

But first it was Aston Villa at Fratton Park and, with Sky deciding to broadcast, a kick-off quirk meant that Pompey could even top the table for an hour or two if they won. Harry Redknapp was well aware of the territory Pompey were now intruding on and was spending the close season in an increasingly feverish search for new blood. Darren Anderton, a Pompey hero of the past, was a prime target and it soon became clear his present club Tottenham would not stand in his way if he decided to leave them. While Anderton disputed his 'sicknote' tag it was widely believed

that part of his Spurs agreement contained a clause in which he earned £500 just for declaring himself fit and available for selection. "Harry has expensive tastes," observed the harassed chairman when it became known his manager was chasing the former Pompey junior who had made his reputation as part of Jim Smith's side which came so close to FA Cup glory in 1992.

At this stage of the summer, there were fears that Shaka Hislop's groin problem might necessitate an operation and it was clear Redknapp would not contemplate going into a Premiership season with any of Yoshikatsu Kawaguchi, Chris Tardif or Craig Bradshaw as Hislop's deputy. A new keeper needed to be found and the search narrowed to Harald Wapenaar, a 33-year old Dutchman. "I saw him play for Utrecht and he looked a good professional," admitted Redknapp. "And he's out of contract." Soon he had become Pompey's fifth new signing and it became clear he was not going to be the only goalkeeper brought to Fratton when, once again, the luckless Kawaguchi was told to look for another club.

Pompey's pre-season hustling was being put in perspective by the almost daily incomings at Chelsea, where Roman Abramovich had taken over and was lavishing his fortune on some of football's biggest names. Chelsea were the envy of the nation, having a chairman prepared to bring in the very best without even once refusing to buy targets identified by manager Claudio Ranieri. How shocking it was, then, to discover the Russian oil magnate would have preferred it if Pompey

Harald Wapenaar was signed as understudy to Shaka Hislop.

had been the object of his massive generosity. According to the Daily Mail, Abramovich's first choice was Pompey. So the story ran, Mandaric was prepared to stand down as chairman but then had second thoughts. Having spent £25m of his own fortune on Pompey at a time when they were at a low ebb, he wanted to sample the Premiership as Pompey's supremo and so the deal collapsed. Portsmouth denied the article but it appeared to be well informed and, if nothing else, it got a few tongues wagging in the pubs and clubs. Think of all the players Chelsea signed and think of how they might have been wearing Pompey blue instead.

Pompey reported for training on July 7 and there was an air of expectancy around the training ground with the new season only five weeks away and a whole new adventure to contemplate. That was the problem, as far as Redknapp was concerned. For far too many players, the Premiership was indeed a whole new adventure because the majority had either never played in it, or had only limited experience of it. Hislop was there, as were last season's long-term crocks, Matt Taylor and Eddie Howe, while Vincent Pericard, the awkward, dreadlocked striker, could only watch while his future was still being decided. Juventus, who had sent him out on a season's loan the year before, were not sure if they wanted him back and tested Pompey's resolve by demanding £1m. Redknapp reckoned he was not worth as much. The talking was continuing as Pompey started the long haul of regaining basic fitness with a host of friendlies to be nego- tiated before the action began in earnest. It was a week or more before Pompey and Juventus finally came to a compromise at around £400,000 and Pericard followed Yakubu in turning a loan deal into a permanent one. Sadly it did not work out for Pericard, who had become such a fans' favourite in the championship year. Injuries ruined his introduction to the top flight; his only start was against Northampton in the Carling Cup and the last of his six substitute appearances was in December 2003 so that Redknapp was never able to discover if the Cameroon- born Frenchman had it in him to become a Premiership player.

Two other issues needed resolv- ing. One concerned Paul Merson, whose future at Pompey was now decidedly wobbly, and the other was Anderton, who, it might be suggested, was being lined up as a replacement of sorts. Nothing with Merson was ever as it seemed. Still battling with his gambling prob- lems and living in the Midlands, the former Arsenal and England player probably had a year or two left in him but whether he could still cope with the Premiership was a ques- tion Redknapp wrestled with for months. There was a war of words developing. Merson said he was being frozen out by the signings of Sheringham and Berger and was no longer valued, Pompey countered with the claim that he was not help- ing himself by living so far away in Sutton Coldfield and was hardly endearing himself to the manage- ment by asking for the occasional extra time off. A parting of the ways

Eddie Howe reported for pre- season training after his long- term absence through injury.

was looking increasingly inevitable, so it was no surprise when Walsall entered the frame offering a possi- ble salvation. But, while Walsall was on his doorstep, there was the small matter of his wages which were well beyond their scope. The only way around it was for Pompey to pay a substantial portion of his salary, an ironic contrast to the previous year when Aston Villa helped Pompey with Merson's wages. Nothing could keep Merson quiet, even as the move to Walsall began to materialise. He claimed the travelling to Pompey for training was not stressful but Redknapp said: "Merse came to me and said he didn't think he could play in the Premiership. Those were his words to me." Amid such a welter of accusations it was clear Merson could not be retained and, with reports of Nottingham Forest now showing an interest, the players headed to Nigel Mansell's Woodbury Park Golf and Country Club near Exeter without him. In the middle of July, Merson became part of Pompey's past when he signed for Walsall with many Pompey fans, mindful of his vast influence in the promotion season, sorry to see him go and all the sorrier because he was going amid such acrimony. Not that Merson could complain. As captain of the championship side he earned a £250,000 bonus. This, on top of a £200,000 pay-off hidden in his Walsall wages, and he was to get another £100,000 if Pompey stayed up. There is no disputing Merson's part in the Pompey success story and there cannot have been many more talented players to have played for the club. But his constant battle against his addictions made him difficult to handle at times and it was probably the right decision for all concerned that he chose to move on.

Fratton Park was a maelstrom of rumours as the pre-season training built up. Sunderland's Kevin Phillips would cost too much in wages, Haydn Mullins at Crystal Palace got more than one mention in the tabloid gossip columns, but the new Merson, the man most coveted by Redknapp, was still Anderton. How Pompey tried. All kinds of deals and compromises were suggested and rejected with Redknapp evidently keener than his chairman. It was reported that Pompey offered him £20,000 a week to sign, which would have made him, comfortably, the highest paid player in the club's history, but he was earning more at White Hart Lane and even that was not enough to tempt him to forsake the last year of his contract at Tottenham to take on a new challenge. Redknapp even enlisted Spurs old boy Sheringham in an attempt to prise Anderton away, and it reached the stage where Mandaric gave the player a deadline to make a decision. The deadline came and went and, although Mandaric then claimed the move was off, Redknapp tried to revive it before even he had to admit defeat. Mandaric was scathing in his condemnation. "It was a substantial deal and we are disappointed he did not take it. But maybe that was for the best." So Merson had gone and Anderton had not arrived.

There was plenty to worry about, therefore, as Pompey prepared for their first friendly as a Premiership 'giant' at Exeter. Later in the season, Pompey would be playing at Newcastle's palatial St James's Park. This was Exeter's St James Park and palatial was not a word used to describe it very often, not even by their most ardent supporters. In many ways it was a strange place to begin a ten-month season. Exeter had lost their place in the Football League and there was an air of pessimism among a small crowd, the home fans bewildered by an array of trialists, most complete-

Gary O'Neil suffered a setback in training in his attempt
to secure a regular first team place.

ly unknown, coming on and going off with an alarming rapidity. Scott Hiley, a Pompey player of the year only three years before, was the one familiar face in the Exeter ranks. Now assistant player-manager, Hiley got a good reception from the travelling Pompey fans when he came on as a substitute with 20 minutes remaining in what proved to be a gentle work-out. Svetoslav Todorov carried on where he left off the previous season with an individual effort, taking a pass from Patrik Berger 35 yards out to run on and score. Sheringham's first Pompey goal was a glancing header just before half-time and Steve Stone supplied the third for Carl Robinson from eight yards. Kevin Harper cut in to score the fourth.

So Pompey were up and away. The result in itself was not significant, but it was a step towards achieving full fitness and supporters were happy enough with what they saw. Sadly, there was a setback. Gary O'Neil, who faced a competitive season attempting to hold down a regular place, went off with a knee injury, joining Howe, Hislop, Taylor and Linvoy Primus on the treatment table - and it was still only July 16. Minor transfer activity continued. Luke Nightingale was wanted on trial by Swindon but took a short-term contract at Southend, Jason Crowe began afresh at Grimsby and five new first year trainees were named, two of them spotted by scout Rob Walker in Northern Ireland. Marc Wilson and Daryl Fordyce were taken on at the start of their apprenticeship and, as a reminder that nothing lasts for ever, news came through of

Jasper Yeuell, a member of Pompey's championship-winning side of 1950, died in July aged 78.

the death of Jasper Yeuell, a member of Pompey's championship-winning side of 1950, at the age of 78.

Training and medical staff are used to dealing with groin strains, ankle injuries, broken hearts and sundry other ailments, real and imagined, but not with malaria. Yakubu Ayegbeni returned for training from a few days at home in Nigeria feeling a little unwell. Tests in hospital revealed that Yakubu had picked up a minor strain of the debilitating and deadly disease, which is rampant in some parts of his native land. Luckily, it was only minor otherwise Yakubu could have been out for the long term. As it happened, after a spell in hospital, he was released and there was time enough for him to regain his health for most of the friendly programme and certainly the visit of Aston Villa, a fixture ringed on every Pompey fan's calendar. It was a scare, nevertheless, which Redknapp could have done without at this stage in the preparations and not one he could ever have expected to cope with. Yakubu, meanwhile, quickly recovered and became the pacy and powerful spearhead Pompey always hoped he would be - even if he did not always know the way to goal.

Matt Taylor was taking a disappointingly long time to get over his ankle operation so Redknapp was forced to turn his attentions to signing a replacement left-back. Graeme Le Saux had become available at Chelsea after the £7m signing of Wayne Bridge but, like Phillips, went instead to Southampton and Redknapp resorted, until Taylor eventually got fit, to shifting players around in his back four to cover the absence. There was also the tricky situation of the captaincy to sort out before the season got much older, and with Merson gone, the natural replacement, a man with similar standing in the game, was Sheringham. There were a few candidates but Redknapp was positive Sheringham should have the job: "I've got a few players in the squad who could be captain. Tim Sherwood has done it before and Boris Zivkovic has led his country, but Teddy is a very experienced player and I feel he is a good choice." For Sheringham it was all part of the welcome-to-Pompey package put together to make him feel wanted after his humiliating exit from Tottenham. Like Sherwood before him, Sheringham was not slow to blast Glenn Hoddle for his undignified departure, and he would have been forgiven a chuckle or two when Hoddle made his own undignified departure from White Hart Lane not long into the season. Sheringham said: "Being captain is nice but the important thing is that I have come here to play and be part of things and first impressions are favourable."

A surge of interest in the club meant that Pompey could have sold many more tickets than they had

The Yak returned from Nigeria with a mild dose of malaria which, fortunately, did not keep him out for long.

The handing of the captaincy armband to Teddy Sheringham went a long way towards him putting his acrimonious exit from White Hart Lane behind him.

available. At least there was scope to add an additional 600 seats to take the capacity above 20,000 but, for all its historic qualities, Fratton Park was proving woefully inadequate already and the season was still a month away.

Harry Redknapp loves Bournemouth. He lives there, played for and managed the local club, taking them into the first division for the first time in their modest history. Later he went back to West Ham but his affection for Bournemouth, the club and the town, was undiminished, so that when Steve Fletcher asked Pompey to provide the opposition for his testimonial Redknapp readily agreed. Fletcher was a contemporary of Jamie Redknapp at Dean Court and they remain close friends and, while Redknapp Snr got a rousing ovation from both sets of fans in a crowd of around 7,000, the match did not go according to plan. Around 2,000 Portsmouth supporters headed home feeling a sense of disquiet after a 5-4 defeat. True, Pompey were not at full strength (Foxe was injured, De Zeeuw rested and Stefanovic was still awaiting work permit clearance) but no Premiership team should let in five against a team two divisions below in the pyramid and, for all his protestations about the match only being a friendly, Harry Redknapp knew it. Pompey gave an outing to Lewis Buxton, later to spend most of the season on loan at Bournemouth, but alongside Primus and Zivkovic, he endured a difficult afternoon. Fletcher scored with a towering header from the edge of the area, one of Pompey's was an own goal and, all in all, it was a thoroughly unpleasant debut for Wapenaar, who mixed two outstanding reflex saves with the sort of unconvincing display which brought a smile to the lips of Kawaguchi on the bench and suggested Hislop had better stay fit.

For the record, apart from Carl Fletcher's own goal, wrongly credited to Sheringham, the Pompey scorers were Sheringham, two, and Lee Bradbury, but Bournemouth might have won by a larger margin. Redknapp admitted: "Jim Smith said don't anyone get injured, but I think we took his advice a little too literally. It's the first game for many of them so it's no big deal. It means nothing. It's about getting fit." But the setback had clearly rattled him and he started a mantra that bright summer day which he was to repeat time and again over the season. "The problem is, I have got no depth whatsoever. I need to get in another three on top of Stefanovic who can play at the highest level. Some of them out there against Bournemouth will not be in my team. Look at my bench, are they Premiership players? No disrespect, some of those cannot play in the premier league. They will go on loan or move permanently, but if they could not get into my first division team, how will they get into my Premiership one? It's going to be a very difficult season, it's a massive leap. Look at West Ham. They beat Bournemouth 4-0 a few days ago and they got relegated." Mollifying words for the Pompey fans, but Mandaric, who had shifted unhappily in his seat in the directors' box, hinted at divine inspiration when he said: "I'm going to give my support to Harry Redknapp and then go into a church and pray we can find a home for these other players."

It was altogether less fraught and worrying a few days later, July 22, at Havant's West Leigh Park when Pompey saw off the Doctor Martens' League side by 6-0. Some 2,500 turned up, many of them Pompey fans, to get a first look at the new Pompey. Chris Clark scored twice and Rowan Vine once, while Mark Burchill got a hat-trick. Burchill could have got ten for all the difference it made to his prospects of forcing his way into the Premiership reckoning. Pompey had not even bothered to give the Scottish international a squad number and there was nothing he could have done which would have persuaded Redknapp to change his mind. As far as Redknapp was concerned, Burchill was a non person. Not that Harry saw two of Burchill's goals. A loudspeaker announcement asked for a vehicle to be removed from where it had been illegally parked in the ground's car park. Once the number plate was read out, a sheepish Redknapp left his seat and made his way along the touchline to the roars of delight from the crowd. Portuguese goalkeeper Sergio Leite impressed without having much to do but Pompey did not offer him a chance and the Porto player moved on to Charlton. It was obvious the management still wanted another keeper - even with five professionals on the books.

Dejan Stefanovic had been forced to wait patiently for his opportunity after his first application for a work permit had been rejected. Pompey were always confident he would win on appeal once he had convinced the authorities that the reason he had not played in enough internationals for Serbia and Montenegro to qualify was that he had been injured. They accepted this explanation and Stefanovic duly completed his move from Vitesse Arnhem for £1.85m in time to watch his new teammates play Swindon in the next of the friendlies. There was speculation he might have been joined by Georgi Kinkladze, who showed up mysteriously at Pompey training, only for Pompey to shoot it down by claiming that the Georgian wonderboy had shown up to regain fitness. Why he should have travelled all the way to Pompey's training ground to get fit was all a bit baffling and the conjecture only increased when he played 45 minutes of a reserve team friendly against Eastleigh. Mandaric said: "He is not on our agenda at all."

And so it proved. Kinkladze, once one of the greatest showmen in English football, never did join Pompey. Nor did the Republic of Ireland winger Steven Reid, who was preciously close to leaving Millwall for Fratton Park for £2m until Blackburn, boosted by the £17m they received for Damien Duff, stepped in first. Had Reid signed he would have been Pompey's record capture 24 hours after Stefanovic had assumed that accolade from Kawaguchi. But it was not to be. Perpetual target Nigel Reo-Coker, meanwhile, was named Wimbledon captain, his move to Pompey now a thing of the past.

The mysterious appearance of former Manchester City star Georgi Kinkladze at the Pompey training ground led to speculation that he was about to move to Fratton Park.

And so to Swindon. The result was 2-2 and it could have been worse with Pompey coming back from two goals down. Swindon were two up after 36 minutes with Steve Robinson and Sam Parkin exposing defensive frailties, but Pompey

came back through a left-foot shot from Zivkovic and another from Todorov. Todorov also hit the woodwork and Pompey had enough chances to win but it was a better performance than at Bournemouth and reassured supporters that Pompey were gradually getting it together.

Norwegian defender Andre Bergdolmo was the latest target. His Dutch club, Ajax, wanted £500,000 and, although Pompey negotiated downwards, Bergdolmo ended up at Borussia Dortmund, apparently unsure that Portsmouth had enough about them to stay in the Premiership more than the one year.

One of the more curious rumours around this time had nothing to do with players or football. It centred around an American tycoon with a name, Sheldon B Adelson, which sounded as though it might have been an invention of Groucho Marx. This latter day Wolf J Flywheel wanted to build a giant casino alongside Fratton Park. As it happened, Pompey had other plans for the land and, in any case, they already had an American tycoon, so the project died before it even had the chance to splutter into life.

Now it was all getting a bit serious. The season was not much more than two weeks away and Pompey were off to Scotland for a series of matches with the fit-again Yakubu and without Tim Sherwood because of a virus. According to physio Gary Sadler, Sherwood woke up one day stone deaf and feeling giddy. Only later did it emerge that Sherwood was quite unwell and could have lost his hearing permanently, but football waits for no man and Kilmarnock loomed. This proved to be the best performance so far. Premier League Kilmarnock were overwhelmed, with Yakubu proving his fitness with two goals and Sheringham showing his quality with a cracking left-foot volley which removed all doubts, if there were any, that the former England player was a spent force. Sheringham added another later and Stone completed the rout and, with the reliable Shaka restored between the posts, the defence looked altogether happier in a 4-4-2 formation. Pompey's fans travel everywhere with them and there was a gaggle at Kilmarnock that Friday night, all of them intrigued by a trialist called Andy Henry. This tall Patrick Vieira-lookalike seemed a decent prospect, but no player by that name could be found in the record books, however intently they were studied. The internet was equally useless. Just who was Andy Henry?

So the pre-season began to draw to a close. Some of it had been good and some of it less so, but the team was taking shape and Redknapp and Mandaric were still committed to bringing in yet more players before the Premiership's big kick-off. Time was running short. This was promising to be a tumultuous year and all at Fratton Park were desperately anxious to make sure it did not end in tears.

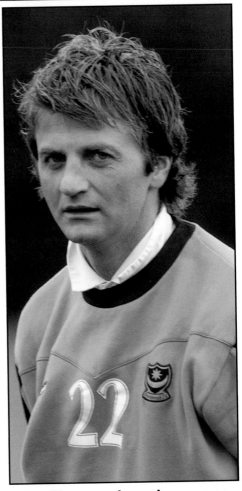

Tim Sherwood - woke up one day stone deaf and feeling giddy. Only later did it emerge that Sherwood was quite unwell and could have lost his hearing permanently.

4.

Andy who?

MARK BURCHILL'S FAILURE TO earn a place in the Portsmouth side mystified supporters as much as it mystified them why Celtic were prepared to let him move to Fratton Park in the first place. Martin O'Neill is an astute manager and it seemed odd, to say the least, that O'Neill was prepared to allow a 21-year old, already capped by Scotland, to join Pompey for as little as £600,000. As usual, a player liked by Graham Rix was not wanted by Redknapp and, although he contributed some important goals in the championship season, he drifted so far out of the reckoning that when Redknapp announced his squad numbers for the forthcoming season, Burchill didn't get one. All kinds of fringe players did, but Burchill was notably frozen out. Later, as Pompey struggled for goals, isolated banners appeared on the terraces demanding his restoration to the team but, privately any-

Mark Burchill's pre-season goals failed to earn him a squad number, let alone a place in the starting line-up.

STAY UP POMPEY!

way, Redknapp would rather have played himself.

Pompey could have done with a goal or two from Burchill - or anyone for that matter - in the next Scottish friendly at Dunfermline where, as a pattern for the season ahead, they had plenty of possession but were unable to do much with it. Redknapp attempted to put it all in perspective after the 1-0 defeat: "I didn't get too excited when we won at Kilmarnock and I'm not getting too despondent now." Barry Nicholson got the only goal and Harald Wapenaar showed signs of improvement after a shaky start to his Pompey career with some important saves, but Pericard, Sheringham and De Zeeuw all missed good chances to give Redknapp and Jim Smith something to mull over.

On the same day, August 2, it was announced that Pompey stalwart Gordon Neave had lost his battle against cancer and had died at his home in Copnor, not far from his beloved Fratton Park, at the age of 78. Neave had been part of the furniture from the moment he was spotted in Egypt, of all places, while on National Service (Do Pompey still have an Egyptian scout?). He was on the club's books in the championship-winning years without establishing a place in the team and got more action at Bournemouth and Aldershot before returning to Pompey in 1959 to become an integral part of the backroom staff, working under 17 managers over the next 40 years as coach, trainer, physio and kitman. Two testimonials in 1974 and 1999 reflected his value to the club and

were richly deserved. Alan Knight first came across the no-nonsense Neave when he joined the staff as a 15-year old fresh from the family home in Balham. "When I first arrived he was in charge of the apprentices. He was a hard taskmaster - but fair. I had great respect for the man, as did everyone. Gordon was also very fit and I only knew him once take time off sick."

The main talking point, though, remained the true identity of Andy Henry, who had played with some distinction in the Kilmarnock friendly. At last it was revealed. Redknapp admitted he had used a false moniker (a ruse which was later to get him into trouble) to throw rivals off the scent. Andy Henry was Amdy Faye, a 26-year old Senegalese international midfielder who had been made available by the French club Auxerre for £1.5m. It was a figure tantalisingly within Pompey's grasp, but it was also, therefore, within the grasp of other Premiership clubs, not least Middlesbrough. Hence the subterfuge. Harry could scarcely contain himself once it became clear Faye would be signing for Pompey ahead of others. "He's an outstanding player and I'm delighted to get him. He's a terrific passer, strong and aggressive. A great box-to-box player." The signing itself was far from easy and had about it elements of comedy which would have defied the imagination of the best of scriptwriters. Faye was suspended at Auxerre the weekend Pompey were in Scotland, so he trained instead with Pompey, looked outstanding,

44

ANDY WHO?

The mysterious appearance of Amdy Faye, alias Andy Henry, at Kilmarnock. The mix-up over the name almost got Harry Redknapp in trouble with the F.A.

**Thierry Henry became the unwitting alibi in Redknapp's
explanation to the F.A. of the Amdy Faye mystery.**

and was drafted in (illegally) against Kilmarnock.

It was said that Middlesbrough, Leeds, Manchester City, Southampton and Wolves were all keen on him, and Middlesbrough had taken their interest a step further by agreeing a fee with Auxerre, as Pompey had done. Arriving back in England after the Scottish jaunt, Faye was ensconced in the Marriott Hotel just outside Portsmouth and Redknapp issued orders to Smith and Kevin Bond to make sure Faye got all he wanted and didn't stray. Redknapp went off to watch Spurs in a friendly with PSV Eindhoven, believing his impending capture was tucked up in a hotel well away from harm's reach. Imagine his horror, then, as he headed home for a family barbecue when he got a panicky phone call to tell him Faye had been smuggled out in a laundry basket (only joking) and had made his way to Heathrow where the breathless Redknapp found him in the departure lounge, minutes away from disappearing from Pompey's life for ever. Had he gone back to Auxerre, Redknapp believes he would have found out about Middlesbrough's counter-bid and become aware also that in salary terms he would have been better off in the north east. Harry was all but clinging on to Faye's legs as he crossed the threshold onto the plane when he managed to sweet-talk him into staying. Once back in the Redknapp limousine and heading for the Sandbanks mansion, this time there was no escape for the wavering Faye.

Smith and Bond had not proved to be the best of minders and at Sandbanks they were substituted by the menacing-looking Redknapp bulldogs (bark worse than bite), who were delegated to keep watch outside Faye's bedroom to prevent any further last-minute change of heart. Faye spent a sleepless night peering through cracks in the door to see if the dogs were still there. (Again, only joking). Next day Faye was taken to Pompey training and duly completed his transfer, much to Middlesbrough's annoyance. Steve McClaren claimed Pompey had destroyed faxes intended to alert Faye to their desire to sign him and sent to their hotel in Troon, but Pompey strongly denied the allegations. Redknapp has signed a multitude of players in more than 20 years of management, probably more than any manager in the game, but even he was surprised at the way the Faye saga unfolded: "I have had a lifetime of doing things like that but I have never used the dog-watching scenario before. He clearly wasn't very keen on them. Now he's joined us and will prove to be a very good footballer. You don't play for Auxerre for five or six years if you are not a good player and in the Champions' League last season he gave Patrick Vieira a hard time."

The Football Association were less amused. They wanted an explanation about 'Andy Henry'. Harry slid out of trouble with his usual panache with an explanation straight from the mouth of Del Boy Trotter: "It was all a bit of a mix-up. His English was not the best. When he said his name was Amdy, I thought he said Andy. Then he kept saying Henry, Henry. I thought that was his second name but he was trying to tell me he knew Thierry Henry. That's what happened." Ah, that's sorted then. Whether the FA believed him or not is another matter, but it's a wonderful story and no action was taken.

Back in England and with the new season approaching with indecent haste, Pompey fielded three trailists at Brentford where they won 1-0. At the back was Rossen Kirilov, a Bulgarian from Todorov's old club at Lech Lovech, Jocelyn Blanchard, a 31-year old midfielder released by Lens, and a certain Georgi Kinkladze. They all made a contribution with the intriguing prospect of a Kinkladze signing improved by a commanding display from the little genius, albeit against second division opposition. Pericard scored the only goal after Pompey had again spurned chances with alarming profligacy. Making an impression for Brentford was goalkeeper Paul Smith, later to have a Pompey trial and even later to join Southampton.

Juan Pablo Sorin was 27 and considered to be one of the best defenders in the world. He was also a target for Pompey. And a very realistic one at that. An Argentinian registered with Brazilian club Cruzeiro, he was a victim of Brazil's two foreigner per club quota and had been loaned to Lazio and Barcelona. Redknapp and Peter Storrie flew to Barcelona to meet the player, his wife and agent to put a strong case as to why he should join Pompey. Redknapp said: "I think we might be able to afford his wages. He was earning decent money at Barcelona but they don't get much in Brazil." Storrie, aware of the escalating wage bill more than anyone, was more cautious on returning to England: "We will have to discuss a fee first before we start talking about wages." Ten days later, the chairman gasping for air, Pompey agreed a club record fee of £2m for the undeniably talented Sorin with Cruzeiro. They also offered him in excess of £20,000 a week, which would have made him the club's best-paid player of all time. Mandaric said: "We have given it our best shot. The important thing is not to go crazy with what we pay."

Pompey needed to know soon because the end of August was a cut-off day. The transfer window would close and would not re-open until the start of January and Sorin was given a deadline of his own. Sign or forget about it. As the player pondered and prevaricated, there was talk of a loan deal and a permanent signing in January but, as August 31 loomed, and after days and weeks of negotiations, Sorin declined and promptly signed for Paris St Germain. Pompey were shocked because they really believed they had him. But that's football, as Redknapp knew from bitter experience only too well.

For every Faye there is a Sorin. One of the drawbacks of long-term contracts is that if a new manager does not like certain players he inherits, as Redknapp had done from Rix, he is lumbered with them whether he wants them or not. By being promoted to the Premiership, the standard of players required by Pompey was much higher than they had ever been. This meant a huge logjam of players built up, some of

ANDY WHO?

Lee Bradbury was one of many under contract in the summer who had little or no chance of being part of Redknapp's plans for the forthcoming season.

whom might be able to play in an emergency but who, in the main, were never going to hold down a place against the likes of Arsenal and Manchester United. But, protected by contracts and apparently unwanted by clubs at an impoverished lower level, they hung on at Fratton Park, adding to an already overloaded payroll and occupying space in the reserves which might have been better used to try out promising youngsters.

In fairness to the players concerned, many of them would have preferred to have left Fratton Park once it became clear they had no future with Pompey but, all the while no other clubs came in for them, they had no alternative but to sit on their contracts. A great list of names like Neil Barrett, Lee Bradbury, Craig Bradshaw, Mark Burchill, Lewis Buxton, Deon Burton, Mark Casey, Shaun Cooper, Kevin Harper, Yoshi Kawaguchi,

STAY UP POMPEY!

Carl Pettefer, Courtney Pitt, Carl Robinson, Chris Tardif, Jamie Vincent and Rowan Vine had no, or little, chance of playing in Redknapp's Premiership team. It would have taken an emergency of catastrophic proportions, and Pompey had a few of those in the months to come, for any of them to have got a chance at Fratton Park, and yet all of them were perfectly capable of playing at a less demanding standard. Some, such as Buxton, Vine and Cooper, had not been written off by Redknapp because they were still young enough to improve but, realistically, they were not going to play in the Premiership in the year ahead. If they could not be sold or permanently offloaded in a dead transfer market, the only way out for Pompey was through the loan system. Having spent the previous year on loan at Brentford with some success, Vine was sent out to Colchester for the season, while pacy left-winger Pitt - much admired and expensively imported by Rix - was borrowed by Luton in the days leading up to the start of the Nationwide season. Bradbury, who once cost Manchester City £3.5m, headed for Derby on the same makeshift basis. Sadly, in his case, the loan lasted a matter of minutes before he was sent back to Fratton Park nursing a broken foot.

A big test for Pompey, the biggest so far, was the visit of the Dutch club Feyenoord to Fratton Park for the final friendly seven days before the start of the league season. Feyenoord were one of the best sides in Holland and had proved themselves in European competi-tion over many years. This was a proper yardstick for Pompey's progress, even allowing for the fact that there was no edge of contest. In sweltering early August conditions, Redknapp's side provided a pleasant surprise for those supporters who feared the worst. Aston Villa were a matter of days away and this was the final dress rehearsal but, in the energy-draining circumstances, it all went remarkably well. Patrik Berger put Pompey ahead in the 43rd minute with a sizzling 25-yarder to show that injury and a prolonged spell outside the Liverpool team had not diminished his skill. Seven substitutions at half-time by Pompey alone did nothing for the flow of the game but Redknapp used the opportunity to look at Rune Pedersen, a goalkeeper from FC Copenhagen, and take a second glance at the Bulgarian Kirilov. Neither got nearer a contract offer but Redknapp liked what he saw of the team performance: "We played some great stuff and I am pleased bearing in mind how hot it was. We scored two great goals and I am confident we can take this form into the Villa game. It's going to be a tough year but let's enjoy it whatever happens." Yakubu got the other Pompey goal, but it was the display of Sheringham, well into his 38th year, that caught the eye of Steve Stone: "Teddy has tremendous quality and he showed it with everything he did. It is the sort of quality we are going to need in the Premiership and I believe he can help us survive."

There were still some finishing touches to be made as the count-

**Todorov tangles with the Feyenoord defence
during the friendly at Fratton Park.**

down to the season began. Redknapp was still obviously concerned about his left-back position. There were unspoken fears about the future of the injured Taylor and, in the week building up to the big kick-off, the Sorin deal was no nearer being resolved. That's why Redknapp noted the penniless plight of Leeds, later to be relegation rivals, and their need to offload the higher wage-earners. One such player was Ian Harte, a left back of note, whom Leeds had made clear was available if anyone could match his salary. This, the Pompey boss, doubted. "I do like Ian Harte, although he's on decent money at Leeds." The controversial Mark Bosnich was invited to train with Pompey because the manager was not convinced the back-up for the ailing Hislop was of a high enough quality, but Bosnich never showed and the search for a third goalkeeper became a priority.

There was one late signing as West Ham's French right-back Sebastien Schemmel came down on a free transfer after falling out with Glenn Roeder and expressing a desire to renew a profitable relationship with Redknapp. Schemmel was player of the year at Upton Park when Redknapp had been manager there and the Upton Park

STAY UP POMPEY!

Redknapp went back to his old club for one late signing before the start of the season. Sebastien Schemmel, the French right-back, had been a player of the year at Upton Park.

crowd liked and admired him. Schemmel was signing number nine and did not waste the opportunity to accuse Roeder of forcing him out.

All appeared to be coming along nicely. The sun was still shining, the signings were rolling in and so too was the cash from the ever-increasing demand for tickets at Fratton Park. In fact, demand exceeded supply by several thousand, if rumour was to be believed. The lucky ones were the 15,000 who bought season tickets. The other 5,000 or so were those who bought tickets when they became available on a match basis. But

suddenly there was a cloud on the horizon, a monumental setback for which no club could have planned or expected. Svetoslav Todorov, on whom so much depended in terms of goals, caught his studs in the turf at training without a player anywhere near him and collapsed in obvious pain and distress. This was just 48 hours before the start of the season - and how do you go about replacing a man who the previous year had scored 26 goals? Even as he lay prone and motionless on the ground Pompey were fearing the worst. Cruciate ligament damage can take months to repair and operations are not always a success. It was a nervous three days before Pompey were told of a torn cartilage - and of the cruciate ligament damage they had suspected. It was a massive blow and Todorov was unable to play much in the season which followed. He may even have attempted to come back before he was ready. The temptation to recall a player of his calibre is always there and understandable but, after playing half a game against Liverpool in March, he disappeared for the remainder of the season with an injury in the same knee, a key personal year all but written off.

Saturday, August 16

PORTSMOUTH (1) 2
ASTON VILLA (0) 1

And so to the big day, August 16, Portsmouth versus Aston Villa. Ever since the last ball of the previous season had been kicked at Bradford an eternity ago in May, this was the occasion every Pompey fan had marked down as the start of a new and exciting adventure. It was another hot, sultry day and Fratton Park was buzzing with anticipation long before kick-off. Television cameras were in place and fans took their seats early, not wanting to miss the chance to sample or become part of an incredible atmosphere. The pundits, many of them ex-players, had decided Pompey would be relegated almost to a man in their newspaper columns and self-styled experts on television had all predicted an instant return to the wastelands of the first division. Redknapp knew they would be favourites to go back down and warned the club's supporters to expect a rough ride, whatever the eventual outcome.

Pompey's best chance was always going to be Fratton Park, its tightness, its hostility, its aggression, and that was why Pompey needed to beat Villa and get the season off to the best possible start. There was the legacy of last season to build on and in a spirit of optimism anything is possible. For Villa reject Stone, it was the chance to get the better of his old club, although the man behind his humbling move to Pompey, Graham Taylor, had since moved on. For Stone, the hurt was still apparent. That was just the sort of spirit Redknapp wanted because five of his new signings would be starting and a sixth, Schemmel, was on the bench. It was part of the learning process for all of them and, in a perfect world, the Pompey manager might have preferred to have kept some of them back to allow them further time to settle but Todorov, Primus, Sherwood, Taylor and Howe were all injured and, having failed to sign a left-back, the ever-willing De Zeeuw filled an unaccustomed position. The match had long been a sell-out and the famous Fratton roar greeted the new season and a whole new era.

Gordon Neave's death was properly observed in a minute's silence as the 12.30 start approached and, when Teddy Sheringham finally released almost four months of pent-up emotion by kicking off, a fantastic burst of energy engulfed the stadium, as if someone had let go of a giant pressure valve. Nerves

STAY UP POMPEY!

Sheringham sweeps the ball into the net for Pompey's
first ever Premiership goal, while Berger (below)
celebrates the second.

were obvious: stray passes marred every progressive move, multi-millionaire footballers fumbled and fiddled, their first touches suddenly as clumsy as those of a Sunday morning parks player. Marcus Allback had a goal disallowed and there were agonising moments when Villa looked slicker and sharper and a world away from the sort of basic fodder of the first division. But Villa had nothing to show for it and after 42 minutes, Faye, Berger and Yakubu broke with pace and precision and a rebound from the goalkeeper was swept into the net with glee and ruthlessness by Sheringham. One-nil Pompey and for a few heady seconds it seemed like the whole of Portsmouth had gone into an orbit of ecstacy. John Westwood almost swallowed his trumpet as fans all around him, crazed by excitement, celebrated with wild abandon. What a moment!

Alpay and, later, Angel missed easy chances for wasteful Villa and it was Pompey who went further in front after 63 minutes. Berger evaded Alpay and Johnsen to rifle a left foot shot wide of Sorensen. Fratton Park erupted into a choking chorus of 'We're top of the league' after news filtered through that Birmingham had beaten Tottenham in an earlier kick off but only by a single goal. Peter Crouch, the money from whom set off the Pompey transfer spree under Redknapp, came on as a sub for Villa and, at that stage of the match, there cannot have been many Pompey fans who wished he still wore the club's royal blue.

Pompey were coasting to victory, fans dancing in their seats, when

Juan Pablo Angel - missed numerous easy chances for Villa.

Gareth Barry tumbled under a Zivkovic challenge, or so it seemed at the time, and the penalty was despatched by the same player. Those watching on television at home saw quite clearly that no contact had been made and a lesson had been learned: This may be the Premiership and the referees are supposed to be the best in the land, but decisions made are every bit as dodgy as those made in, well, Sunday morning parks matches. Barry was sent off for complaining about a throw-in decision, taking the wind out of Villa's late rally in which Pompey were seen to be hanging on grimly and with faltering resolution. Graham Barber at last cut through the tension with a shrill blast of his whistle and joy was unconfined. While Redknapp noted the excellence of the team spirit and the determination, the day belonged to chairman Mandaric, who wiped away a tear from the eye in noting the club's position at the top of the Premiership after years of failure and waste. "This is just the start of the adventure," he said.

Portsmouth (4-4-2): Hislop; Zivkovic, Foxe, Stefanovic, De Zeeuw; Stone, Faye (Schemmel 90), Quashie, Berger; Sheringham, Yakubu (Pericard 76).
Subs not used: Wapenaar, O'Neil, Burton
Booked: Stefanovic, Faye.
Goals: Sheringham 42, Berger 63.

Aston Villa (4-4-2): Sorensen; Delaney, Johnsen, Alpay, Samuel; Hendrie, McCann, Barry, Whittingham (Hitzlsperger 59); Allback, Angel (Crouch 77).
Subs not used: Mellberg, De La Cruz, Postma.
Sent Off: Barry (87).
Booked: McCann.
Goals: Barry 84 pen.

Att: 20,101
Ref: G Barber (Hertfordshire).

Stats:
Shots on target: Pompey 6 Aston Villa 4
Shots off target: Pompey 2 Aston Villa 3
Corners: Pompey 7 Aston Villa 9
Fouls: Pompey 20 Aston Villa 25
Offside: Pompey 1 Aston Villa 1

As a sort of post-debut torpor settled over Fratton Park in the days after the Villa match, there was more good news for Pompey in the shape of Matt Taylor, who confounded sceptics by returning to the lightest of training. Even that had not been anticipated a couple of weeks earlier when footballing obituaries were being prepared for one of the brightest young talents in the game. Strange rumours surfaced about Alexei Smertin, the Russian captain, whom Chelsea apparently wanted to buy and then loan out instantly. It all sounded very odd. Meanwhile Redknapp denied any interest at all in Lomana Lua-Lua of Newcastle. Fair enough.

Saturday August 23

MANCHESTER CITY (0) 1
PORTSMOUTH (1) 1

The City of Manchester Stadium is one of Britain's finest, a state-of-the-art tribute to the best of 21st century architecture and construction. For Manchester City, it was now home and Pompey had the privilege of being the first league visitors to this magnificent arena - almost spoiling City's big day in the sun. Not that talisman fan Westwood and drummers Simon Mill and Alan Fuller saw the last 20 minutes. They were ejected for making too much noise. At a football match! At this stage Pompey were leading 1-0 and Westwood said: "I think it was sour grapes on their part because 3,000 fans were outsinging 43,000."

Even outside, the Pompey band might have had something to cele-

ANDY WHO?

Superfan John Westwood was less than impressed by his ejection from the City of Manchester Stadium with 20 minutes to go for "making too much noise".

brate had Pompey been able to hold on to a lead given them after 24 minutes by Yakubu, who used his pace and power to muscle past a challenge from Distin and then beat Seaman with a shot. Manchester City didn't do anything to suggest they had an answer and, as time ticked away, it began to look as if Pompey might follow that first home win with another away. Then, agonisingly, with seconds remaining, David Sommeil headed in a Joey Barton free kick to rescue a point for City and set up a hectic last five minutes when only some desperate defending enabled Pompey to escape with a draw. The disappointment of conceding such a late goal aside, Pompey fans were pleased

STAY UP POMPEY!

with the point, the performance and the promise. Little did anyone know it would be eight months before Pompey finally won on an opponent's ground, or that Manchester City would accompany Pompey in a relegation battle. Redknapp was never one to mask his emotions: "When you're so close to winning, it's a shame to draw. I thought we deserved to win because Shaka didn't have much to do. I need to get in two players this week, a left-sided midfield player and a forward because we're short there." But the manager had a firm riposte for telly pundit Andy Townsend, who suggested Pompey's philosophy was based on a crude kick-and-run tactic: "He must think I'm Harry Bassett from Wimbledon, not Harry Redknapp. I've been a manager 25 years and none of my teams played that way."

Man City (4-4-2): Seaman; Jihai, Sommeil, Distin, Tarnat; Wright-Phillips, Barton, Sibierski (Berkovic 64), Sinclair; Anelka, Fowler (Wanchope 45).
Subs Not Used: Weaver, Wiekens, Tiatto.
Booked: Barton, Tarnat.
Goals: Sommeil 90.

Portsmouth (4-4-2): Hislop; Schemmel, De Zeeuw, Stefanovic, Zivkovic; Stone, Faye, Quashie, Berger (Harper 82); Sheringham, Yakubu (Pericard 74).
Subs Not Used: Wapenaar, Primus, O'Neil.
Booked: Faye, Pericard, Zivkovic.
Goals: Yakubu 24.

Att: 46,287
Ref: M Messias (N Yorkshire).

Stats:
Shots on target: Man City 5 Pompey 2
Shots off target: Man City 11 Pompey 2
Corners: Man City 10 Pompey 7
Fouls: Man City 9 Pompey 21
Offside: Man City 4 Pompey 3

Games were coming thick and fast now and it was to Pompey's advantage to have a comparatively gentle start to life in the Premiership. Villa, Manchester City and now Bolton at Fratton Park were nobody's idea of championship challengers, not that Pompey could

Alexei Smertin, the captain of Russia, found himself part of the Pompey Premiership machine on the night of the Bolton game after being bought by Roman Abramovich at Chelsea and immediately loaned out to Pompey.

afford to take any of them lightly. There was an added dimension to the Bolton game that Tuesday night. Sitting in the stands was little, long-haired Smertin, whose world had been turned upside down by a £3.5m transfer from his French club to Abramovich's Chelsea. Why Chelsea needed him, after a summer of collosal spending, was never clear and it appeared they didn't because no sooner was the ink dry on his contract than he was shipped out on loan to grateful Pompey. What a present. Russia's captain, a player way beyond even Mandaric's purse, handed to Redknapp for the season. Shame Chelsea did not let them have someone like Hasselbaink as well, but who's complaining?

Tuesday August 26

PORTSMOUTH (0) 4
BOLTON WANDERERS (0) 0

Smertin witnessed one of the great nights in modern Pompey history. After a keenly contested first hour,

It was a sensational night at Fratton Park - and for Teddy Sheringham - when Bolton visited at the end of August. A superb 4-0 victory put Pompey top of the Premiership, while Sheringham bagged a hat-trick.

Bolton were swept aside with some scintillating football in which Sheringham, oozing class with every touch, scored his first hat-trick for three years. How that went down at White Hart Lane we can only guess, but it can have done nothing for Glenn Hoddle's already perilous grip on the managerial chair. At the end of a glorious evening, after Pompey had won 4-0, Redknapp's men found themselves top of the table on merit, no early kick-off fluke this time, for the first time since January 1952, when they beat Huddersfield 3-1. Sam Allardyce promised to teach the upstarts a lesson or two about life in the fast lane and for 52 minutes there was little to choose between the teams. The turning point was an exceptional save by Hislop from Kevin Davies. Bolton were still bemoaning their luck when Stone bundled in a rebound to put Pompey in front. Florent Laville somehow shot over from three yards when an equaliser looked imminent and the derisive cheers had scarcely died when Berger, Quashie and Zivkovic combined for Sheringham to score with a bullet header. Celebrations were well under way when, with two minutes remaining, Stone pulled a pass back for Sheringham to convert his second from ten yards and then, in injury time, a careless and pre-meditated hack by Campo on Pericard in an effort to retrieve his own error resulted in a penalty which Sheringham placed to the keeper's left to complete his hat-trick. His last had been for Manchester United against Saints and his final goal took Pompey to the Premiership zenith, albeit for 24 hours until Arsenal and Manchester United restored the status quo.

Portsmouth (4-4-2): Hislop; Schemmel (Primus 81), De Zeeuw, Stefanovic, Zivkovic; Stone, Faye, Quashie, Berger Sheringham, Yakubu (Pericard 84).
Subs Not Used: Wapenaar, O'Neil, Harper.
Booked: Zivkovic, Quashie.
Goals: Stone 48, Sheringham 57, 88, 90 pen.

Bolton (4-5-1): Jaaskelainen; Barness (Charlton 41), N'Gotty, Laville, Gardner; Okocha, Pedersen, Campo, Frandsen (Jardel 63), Djorkaeff; Davies (Giannakopoulos 64).
Subs Not Used: Poole, Nolan.
Booked: Laville, Davies, Charlton, Giannakopoulos.

Att: 20,113
Ref: D Gallagher (Oxfordshire).

Stats:
Shots on target: Pompey 8 Bolton 4
Shots off target: Pompey 5 Bolton 9
Corners: Pompey 0 Bolton 3
Fouls: Pompey 10 Bolton 13
Offside: Pompey 8 Bolton 1

For Redknapp, being top of the league was something he had never before experienced, even for a day or two at West Ham: "We're not getting carried away, but nothing beats this feeling, looking down on everyone else. You don't get time to enjoy these moments for long but it's still nice. I have told the lads they were rejected by others who didn't think they could make it in the Premiership but they are now proving them wrong. I'm happy to send the punters home happy." Sheringham noted the excitement of the fans but also indicated that he was now more motivated than for years. At his age, he needed that. Smertin saw the passion in the fans, the fierce determination of the players and wanted to be part of it. Within 48 hours of being signed from Bordeaux, and never having spoken to Claudio Ranieri, he was on his way to England's south coast. Quite how this came about we might never know. There were dark rumours of Abramovich buying Smertin to help a Russian friend but no explanation was sought or given. Not that Redknapp was complaining as he contemplated the prospect of a world class player being added to a squad short of world class players: "Once he's got his work permit, he will go straight into the team. No doubt about that." Paul Konchesky was briefly a Pompey target to fill that pesky left-back slot, but when Charlton wanted a fee, the deal, such as it was, fell flat. The Smertin work permit duly arrived and, for a few incredible days, Fratton Park was the happy valley, a place of smiles: top of the table and now reinforced by an international captain - for nothing. Not even the sight of the stricken Todorov heading for Dr Steadman's clinic in the United States could alter an atmosphere bordering on incredulity.

Paul Ince caused the major talking point in the dire 0-0 draw with Wolves. He felled The Yak during the second half and Redknapp's protests led to him being dismissed from the dugout.

Saturday, August 30

WOLVERHAMPTON WDRS (0) 0
PORTSMOUTH (0) 0

Wolves had accompanied Pompey into the Premiership by the skin of their black and gold teeth through the play off system and were the club most fancied to finish bottom, even in August. They were already doing a decent impression of a team hopelessly out of their depth when Pompey travelled to Molineux in search of that first away win on August 30. Wolves are nothing if not battlers and, in a match reminiscent of the first division both clubs had just left, a goalless draw was about right. At least Pompey ended the month unbeaten - but there were drawbacks. Five players were booked, some harshly, and Redknapp was banished to the stands by card-happy referee Andy D'Urso. Stone, Sheringham and Berger, with a header into the side-netting, all went close to snatching a goal but Wolves, who sensed this was a chance to claim their first win, were spurred on by a noisy and clamouring home crowd who deserved better than some sloppy finishing by Henri Camara and Nathan Blake.

The major talking point came in the second half when Yakubu was felled by the ageing and aggressive Paul Ince and after an angry Redknapp had remonstrated with the fourth official, D'Urso was called to the touch-line from where the unre-pentant Redknapp was sent packing. Smertin came on for the final 22 minutes and Shering-ham had a shot cleared from the line by Paul Butler, but overall it was a poorish match unde-serving of a goal. Not that Redknapp was too con-cerned about the match, it seemed: "I thought the referee was inept. I told the fourth official what I thought of the ref's per-formance and then he told the ref. Maybe I shouldn't have said any-

Redknapp's views on refereeing in the Premiership were loudly advanced following the Wolves game.

thing, but I thought the official should have been a bit more manly about the whole thing. I could see the referee was going to send me off and I told Jim to speak to him but he was too slow in getting over. Jim's not as quick as he used to be." Warming to his theme, Redknapp launched into a wither-ing series of comments about the standard of Premiership officialdom

which he felt should have been much better. "The standard of ref-ereeing so far this season is fright-ening even though refs are sup-posed to be getting better. It drives me mad because all we want is a sensible performance. We had bet-ter referees in the first division. At this rate we're not going to have a team by next month with all the suspensions we are going to get. I

ANDY WHO?

don't normally get involved with referees. I didn't even know his name. In fact, I thought it was the Pompey lad, Rob Styles. The fourth official could have told me to calm down. He could have said he agreed with my assessment of the ref but tell me to keep it quiet." And the match, Harry? "It was a good point. Overall we've made a great start. Eight points in August, not at all bad." By Harry's standards, this was a major rant against referees and little did he or any of us know of the Robert Pires incident still to come.

Wolverhampton (4-5-1): Oakes; Irwin, Butler, Craddock, Naylor; Newton, Rae (Gudjonsson 80), Ince, Cameron, Camara; Blake.
Subs Not Used: Murray, Iversen, Silas, Okoronkwo.
Booked: Butler, Rae, Ince.

Portsmouth (4-4-2): Hislop; Schemmel, De Zeeuw, Stefanovic, Zivkovic; Stone (Smertin 68), Faye, Quashie, Berger; Yakubu (Pericard 85), Sheringham.
Subs Not Used: Wapenaar, Primus, Harper.
Booked: Quashie, Stone, Schemmel, Zivkovic, Yakubu.

Att: 28,860
Ref: A D'Urso (Essex).

Stats:
Shots on target: Wolves 3 Pompey 4
Shots off target: Wolves 7 Pompey 5
Corners: Wolves 4 Pompey 6
Fouls: Wolves 15 Pompey 18
Offside: Wolves 5 Pompey 6

But there was one day before the transfer window closed, one day to do business and, true to form, the manager did not waste it. Jason Roberts was driving up the motorway to Wigan from disillusionment at West Bromwich when Harry told him to turn around and head south. A deal whereby the pacy Roberts joined Pompey on loan for a season had been agreed. Pompey were to pay £100,000 for each half of the season he played for them and, if all went well, there was a £2.25m permanent transfer at the end of it. Roberts liked the prospect of Premiership football and spurned Wigan (temporarily as it turned out) but still the manager was not satisfied that his squad was strong enough to withstand four months at the highest domestic level. Experienced keeper Pavel Srnicek, most recently of Brescia and training at Wolves, was recruited as the third keeper and that meant a sorry farewell to the ever-optimistic Kawaguchi. Danish club FC Nordsjaelland had somehow been alerted to him after months on the transfer list and paid around £200,000 to take him away from Fratton Park.

Whether or not Pompey had done their best by Kawaguchi remains a debating point among fans, some of whom believed he had been made a scapegoat and deserved better than the treatment he got. There is no doubt he had been signed originally as a crude commercial tool, Pompey hoping to tap into the huge Japanese market with replica shirts and other paraphernalia but, when that failed to happen, he was dumped. Mandaric had the good grace to admit a mistake had been made: "I have learned a lot from the whole episode. I realise it was an error and the buck stops with me." At least his transfer thinned the number of Japanese journalists in the already overwhelmed and inadequate edifice that passed for a press

STAY UP POMPEY!

Would the departure of Kawaguchi mean that Fratton Park would no longer play host to a significant number of Japanese fans?

box at Fratton Park. They chronicled his trials and tribulations in England in faithful hordes, hanging on to his every word even when he was not playing, which was most of the time. Yoshi loved his time in England, blamed no one for his failure and left smiling. Everyone else was smiling, too, at Fratton Park, but for different reasons. August 2003 was that sort of month.

The Premiership
TOP 6 AT END OF AUGUST 2003

	P	W	D	L	F	A	Pts
Arsenal	4	4	0	0	10	2	12
Manchester United	4	3	0	1	7	2	9
PORTSMOUTH	**4**	**2**	**2**	**0**	**7**	**2**	**8**
Manchester City	4	2	1	1	8	5	7
Chelsea	3	2	1	0	6	4	7
Birmingham City	3	2	1	0	2	0	7

5.

Reality Bites

IN 20 YEARS OF TOUCHLINE hollering and the occasional ref-rant, Harry Redknapp had never been in trouble. So to be charged with abusive and/or insulting words towards the referee at the Wolves match by the Football Association was something of a disciplinary low point in his career and not easily shrugged off by a man who prided himself on his integrity. If the performance of the Molineux referee upset him enough to earn a touchline ban and a fine, then one or two incidents in September would try his patience still further, not least the infamous Pires Dive at Highbury. More on that later.

After such a stunning August, there was time for reflection in the early part of September, international commitments giving Pompey time to catch their breath and, for one or two injury victims, the opportunity to begin the process of recovery. Tim Sherwood, his ear problem improving, played in a friendly at Bashley and Matt Taylor, coming back earlier than expected, turned out for an hour at Watford for the reserves. "Just to get 60 minutes under my belt has given me a lift," he said.

Money remained tight at Fratton Park, even with the Sky cash now available. The chairman admitted he had been forced to spend rather

Matt Taylor took his first steps on the road to recovery with a reserve outing at Watford in early September.

more than he had anticipated since promotion and, while he was happy to go along with Redknapp's expansionist plans, it didn't help him sleep any easier when Pompey were obliged to stump up £10,000 after failing to sell all their 3,000 allocation of tickets for the Wolves trip. Worried Pompey decided, on that basis, to take the full allocation only for the big matches with a reduced number for the others.

How Redknapp would have liked Svetoslav Todorov for those opening matches, even allowing for the fact that Pompey had made a more than satisfactory start to life in the Premiership. His sharpness and economy in front of goal had been every bit as important to Pompey in their sprint to the championship as Merson's accomplished midfield cajolings, Taylor's athletic surges down the left and the imperious defensive authority of Primus and De Zeeuw. Now he was in a Colorado clinic recovering from his cruciate knee ligament operation and the prognosis was good. Physio Gary Sadler was able to report: "It's very positive news, much better than we had hoped. He will stay in America for another two or three months until his review with a consultant because he would not be fit to travel on a plane." Pompey were left with the firm impression that Todorov, providing there was no reaction, could be available at some stage in the New Year, perhaps for the final two months of the season.

Teddy Sheringham's outstanding contribution to Pompey's flying start did nothing to appease angry Tottenham fans, for whom he was still an icon, or for Glenn Hoddle whose decision it was to eject him from White Hart Lane. Sheringham had taken a pay cut to join Pompey to prove a point or two, especially to Hoddle, and smiles did not come much wider than Sheringham's when he was named Barclaycard Player of the Month for August. The

Svetoslav Todorov was recovering from his cruciate knee ligament operation in America whilst Pompey made their excellent start to the season.

REALITY BITES

Teddy Sheringham had put one over his old boss at Spurs, Glenn Hoddle, who had demonstrated by his actions that he thought Teddy was no longer of Premiership standard, by being named Barclaycard Premiership Player of the Month for August.

distinguished former England international had said his piece about Spurs and Hoddle earlier and, instead, praised the part played by the largely unsung De Zeeuw in the heart of Pompey's defence. "I think Arjan has been head and shoulders above everyone this season," he said.

Redknapp, one eye on the Arsenal match, was far from happy when he discovered that Amdy Faye, now free from the attention of his dogs, would be late back from Japan where he would be playing for Senegal just three days before Pompey's biggest fixture so far.

Hardly ideal preparation, but one of the inevitable hazards of signing international players. Kevin Harper, a fringe player the previous year, was still a fringe player this season and, although he was somewhat surprisingly selected for the full Scotland squad by the increasingly desperate Berti Vogts, Pompey were quite happy to let him join Norwich on loan and would not have stood in his way had a permanent deal been suggested. Deon Burton's second spell as a Pompey player had so far not been as successful as his first. It began to look as if he had been a Jim Smith-inspired signing, brought in at the start of the championship season as a stop-gap from Smith's old club Derby but who had now slipped well down the pecking order. Burton's link with Merson at Walsall for a month on loan did not provoke much comment and certainly no criticism.

Saturday September 13

ARSENAL (1) 1 PORTSMOUTH (1) 1

If Aston Villa was the big game of August, the comparatively short journey to North London to Arsenal's hallowed Highbury was the top date for Pompey fans for September. Many of them made the trip more in hope than expectation of a point or three. Damage limitation is normally the theme of the day even for teams with greater Premiership experience but, in what proved to be another season of tremendous achievement by Arsenal, Pompey's performance there on a bright September 13 afternoon deserved more than the draw they finally got after much, much controversy. Had it not been for the intercession of referee Alan Wiley, Pompey might well have inflicted on stuttering, lethargic Arsenal a rare home defeat, one which might - just possibly - have altered the course of the London side's entire season.

Redknapp stuck to a 4-4-2 formation and had Sherwood and Foxe on the bench alongside new loan signing Jason Roberts. Those expecting an avalanche of Arsenal attacks engulfing an overworked Pompey defence were wrong. Faye showed no signs of jet lag as

Pompey seized the initiative with a series of well-planned and exciting attacks. Berger, Quashie and Yakubu all went too close for comfort for Gooners' fans and, in the 26th minute, huge portions of the famous old stadium were hushed when Schemmel sent Stone overlapping down the right and Sheringham met the cross perfectly from three yards. Pompey supporters went berserk, the goal having exceeded their wildest dreams, and no one could say it had come

Steve Stone provided the cross for Sheringham to put Pompey 1-0 up at Highbury - not bad for two supposed Premiership rejects.

Dejan Stefanovic was on the wrong end of some Robert Pires gamesmanship which led to Arsenal's fortunate eqauliser.

against the run of play. For their Arsenal counterparts it was all the harder to bear because the scorer had been Sheringham, a Spurs man through and through despite his spat with the present regime at White Hart Lane.

Arsenal were rattled and, although Berger stepped from the fray with a groin injury, it was going to need something special to get them back into the match. It was then that Mr Wiley, a respected and dedicated official, made his foray into Pompey history. With 35 minutes gone on the old historic timepiece at the Clock End, Robert Pires, who normally needs no help from any referee to perform his wondrous skills, attempted to run past Dejan Stefanovic in the Pompey area only to tumble spectacularly. From some angles it might have looked a penalty but, from the majority of vantage points, it looked more like an outrageous dive by the Frenchman. Even Arsenal fans, appealing hopefully, were surprised when referee Wiley pointed to the spot instead of booking Pires for diving. Disbelief turned to anger and then belated acceptance as Wiley refused to change his mind or his decision. Stefanovic, who had not even waved a leg at the passing Pires, was further humiliated when Wiley booked him for the foul. Admittedly, with the benefit of numerous television replays, it was clear that Pires had been cunning enough to run into Stefanovic rather than the other way around. Highbury was still a cauldron of conflicting emotions as Thierry Henry converted a twice-taken penalty to get Arsenal back into a match in which they had so far been distinctly second best.

The second half was a different game, Arsenal pouring forward in more familiar fashion with the reliable Hislop denying Dennis Bergkamp and Henry and Kolo Toure contriving the miss of the day from close range. But Pompey gave as good as they got, and if only Yakubu's pace had been matched by his finishing qualities. As the beleaguered Wiley blew his final whistle, Pompey's 2,600 travelling army temporarily forgot their grievance to chant: "We are going to win the league" and even rabid Arsenal fans could not, overall, begrudge them their moment of glory. Pompey were still unbeaten. Not that Redknapp could be calmed from the fury and injustice he felt about the Pires penalty, risking more trouble a matter of days after the Wolves brush with authority. Redknapp said: "When I saw what had happened I turned to my chairman and said 'He's booking Pires for diving'. Then I saw he had given a penalty and I was absolutely shocked. No way was it a penalty. It's crazy. Every week I'm seeing penalty decisions which make me laugh. I've watched it on television and it wasn't a penalty. Stefanovic has got his foot firmly to the ground and never lifted it. Pires came in and kicked Dejan's foot and went over the top of him. It was a terrible, terrible decision. It was embarrassing. Pires is a fantastic player and I don't know if he kicked Stefanovic's foot on purpose. The trouble is that decisions like that change games." Redknapp was left to contemplate an injury to Berger which looked at that stage to be long term and a performance which bordered on the miraculous, bearing in mind that Pompey had made no special plans or changed formation to accommodate Arsenal's collective genius. There was special praise for Faye, who had got back from Japan only on Friday lunchtime, and for Yakubu who posed all kinds of problems while still suffering from the after-effects of malaria. Even Arsene Wenger, not noted for praising opponents, was forced to concede that Pompey had made life uncomfortable. "Portsmouth deserved to be 1-0 up. Yakubu gave us big problems at the back. We couldn't handle him or get near him throughout the game. He gave both centre halves, Campbell and Toure, a difficult afternoon."

Arsenal (4-4-2): Lehmann; Lauren, Campbell, Toure, Cole; Parlour, Vieira, Edu (Ljungberg 70), Pires; Bergkamp (Wiltord 74), Henry.
Subs Not Used: Stack, Keown, Aliadiere.
Booked: Campbell, Toure.
Goals: Henry 40 pen.

Portsmouth (4-4-2): Hislop; Schemmel, De Zeeuw, Stefanovic, Zivkovic; Stone, Faye, Quashie, Berger (Smertin 34); Sheringham (Sherwood 90), Yakubu (Roberts 72).

Subs Not Used: Wapenaar, Foxe.
Booked: De Zeeuw, Stefanovic, Schemmel.
Goals: Sheringham 26.

Att: 38,052
Ref: A Wiley (Staffordshire)

STATS:
Shots on target: Arsenal 7 Pompey 2
Shots off target: Arsenal 8 Pompey 6
Corners: Arsenal 8 Pompey 0
Fouls: Arsenal 11 Pompey 23
Offside: Arsenal 0 Pompey 3

Where would Pompey have been without Milan Mandaric? Probably in their old position, vying with Port Vale, Grimsby and Walsall for the right to stay out of the second division. Pompey needed a mega-rich godfather and that's exactly what they got in the Serbian-born American, whose fortune might well have been depleted by the fall of share prices on the Stock Exchange but not nearly as much as by Pompey's seemingly bottomless well of debt and wage demands. Pompey fans had long realised that it paid to keep him onside with an occasional: "Milan, Milan, give us a wave" and there was general

Milan Mandaric was granted the Freedom of the City by Portsmouth City Council in recognition of the key role he had played in the revival of Portsmouth Football Club, something he could reflect on while grazing his goats on Southsea Common.

acknowledgement that Portsmouth City Council had got it right by granting him the Freedom of the City, an ancient ceremonial award which entitled him to graze his goats on Southsea Common and to drive them over Fratton Bridge when he felt they needed a change of scenery. It was a civic recognition of Mandaric's achievements for the club and for helping to restore much-needed pride in the city itself. The club was similarly recognised by the council as Portsmouth, as a whole, still basked in the glory of first division promotion, forever grateful that Mandaric had chosen Pompey to fulfil his ambitions to own and develop a football club.

Mandaric was as committed as ever to building a new stadium at Fratton Park but there had been delays in proposals to replace it with a gleaming new edifice on the same site. One of the problems had been in buying a sliver of land behind the present ground which Pompey needed to acquire in order to develop what they already owned. It was owned by the Sellar Group of developers who, sensing Pompey's desire to make progress with the project, were demanding £2m for the land; Pompey felt it was worth £900,000. The matter went to the High Court for arbitration and Pompey duly triumphed. However, Mandaric's moment of delight was tempered by the knowledge that his courtroom opponents were being advised by David Deacon, son of the former Pompey chairman and the man credited with bringing Mandaric to the club in the first place. Deacon was now working for the Sellar Group after

originally negotiating the deal on behalf of the club when managing director. The chairman remarked: "It was a very good day because justice has prevailed and the obstacle to our progress removed. He was a highly-paid employee of the club and it deeply disappoints me he went to the court and spoke against us in this way. I am happy with the way things have turned out."

Mandaric found his manager was in demand, if rumours were to be believed, after Spurs had dispensed with Glenn Hoddle. All kinds of people, real and imagined, were linked with the vacancy and the strongest of all whispers was that Redknapp would become manager at White Hart Lane and Sheringham would be his coach. This never developed. Spurs never did make an approach for Redknapp and, in any case, Mandaric would have resisted all overtures. The Premiership was always awash with tittle-tattle but there was one doing the rounds which suggested that chairman and manager did not always see eye-to-eye. While admitting there had been some healthy dialogue over the spending of money, Mandaric was at pains to point out that relations were not strained to breaking point and each had a proper respect for the value of the other. In the meantime Redknapp, well settled at Pompey and enjoying his Premiership resurrection, made it clear he was not interested in bailing out Tottenham from their self-created chaos.

Alan Wiley, in a fit of remorse after his decision to award a penalty against Pompey at Arsenal had been cruelly exposed by television as inept, attempted to balance his indiscretion by sending a letter to the Football Association asking them to drop the yellow card against Stefanovic, but the FA made it clear they didn't like to tamper with the disciplinary system by ignoring it. Wiley had the good grace to admit his error after such a public humiliation but the FA were not budging, even after Stefanovic had launched a separate appeal and Wiley had despatched a second letter to his employers. None of which made the Highbury penalty-that-never-was any easier to take for Pompey fans and Wiley, for all his good intentions, might have been better off saying nothing because all he had done was exacerbate an unhappy episode in Premiership history.

Saturday September 20

PORTSMOUTH (0) 1
BLACKBURN ROVERS (2) 2

Blackburn came to the south coast on September 20 to find Pompey unbeaten despite gloomy predictions, and fancying their own chances of breaking the monopoly of the Premiership's big three. Graeme Souness had assembled, from a distance, a team of some quality and it was hard to imagine six months down the line that both sides would be locked in a grim battle for survival. There was no Berger and Sherwood was preferred to Smertin and there was an air of expectancy about Fratton Park as the teams kicked off. But, rather than feed on the atmosphere, it was as if Pompey

Tim Sherwood made a welcome return to the starting line-up against Blackburn.

were drained of the energy which had made them the surprise team of the season so far. Blackburn, without ever looking a class apart, strode into the lead through their Australian full-back Lucas Neill, whose leg-breaking challenge on Liverpool's Jamie Carragher had consumed vast quantities of newsprint in the week leading up to the Pompey clash. It got worse two minutes before half-time when Andy Cole turned past Arjan De Zeeuw to put Blackburn two ahead. Yakubu appeared to be brought down by Brad Friedel and, when Sheringham missed from six yards, it began to look bleak for Pompey.

STAY UP POMPEY!

Arjan De Zeeuw heads home Steve Stone's corner to pull a goal back for Pompey after a rather lacklustre first half had seen the visitors stroll into a two-goal lead.

Redknapp sent on Roberts and told Sheringham to drop deeper and suddenly Pompey began to improve. Almost immediately, De Zeeuw headed in Stone's corner and then shot over from eight yards. Brett Emerton hit the Pompey bar but Blackburn held on, Paul Durkin posing more questions about the standard of refereeing in the Premiership by not using all the available stoppage time as Blackburn did what they could to waste it. Stadium manager Mick Coleman was obliged to eject some fans from the Ty Europe Stand for refusing to sit down, as required by Premiership legislation, so it was an afternoon to forget for most Pompey fans who, upon digesting the result, would have realised that in the top flight there are some nasty twists and turns. Ever-honest De Zeeuw rejected the traditional bottle of champagne from sponsors who had named him man of the match because he did not feel he had deserved it, while Redknapp refused to get down-hearted. "I thought we played fantastically well in the second half but paid for starting slowly. We've got a smashing spirit and we had a go at them after the break. I told the players not to feel sorry for themselves but to have a go at Blackburn - and they did. I think we missed Berger but I don't know if I was watching the same game as everyone else, but even without him I thought we murdered them in the second half." Redknapp was happy enough with nine points from six opening matches, even if some fans were not. "I don't know what some people are expecting from us. Anyone would think we had our sights set on the Champions' League," said the Pompey manager who, in issuing a note of caution to those carried away by Pompey's excellent beginning, reminded them that Premiership safety was the only aim. "We are Portsmouth and we don't want anyone thinking differently. Blackburn are a top six side and I thought we had 85 per cent of the play and were unlucky not to win."

Portsmouth (4-4-2): Hislop; Schemmel, De Zeeuw, Stefanovic, Zivkovic; Stone, Sherwood (Roberts 55), Faye, Quashie (Pericard 84); Sheringham, Yakubu.
Subs Not Used: Wapenaar, Foxe, Smertin.
Booked: Quashie, Schemmel.
Goals: De Zeeuw 57.

Blackburn (4-4-2): Friedel; Neill (Johansson 90), Babbel, Amoruso, Gresko; Emerton, Ferguson, Tugay (Baggio 64), Thompson; Jansen, (Yorke 64), Cole.
Subs Not Used: Kelly, Grabbi.
Booked: Gresko, Thompson, Cole.
Goals: Neill 35, Cole 43.

Att: 20,024
Ref: P Durkin (Dorset).

STATS:
Shots on target: Pompey 3 Blackburn 4
Shots off target: Pompey 3 Blackburn 3
Corners: Pompey 7 Blackburn 6
Fouls: Pompey 17 Blackburn 19
Offside: Pompey 2 Blackburn 2

Fratton Park's musical chairs continued with Carl Robinson heading for Rotherham on yet another loan. Later in the month Gary O'Neil joined Burton and Merson for a few weeks at Walsall in preference to Tony Pulis's Stoke and the luckless Burchill was sent back by Wigan whose manager Paul Jewell claimed he was not fit enough. There was news also that yesterday's man Graham Rix was a contender for the managerial vacancy at Reading, a job he did not get, and it was another six months before Rix finally returned to management at Oxford in the turmoil surrounding Ian Atkins' bizarre departure on the threshold of third division promotion. Eddie Howe began a spot of light training 13 months after his home debut on the opening day of the season had ended five minutes after it had started. His knee injury had required operations and, even in September, it was evident there was a long road ahead of him in attempting to regain full fitness.

Tuesday September 23

PORTSMOUTH (3) 5
NORTHAMPTON TOWN (0) 2
(Carling Cup 2nd Round)

After the nervous exhaustion engendered by life in the Premiership, it was almost a relief to be playing lower division opposition in the second round of the Carling Cup. Third division Northampton even came down on the back of an injury crisis which deprived them of half a dozen first-choice players so Pompey were firm favourites to progress. It had not been a competition in which Pompey had historically excelled and a win over Northampton would take them into the third round for the first time in nine years. Redknapp showed his feelings for the cup by making seven changes from the side beaten by Blackburn, not as a punishment but to rest his best players and to try out other members of the squad. The most interesting was the first competitive chance for Harald Wapenaar against a background of continuing speculation about Hislop's groin problem. Pavel Srnicek, keeper number three, advanced to the subs bench. The biggest cheer from a sparse crowd was reserved for Matt Taylor, who defied medical opinion to make his first appearance of the season. A month earlier, real doubts were being expressed about his capacity to play again. It was always going to be Pompey's night when already-weakened Northampton had their defender Paul Reid sent off, somewhat harshly, for hauling down Roberts 30 yards out.

Referee David Crick added to Pompey's catalogue of strange decisions already accumulated for and against them by saying Roberts had been denied a scoring opportunity. This, after just ten minutes, destroyed the match as a potential spectacle. Sherwood scored Pompey's first three minutes later and Roberts scored his first goal in eleven months after 17 minutes. Northampton goalkeeper Lee Harper made some top class saves and an offside flag prevented Sheringham claiming a goal of the season after Smertin and Schemmel had opened the defence. Another loud cheer greeted Taylor's typical left-foot drive for the third in the 41st minute from outside the area and a rout looked possible when, on the hour, Roberts volleyed in his second. Another offside decision saved Northampton soon afterwards and Harper made a magnificent save to turn a Sheringham effort against the bar. It was no exaggeration to say that Pompey, looking every inch a Premiership side, might have been ten ahead by the time Lawrie Dudfield, whose pace had troubled Pompey all evening, was brought down in the area by Wapenaar. Bearing in mind what had happened to Reid, Wapenaar was lucky to escape with a yellow card. The Dutch keeper then made an excellent save from Chris Hargreaves' spot-kick, only for Crick to order it to be retaken because he had moved. This time Hargreaves made no mistake. It was a minor setback and Sherwood quickly restored Pompey's four-goal advantage, finishing off a move of crisp, one-touch passing. In stoppage time, a cross from the left by Chris Carruthers was deflected by Linvoy Primus over Wapenaar and Dudfield scored from a yard. The final 5-2 scoreline flattered Northampton but the match had served its purpose for Redknapp, who was most impressed by the way Taylor, though obviously ring-rusty, had come through the full 90

Jason Roberts volleys home his second goal of the night against Northampton Town. These were his first goals for 11 months.

minutes rather than the intended hour. Harry enthused: "Matt's a fantastic player and it's great to have him back. He works so hard on the pitch and in training because that is the type of player he is. It would be nice to have a good cup run and it is a sad state of affairs to think this is as far as we have been in nine years. Northampton were unlucky to have a player sent off and it changed the game. Technically, the defender was the last man so he had to go but it was unfortunate for the lad." Redknapp departed, toying with the idea of recalling Taylor to his Premiership squad for the impending trip to Birmingham with Berger still not fit. The opposition may not have been much, but it was a good night for Pompey.

STAY UP POMPEY!

**The biggest cheer of the night was reserved
for the return of Matt Taylor.**

Portsmouth (4-4-2): Wapenaar; Schemmel
(Stone 64), Primus, Foxe, Taylor;
O'Neil, Sherwood, Smertin, Pericard;
Sheringham, Roberts.
Subs Not Used: Srnicek, De Zeeuw, Stefanovic,
Yakubu.
Goals: Sherwood 13, 83, Roberts 17, 60,
Taylor 41.

Northampton (4-4-2): Harper; Chambers,
Willmott (Sampson 65), Reid,
Carruthers; Youngs, Trollope, Harsley (Rickers
74), Hargreaves; Richards
(Burgess 65), Dudfield.
Subs Not Used: Thompson, Asamoah.
Sent Off: Reid (10).
Booked: Chambers.
Goals: Hargreaves 77, Dudfield 90.

Att: 11,130
Ref: D Crick (Surrey).

STATS:
Shots on target: Pompey 10 Northampton 4
Shots off target: Pompey 7 Northampton 1
Corners: Pompey 4 Northampton 2
Fouls: Pompey 7 Northampton 8
Offside: Pompey 6 Northampton 1

For Jason Roberts it was a relief
simply to get his name on a score-
sheet again, something he didn't
often do for West Bromwich, whose
fans made it abundantly clear they
had no time for him. Rather more,
in fact, they detested him - if his

postbag was a representative sample of Baggie fury. Roberts found himself inundated by hate mail from West Bromwich, every letter advising him not to return to the Hawthorns when his loan spell ended. This at least gave him something to think about over four months of his initial loan period, but left Pompey fans wondering how deep had been his dispute with West Bromwich manager Gary Megson. Only later did Megson reveal that when Roberts handed in a written transfer request he had spelt his own name wrongly.

Saturday September 27

BIRMINGHAM CITY (1) 2
PORTSMOUTH (0) 0

Redknapp was as good as his word when Pompey travelled to St Andrews to take on Birmingham. Taylor, who was meeting boot manufacturers Umbro to find a way of protecting his vulnerable heel, got his first Premiership start with Smertin. Quashie and Sherwood were left out and Hislop regained his place at Wapenaar's expense. For the first 20 minutes, Pompey coped comfortably enough but then a tiny error, Faye failing to pick up his man at a free kick, allowed Stephen Clemence to head in a free kick from Stan Lazaridis from two yards. It was enough to change the match as Birmingham got on top, Dugarry having a header cleared from the line by Stone, but the turning point came when Yakubu turned in a Taylor pass only to be ruled offside. Television replays suggested Yakubu had been onside so that, yet again,

Smertin - came in for his first Premiership start at Birmingham.

Pompey had been victims of an incorrect refereeing decision. Five minutes after the break, Lazaridis reacted quickest to Dugarry's pass to beat the onrushing Hislop. Pompey still refused to accept defeat and Smertin forced an outstanding save from Maik Taylor while Sheringham hit the woodwork. Matt Taylor was replaced by Roberts after suffering a reaction from several hefty challenges from the combative Robbie Savage. When Pompey did mount a series of attacks they met in Kenny Cunningham and Matthew Upson, both former Redknapp targets, a formidable barrier and Birmingham held on to win 2-0. Redknapp thought the Yakubu offside 'goal' and Sheringham hitting a post were turning points because there was not, he believed, much between the sides otherwise. He added: "We're going to get back-to-back defeats this season, for sure. It will happen to Birmingham. Steve Bruce has done an excellent job and Birmingham have established themselves as a decent Premiership side. The clubs cannot be compared because Birmingham have spent a lot more money than Pompey can afford."

Birmingham (4-4-2): Taylor; Johnson, Cunningham, Upson, Clapham; Dunn, Savage, Clemence, Lazaridis (Tebily 84); Dugarry (Cisse 71), Forssell (Figueroa 87).
Subs Not Used: Bennett, Morrison.
Booked: Cisse.
Goals: Clemence 21, Lazaridis 50.

Portsmouth (4-4-2): Hislop; Schemmel, De Zeeuw, Stefanovic, Zivkovic; Stone, Smertin, Faye (Sherwood 65), Taylor (Roberts 55); Sheringham, Yakubu.
Subs Not Used: Wapenaar, Foxe, Primus.
Booked: Faye, Sheringham, Sherwood.
Att: 29,057
Ref: S Bennett (Kent).

STATS:
Shots on target: Birmingham 5 Pompey 4
Shots off target: Birmingham 5 Pompey 7
Corners: Birmingham 4 Pompey 4
Fouls: Birmingham 14 Pompey 16
Offside: Birmingham 0 Pompey 6

While the Pompey manager had reason to feel that his team perhaps deserved a share of the points, Birmingham had given them a lesson in how to finish, the ruthlessness of which was a major difference between the division in which Pompey were now competing and the division they had just left. It was now four games without a win, ominously, and after the visit of Charlton - a match Pompey would be expected to win - the following three fixtures took in Liverpool, Newcastle and Manchester United. Welcome to the big time.

The Premiership
TOP 10 AT END OF SEPTEMBER 2003

	P	W	D	L	F	A	Pts
Arsenal	7	5	2	0	14	5	17
Chelsea	6	5	1	0	16	6	16
Manchester United	7	5	1	1	13	3	16
Birmingham City	6	4	2	0	8	2	14
Manchester City	7	3	3	1	14	8	12
Southampton	7	3	3	1	8	4	12
Fulham	6	3	2	1	13	9	11
Liverpool	7	3	2	2	11	7	11
PORTSMOUTH	7	2	3	2	9	7	9
Everton	7	2	2	3	12	11	8

6.

Welcome to the Big Time

ONE PHRASE WHICH IRRITATED Harry Redknapp more than being described as a 'wheeler-dealer', as he often was in the Tabloid Press, was 'bargain basement' when applied to the team he had assembled at Fratton Park. Redknapp felt it implied that his was a cheap-jack outfit made up of ageing players on their last legs or unknown foreigners who cost him nothing. It was true that, by the standards of his Premiership competitors, Pompey's squad had been put together less expensively than most but Redknapp and his chairman were not always happy with the club's public portrayal, so it was a question of putting the record straight when Mandaric revealed that Pompey's wage bill had soared to £17million (it was to go even higher later) and was rising by the day with every new arrival. Mandaric pointed out that this was some £7m more than Wolves and, while he was intent on being cautious with his money, £6m had been spent necessarily on transfer and agent fees in the wake of the dozen signings made since the end of the previous season. High wages were one of the reasons why Redknapp had not pursued his interest in Paolo Di Canio during the close season, something he now regretted, but at the time when the great man was

available he felt Sheringham and Di Canio might not be compatible. On such whims are whole seasons decided and so far Sheringham was doing the business. Sometimes it is an expensive job just keeping players already on the staff but Pompey did not mind reaching for the cheque book to ensure Matt Taylor signed a four-year contract. Whatever it cost was money well spent in Taylor's case, even if he was still some way off full fitness and being the marauding wing-back of the previous year.

Portsmouth's links with the Royal Navy have always been strong, even if it had been the army which had supplied in recent years Guy Whittingham and Lee Bradbury. Jimmy Scoular and Len Phillips had come to Pompey from the Navy to play a full part in a golden era and it is not often remembered that Chris Kamara was bought out of the senior service by Pompey as a 16-year old, once he had come to their attention playing against one of the club's junior sides. But, as a healthy diversion from Premiership stresses early in October, the present staff and players were given a tour of the aircraft carrier Ark Royal in the naval base. The Russian Alexei Smertin feared he might be classified as a security risk (as his team-mates were not

STAY UP POMPEY!

The Ark Royal sails into Portsmouth harbour - Pompey's links with the Royal Navy have always been strong. The squad were given a tour of the aircraft carrier early in October.

slow to remind him) but it was all good-natured stuff and appreciated by the club who had invited the crew to be their guests for the Northampton match. Gestures don't come much more magnanimous than that, incidentally. Six months earlier in the Iraq war, it was apparent that there were many Pompey fans aboard Gulf-bound ships and the club had sent videos of their march to the first division title to help maintain morale, as Mandaric observed. "When we were fighting for the championship, some Pompey fans were defending their country. It puts things in perspective and makes us all the more determined to perform well for them."

Saturday October 4

PORTSMOUTH (1) 1
CHARLTON ATHLETIC (0) 2

Charlton were the next visitors to Fratton Park on October 4 and with them, of course, came Di Canio, though only, mysteriously, as a substitute. To survive and prosper in the Premiership, this was the sort of match Pompey would be expected to win and, with Berger fit to return in place of Taylor, there was an air of optimism at Fratton Park, albeit tinged with nervousness as Pompey's recent results had not been good. Charlton had just beaten Liverpool 3-2, which showed their ability - or Liverpool's lack of it depending on your point of view - and what proved to be the biggest cheer of the afternoon came before the start when Linvoy Primus was presented with the Nationwide PFA Player of the Year award for the season just gone. For an hour, maybe more, Pompey blitzed the Charlton goal with some brilliant football. Dean Kiely made a great save from Sheringham, Berger shot over and Yakubu also pressed the goalkeeper into meaningful action, but even the loss of Smertin with a knee injury after 26 minutes failed to destroy the momentum. A goal had to come and it did after 34 minutes, Sheringham using his stealth to glance home a Sherwood corner. It was Sheringham's sixth (out of Pompey's total of ten) and

Linvoy Primus provided the biggest cheers of what was to prove a disappointing afternoon for Pompey when he was named Nationwide PFA Player of the Year for the previous season.

STAY UP POMPEY!

The players celebrate Sheringham's sixth goal of the season.

Young had caused chaos in the Pompey defence. All of a sudden there was only one team in it, and it wasn't Pompey. The underworked Hislop saved Kevin Lisbie's header from six yards, Fortune headed over and only an interruption caused by plastic bottles being thrown on to the pitch, aimed at a linesman, halted Charlton's late and unexpected charge. There was a minute left when Shaun Bartlett headed in Di Canio's corner and, from being in total control, Pompey were being left to consider the consequences of their third successive league defeat.

Portsmouth (4-4-2): Hislop; Schemmel, De Zeeuw, Stefanovic, Zivkovic; Stone, Faye, Smertin (Sherwood 26), Berger (Taylor 85); Sheringham, Yakubu (Roberts 76).
Subs Not Used: Wapenaar, Foxe.
Booked: De Zeeuw, Sheringham, Sherwood.
Goals: Sheringham 34.

Charlton (4-4-2): Kiely; Young, Perry, Fish (Fortune 64), Powell; Stuart, Holland, Parker, Jensen (Di Canio 64); Lisbie, Bartlett.
Subs Not Used: Royce, Kishishev, Johansson.
Booked: Perry, Bartlett.
Goals: Fortune 77, Bartlett 90.

Att: 20,106
Ref: G Poll (Hertfordshire).

STATS:
Shots on target: Pompey 4 Charlton 6
Shots off target: Pompey 10 Charlton 5
Corners: Pompey 6 Charlton 9
Fouls: Pompey 3 Charlton 14
Offside: Pompey 2 Charlton 3

there looked to be more to come in a one-sided match. Kiely saved again from Sheringham, Berger headed over and then came the moment Redknapp must have dreaded: Di Canio began warming up and, with three quarters of the match gone, Alan Curbishley sent him on and played with three strikers. No game is safe at 1-0 and in the Premiership no game is ever safe with so many quality strikers around. So it proved. With 13 minutes remaining of what had been a Pompey-dominated game, Charlton equalised when another substitute, Jonathan Fortune, scrambled the ball in after a long throw from Luke

Redknapp surveyed the damage before declaring: "Di Canio is an absolute genius. I have never seen a better player in my life. He is a fantastic talent with incredible ability and is a true master of football

WELCOME TO THE BIG TIME

Agony for Pompey as Shaun Bartlett heads in Paolo Di Canio's corner. "Di Canio is an absolute genius," said Redknapp, who had long been an admirer of the quixotic Italian.

because he can score and make goals." Tributes aside, what perplexed Redknapp was the way his team had let slip a match they had commanded from the start. "I really don't know how we lost the game. We took them apart for 60 minutes but you always need a second goal when you are on top and we didn't get it. To concede a goal from a throw-in was scandalous. The centre half has hardly scored in his life." Harry was not far wrong. It was Fortune's second goal and Curbishley conceded that his team had been lucky to go home with the three points. "Portsmouth out-played, out-ran and out-fought us for 60 minutes. We were hanging on. They were all over us and we were getting battered." Matt Taylor

gave a hint as to what Redknapp had said immediately post-match. "I don't want to repeat what was said in the dressing room but I don't think Harry was very happy."

There were two precious weeks to recover from this setback and to analyse why the season had suddenly turned so sour after such a promising start. It was not as though Pompey were playing badly, or that the opposition was in any way superior, but results were all that mattered and there was no denying that, from the pinnacle in late August, Pompey were on the slide. It didn't help when Wapenaar needed ten stitches in a jaw wound after colliding with Yakubu. As a measure of Pompey's progress in terms of player-quality, there were also international calls to consider: Taylor was called into England's under-21 squad and Smertin, Stefanovic and Zivkovic were all required by their countries, all of which was a worry to the management because there was always the danger of the players concerned coming home with injuries. Numbers were boosted by the return of Burton from an abortive month at Walsall where he failed to impress and there was an FA probe into the Charlton bottle-throwing incident from which no charges emanated, although it was a sharp reminder that the hooligan problem could never be completely subdued nor underestimated, as the visit of Saints was later to prove.

Liverpool were due at Fratton Park in what was going to be something of a tester for Pompey. Their recent run had been poor and in past years the prospect of Liverpool up next would have sent a shiver of apprehension through every Pompey spine. At least Redknapp would be on the bench for that one, as opposed to the Carling Cup tie at Nottingham Forest and the trip to Manchester United in the league as the FA had decided to punish him for his uncharacteristically ill-judged remarks about referee Andy D'Urso at Molineux via the fourth official. A two-match ban was added to a fine of £3,000 but it was a sad way to sully a previously unblemished disciplinary record and not like Redknapp at all.

Much as Fratton Park was cherished by fans for sentimental reasons, it was not much help when it came to raising money. Even second division clubs now had hospi-

tality boxes and, while the Sky TV money was crucial, so too was the cash provided from the personal fortune of the chairman. Playing in the Premiership represented a big opportunity to make money on a grand scale. Even moderate-sized clubs in the Premiership were reporting turnovers of between £40m and £50m and Pompey showed they recognised the potential by appointing Andy Wilding, 48, as financial controller in a bid to boost their earnings from all sources. Mandaric, acutely aware of the club's dependence on him, said: "With all the great things happening on the field, we want to maximise turnover and profits off it. Andy, working alongside Peter Storrie and myself, is the perfect man to ensure this happens."

The former Coventry and Hereford goalkeeper David Icke, later a television sports presenter and pundit, was better known, perhaps, for his turquoise shellsuits, his books on politicians and royalty turning into giant lizards and for his theories on world domination conspiracies. Icke was now living in Ryde, Isle of Wight and there was news that his 10-year-old son, Jamie, had been signed by Pompey after being spotted as a promising talent in coaching sessions. The progress of young Jamie was being monitored. Meanwhile, Steve Stone needed to have his spine clicked back into place after becoming the latest player to collide with the Yak and Jamie Vincent headed a growing list of Pompey players sent out on loan, in his case to Walsall. Burton disappeared again to Swindon, Shaun Cooper to Leyton

WELCOME TO THE BIG TIME

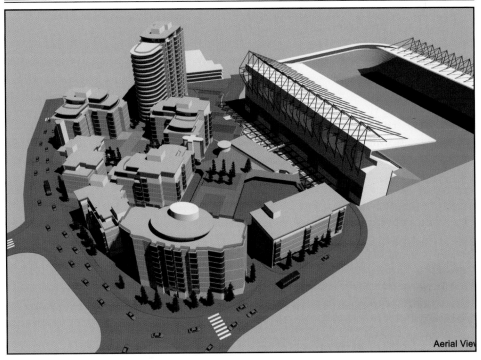

Aerial View

**An aerial view of the design of the proposed
new stadium with Pompey Village.**

Orient and Carl Robinson to Rotherham. Coming back in the other direction from Luton was Courtney Pitt, another loan apparently unsuccessful in finding him a new permanent home.

Billy Barr is the chairman of Ayr United and as such knows what it takes to make a club successful. He is also owner of Barr Construction Limited who have specialised in building sports stadia. His company created the Walkers Stadium at Leicester, Southampton's St Mary's and the Fitness First at Bournemouth, among others. At a press conference at Fratton Park on October 17, Mandaric, Peter Storrie and representatives of Barr's gathered to discuss what could be done for Pompey in the way of a new sta-

dium. The idea was to transform the present 20,200-seater into a 35,000-capacity arena (fractionally bigger than Saints', of course). The project was to begin in April 2004 and involved a step-by-step development of the existing site over four phases. The initial phase was to see the industrial sites behind the North Stand demolished to allow a new stand to rise in its place, beginning in six months. Work was to continue throughout 2004-05 without affecting the capacity of the existing stadium. Two new corner stands in the north west and north east of the ground were to be built while the plan was for Milton Lane to be re-aligned to the north of these new stands. This was to be completed by March 2005 and the new North Stand would include corporate boxes for 414 people and executive lounges for a further 350. The big talking point was the pitch itself, which was being turned round 90 degrees, allowing the West Stand, sponsored by Ty, to be extended. More hospitality lounges, directors' accommodation and players' dressing rooms were to be sited there and the old South Stand reduced in capacity while the new East Stand was being constructed. The completion of phase two would give a capacity of 28,000 and the further two, optional, phases would take it up to a St Mary's-beating 35,000 by adding stands to the corners. This was all wonderful news, not least to Mandaric who said: "We are moving nearer to the time when this fine city and its magnificent supporters will be Premier League in every sense." At this stage, there was no mention of who was going to pay for it all but there were also plans afoot to develop land near Fratton Park to create Pompey Village, so that the whole project was going to be self-financing to some extent. First, detailed plans had to be drawn up and presented to the city council for their consultation and consideration and that was going to take time and patience. But it was a start, much needed in the circumstances and for those fans sceptical about it ever becoming a reality, Mandaric had so far delivered on all his promises.

Saturday October 18

PORTSMOUTH (1) 1
LIVERPOOL (0) 0

Patrik Berger was once a big favourite at Anfield, his dark locks flowing as he ran with pace, vigour and purpose on Liverpool's behalf for half a dozen years and, on his day, his left foot was as potent as any in the English top flight. But injuries and a disaffection with the Houllier regime led to a free transfer in the summer of 2003 and Redknapp moved swiftly to bring him to the south coast just as he pondered a move to Germany. The fear was that Berger's best days were behind him, that Redknapp had bought an injury-prone big name who had joined Pompey for one last major payday. But Harry knew his man, sensed that Berger had a bit to prove and still had plenty of high quality football in him. There was revenge in the air, then, on October 18 when Liverpool came to Fratton Park as there was no doubting that the Czech star nursed a grievance. Within 190 seconds he had gained the ultimate in satisfaction, scoring what proved to be the only goal to raise questions about Houllier's decision to release him and send 3,000 Scousers home dejected, deflated and disbelieving that one of their rejects could return to haunt them so soon. Liverpool were without the injured Michael Owen, admittedly, and it might have been different had Emile Heskey, getting away from Arjan De Zeeuw, not shot against the post inside the first minute. But Sheringham and Schemmel combined down the right and Berger turned the ball in at the near post. Liverpool were stunned as the old Fratton End burst into an ecstatic roar. The test of a great side is the ability to retaliate but this Liverpool team simply did not have it in them to do so. No wonder Liverpool stars of old were quick to rush into print their condemnation of the team now wearing the famous red shirts. Harry Kewell had a free kick cleared from the line but it was Pompey who went closest to scoring again, Dudek making some important saves while Igor Biscan headed a Schemmel free kick against his own bar and Yakubu hit the underside from 30 yards. There was time in those anxious last minutes for Florent Sinama-Pongolle to slip clear but he shot wide with just Hislop to beat, though it would have been a gigantic injustice had Liverpool equalised; they had not deserved to.

It took just three minutes for Patrik Berger to make Liverpool, and Gerard Houllier, regret their decision to sideline him at Anfield.

Portsmouth (4-4-2): Hislop; Schemmel, De Zeeuw, Stefanovic (Foxe 35), Zivkovic; Stone, Faye, Quashie (Sherwood 90), Berger; Sheringham, Yakubu.
Subs Not Used: Wapenaar, Taylor, Roberts.
Booked: Berger, Faye.
Goals: Berger 4.

Liverpool (4-4-2): Dudek; Finnan, Henchoz, Hyypia, Riise; Diouf (Sinama-Pongolle 64), Gerrard, Biscan, Smicer (Le Tallec 60); Heskey, Kewell.
Subs Not Used: Kirkland, Traore, Welsh.
Booked: Diouf, Biscan.

Att: 20,123
Ref: S Dunn (Gloucestershire).

STATS:
Shots on target: Pompey 2 Liverpool 4
Shots off target: Pompey 6 Liverpool 7
Corners: Pompey 5 Liverpool 3
Fouls: Pompey 21 Liverpool 11
Offside: Pompey 10 Liverpool 3

There was a huge outpouring of relief at the final whistle as Pompey fans celebrated an unlikely victory, one they had certainly not counted on when the fixtures were published. For Mandaric, it was his biggest single triumph yet as chairman. "The draw at Arsenal was good but I'm ranking this as number one. It is great for Patrik because he is a top player and a top man. I just hope I have got enough pills for my blood pressure. Those last ten minutes were the longest of my life." Berger is not a man of many public words. He steadfastly refuses to do interviews on the basis that he was once misquoted by a journalist in the Czech Republic, so his recollection of the match will go for ever unrecorded. Redknapp was less reticent, thank goodness, praising substitute Foxe, Yakubu for his unrewarded effort and the team generally for putting behind them so emphatically the disappointment of losing all the points to Charlton. "I was pleased for Patrik. He's been in good form since he has been here and he seems to be enjoying his football again. He hardly played at all last season so the important thing for him was to stay injury-free and get games under his belt. It was a good day for him and I'm sure he enjoyed scoring against his old club. I can't spend millions so I have to take a few chances on players like him. I would rather take people like him, Teddy and Steve Stone over untried footballers. Stoney never stopped running. The physio wanted him to come off after an hour in case he aggravated his training injury but he was playing too well."

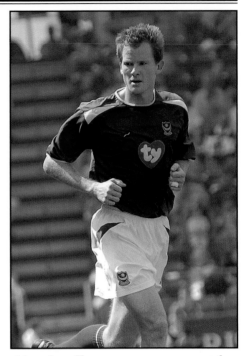

Hayden Foxe came on as substitute for Stefanovic in the first half against Liverpool and did a magnificent job.

The only dampener on what was seen as something of a landmark victory for Pompey, in their quest to be considered a Premiership side on merit, was another coin-throwing incident. Once more the FA were asked to investigate and once more they decided there was no case to answer. Stadium manager Mick Coleman had a more difficult job than many of his contemporaries because new stadia have seats well removed from the playing area, as opposed to Fratton Park where such acts as coin-throwing are harder to deter and detect and are more likely to hit their target. Coleman, perhaps more than most, must have welcomed news of a new Fratton Park.

WELCOME TO THE BIG TIME

Saturday October 25

NEWCASTLE UNITED (2) 3
PORTSMOUTH (0) 0

And so to Newcastle on October 25. Up to this stage of the season, Pompey had always given a good account of themselves, even in defeat. After the Liverpool win, spirits were high and self-belief restored following a run of disappointing results, but Newcastle are a formidable side on their own pitch and for the first time Pompey failed to perform. They were outfought and overwhelmed and lucky to come away from St James' Park with a 3-0 defeat. The determination, the will to survive and the sheer energy of the display against Liverpool were all sadly missing, left behind on the south coast as Newcastle swept Redknapp's team aside with contemptuous efficiency. From the moment Hislop made a great save with his foot to keep out Shola Ameobi after 28 seconds, Pompey were on the defensive and it needed all the great experience of the likes of ex-Newcastle keeper Hislop and De Zeeuw to prevent a truly major setback. Alan Shearer had a strong penalty appeal rejected when Zivkovic appeared to foul him and Ameobi headed over the bar with the goal at his mercy. The 3,000 travelling fans, who had made a journey the length of England, were strangely subdued as it became a question of when, not if, Newcastle would score. It had to happen and it did after 17 minutes. Ameobi outpaced Schemmel and crossed for Lee Bowyer and

Laurent Robert to combine in a move which saw Gary Speed fire low past Hislop. Worse followed. Paul Durkin, having turned down the earlier, more obvious spot-kick appeal, gave one far less clear-cut. Bowyer's drive struck the hand of the grounded Stefanovic and Durkin decided there was a deliberate handball. Shearer, not at all put off by those Pompey fans who remembered his Saints ancestry, made no mistake in converting his 155th Newcastle goal. Pompey retaliated only too briefly when Shay Given saved from Yakubu and then, superbly, from Sheringham but the rally did not last long or produce any impact. The game was

Only the expertise of Pompey's former Newcastle goalkeeper Shaka Hislop kept the score down at St James' Park.

STAY UP POMPEY!

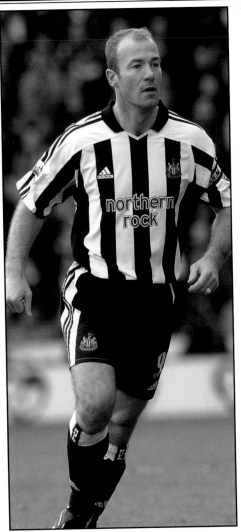

Pompey fans were very aware of the Saints' ancestry of Newcastle's Alan Shearer as he scored Newcastle's second.

been all season. It's the first time anyone has turned us over. The best team by far won. We looked too open, were run off our feet in midfield and didn't hold the ball up front. I'm afraid there was a gulf in class but Newcastle are a top-five side. When the referee didn't give the first penalty that Shearer was calling for I feared he might give the next one. The first one looked a penalty but the one he gave looked harsh."

Newcastle (4-4-2): Given; Hughes, O'Brien, Bramble, Bernard; Bowyer (Ambrose 79), Jenas, Speed, Robert (Viana 80); Shearer, Ameobi (Lua-Lua 80).
Subs Not Used: Harper, Caldwell.
Goals: Speed 17, Shearer 28 pen, Ameobi 61.

Portsmouth (4-4-2): Hislop; Schemmel (Taylor 51), De Zeeuw, Stefanovic, Zivkovic (Foxe 72); Stone, Quashie, Faye (Sherwood 76), Berger; Sheringham, Yakubu.
Subs Not Used: Wapenaar, Roberts.
Booked: Sheringham.

Att: 52,161
Ref: P Durkin (Dorset).

STATS:
Shots on target: Newcastle 5 Pompey 2
Shots off target: Newcastle 3 Pompey 6
Corners: Newcastle 6 Pompey 6
Fouls: Newcastle 11 Pompey 15
Offside: Newcastle 2 Pompey 3

all over in the 61st minute when Ameobi beat De Zeeuw in the air to reach Speed's cross and his looping header beat Hislop and went in off the underside of the bar. The rest was a sorry formality, as Redknapp had no option but to admit afterwards. "It was the poorest we have

Homegrown Gary O'Neil was finding it difficult to break into the Pompey team at this juncture of the season. There was a long queue of more celebrated players ahead of him for a place in midfield, although he had packed away a fair bit of experience of his own considering he was still only 20 and had been in and around the Pompey team since he was 16. It was considered best for him to be sent out on loan and a further month was arranged for him at Walsall. Better to be playing at that level than in Pompey's reserves, but there was a clause in the temporary transfer which enabled him to be recalled to Fratton Park at a moment's notice. Little did anyone realise he would be back within days at Nottingham Forest in the third round of the Carling Cup. Meanwhile, Lewis Buxton, another to come through the youth system, was also allowed to go out on loan, this time for the whole season to Bournemouth where he had spent part of the previous year. Buxton had done well in his debut season for Pompey, looking calm and assured, but Redknapp decided he needed more battle-hardened campaigners at the back and the Isle of Wight-born defender made only one brief substitute appearance in the promotion year. Once more he was well down the pecking order so the move to Bournemouth suited all concerned.

O'Neil's second month at Walsall had barely begun when he was involved in a mini-drama as Pompey surprisingly recalled him for the Forest match. O'Neil had trained with Walsall on Monday and Tuesday and had been given the Wednesday off by their manager Colin Lee. Turning off his mobile, O'Neil headed for the golf course (so it was thought), oblivious to the fact that Pompey needed him to go that day to Nottingham. Only after a series of increasingly frantic calls did O'Neil respond, telling chief executive Storrie that he had been asleep at the family home in Bromley and had not been on the golf course at all. O'Neil promptly

drove up from South London to reacquaint himself with the Pompey players and then spent most of the evening on the bench. At least O'Neil's car worked, which was more than could be said for the top of the range £45,000 Porsche 911 Carrera owned by Matt Taylor. The car flipped as Taylor made his way

Gary O'Neil made a surprise re-appearance in the Pompey first team for the Carling Cup tie with Nottingham Forest.

to the Solent Hotel at Whiteley to meet his team-mates at the start of the journey to Nottingham. Taylor was lucky to get out with little more than a cut wrist and a severe shaking but it did not stop him turning in a typically wholehearted performance later in the day at the City Ground. Redknapp, who had himself once been severely injured in a coach crash in Milan, said: "Matt had a bad day. He had a car accident and how he got out of it alive, I don't know. But you would never have known it by the way he played. He showed great attitude." The memory of the car crash which killed Aaron Flahavan only a couple of years earlier was still vivid in the minds of many Pompey fans, including Redknapp, who visited the site of Flahavan's death near Bournemouth only hours after it had happened in the early hours of a summer Saturday morning. The shock and disbelief were not easily forgotten.

Wednesday October 29

NOTTINGHAM FOREST (1) 2
PORTSMOUTH (0) 4
(Carling Cup 3rd Round)
After Extra Time; 90 mins 2-2

The match itself was won 4-2 by Pompey after extra-time and it was hard to gauge just how seriously the Pompey manager was taking the competition. This was the third round but Redknapp still made five changes from the team beaten at Newcastle with Wapenaar returning in goal and, in a 3-5-2 formation which had served Pompey so well the previous sea-

son, Taylor got a chance at wing-back and Jason Roberts started up front. Berger, the Yak and the much-travelled O'Neil were among the subs. It did not work at first. For 45 minutes Pompey got nowhere, failed to muster a shot and trailed by a goal scored after

Matt Taylor had a frightening experience when his Porsche 911 Carrera flipped on the day of the Carling Cup game at Forest - but he still put in his usual wholehearted performance.

WELCOME TO THE BIG TIME

42 minutes by Eugene Bopp from eight yards. Redknapp switched back to a more conventional 4-4-2 formation after the break and brought on Berger and Yakubu in place of Quashie and Stefanovic. Within 12 minutes of the restart, Berger was involved in a move with Sheringham and Schemmel which ended in Forest's veteran defender Des Walker turning the ball into his own net under pressure from former Forest player Steve Stone. Then, in the 64th minute, Berger found Yakubu on the edge of the box where he took one touch before firing left-footed just under the bar and beyond the reach of goalkeeper Darren Ward. First Division Forest, who had fallen on hard times since the glory days of Clough and Taylor, equalised three minutes later when Bopp got his second, turning in a cross from Marlon Harewood which had taken a deflection off De Zeeuw. Pompey did not want extra-time but that's what they got and it wasn't until the 101st minute that the Premiership side at last nudged in front, Berger and Yakubu setting up Roberts to swivel and fire past Ward. Seven minutes later the game was made safe when Yakubu, at last shaking off his goal drought, got his second, a classy affair as he shook off the attentions of four back-tracking defenders before drawing Ward and placing his shot into the corner of the net.

Nottm Forest (4-4-2): Ward; Louis-Jean, Thompson, Walker (Robertson 99), Morgan; Sonner (Williams 69), Bopp, McPhail (Jess 104), Reid; Taylor, Harewood.

The Yak's goal drought ended at Forest.

Subs Not Used: Roche, Stewart.
Booked: McPhail.
Goals: Bopp 42, 67.

Portsmouth (3-5-2): Wapenaar; Foxe, De Zeeuw, Stefanovic (Yakubu 45); Schemmel, Stone, Sherwood, Quashie (Berger 45), Taylor; Sheringham (O'Neil 110), Roberts.
Subs Not Used: Srnicek, Primus.
Booked: Quashie.
Goals: Walker 57 o.g, Yakubu 64, 108, Roberts 101.
After Extra Time

Att: 20,078
Ref: H Webb (S Yorkshire).

95

STAY UP POMPEY!

STATS:
Shots on target: Nottm Forest 6 Pompey 6
Shots off target: Nottm Forest 7 Pompey 10
Corners: Nottm Forest 6 Pompey 6
Fouls: Nottm Forest 14 Pompey 15
Offside: Nottm Forest 1 Pompey 6

Only afterwards did Redknapp confirm that Pompey were giving the Carling Cup their fullest consideration. "Yakubu's goals were incredible," he said. "We've got Manchester United at the weekend and the last thing I wanted to do was go to Old Trafford on the back of two successive defeats. Forest are a great side and Paul Hart is doing a grand job." The significance of the result become apparent when the draw was made for the fourth round, pairing Pompey with Saints at St Mary's. After years of avoiding each other, the two clubs would now be meeting twice in a matter of three weeks in December. No wonder there were huge cheers among the Pompey fans at the City Ground, although there was some disbelief among the Fratton Park hierarchy when it became known. Mandaric, for one, struggled to come to terms with the news. Storrie it was who broke the news after discovering that in the Forest boardroom there was no Sky Sports 2, who were doing the draw live. Storrie rang his wife Frances to find out who Pompey would be meeting and, when the information was passed on to the chairman, he thought it was a joke at his expense. "It should be a great evening," he said later, recovering his poise. Redknapp was more effusive. "It will be a big match for everyone on the south coast. You could say

there wasn't Carling Cup fever before down here, but there is now." But first there was Manchester United at Old Trafford and Redknapp urged caution as there were many other important matches before the Saints double-header. Amdy Faye reported damaged medial ligaments from a training incident and, not for the first time, the Pompey manager talked of being "down to the bare bones".

The Premiership
BOTTOM 10 AT END OF OCTOBER 2003

	P	W	D	L	F	A	Pts
PORTSMOUTH	**10**	**3**	**3**	**4**	**11**	**12**	**12**
Tottenham Hotspur	10	3	3	4	10	13	12
Everton	10	2	4	4	12	14	10
Aston Villa	10	2	4	4	8	12	10
Wolverhampton Wdrs	10	2	3	5	7	21	9
Blackburn Rovers	10	2	2	6	15	19	8
Middlesbrough	10	2	2	6	7	15	8
Bolton Wanderers	10	1	5	4	8	19	8
Leeds United	10	2	2	6	9	21	8
Leicester City	10	1	2	7	14	21	5

7.

A Tale of two Uniteds

AUGUST HAD BEEN BRILLIANT, September not bad, October a bit of a disappointment. What would November bring? Four defeats in five matches was a fair indication that not only were Pompey coming to terms with the Premiership, but that the Premiership was coming to terms with Pompey. The rush of adrenaline on which Pompey surged into the big time was beginning to wear off and, as Redknapp prophesised it would be, life was becoming hard. After the poor display at Newcastle, undisputably Pompey's worst so far, Old Trafford was hardly the sort of place they would have chosen to visit next.

Saturday November 1

MANCHESTER UNITED (1) 3
PORTSMOUTH (0) 0

This was not quite the Manchester United of old, not even of last season when they beat Pompey in the FA Cup. Sir Alex Ferguson appeared to be distracted by the fate of a racehorse and United without Beckham were giving the impression of a team, collectively, no longer at its best. The aura of invincibility built by Ferguson at Old Trafford was wearing a bit thin and when Pompey headed for Old Trafford, backed by their formida-ble army of fans, United had just lost at home to Fulham. Such a defeat would have been unthink-able a year earlier. So there were grounds for optimism.

Redknapp replaced the injured Faye with Sherwood and Foxe, fit again, was recalled in place of Schemmel. Zivkovic moved to right-back and the dependable and ver-satile De Zeeuw shuffled across to the left. Sadly, the result was another 3-0 setback, but at least the performance was a vast improvement on that at Newcastle and in no way did it reflect the bal-ance of play. For 80 minutes, Pompey were a match for United before two late goals gave the score-line a flattering look. It was a mov-ing occasion for Sheringham, who received an ovation from both sets of fans when he led out Pompey. Sheringham had so far proved to be an inspired signing by Redknapp and United fans, perhaps aware of a slight but perceptible decline, remembered him as part of a team which won an extraordinary treble when United were almost certainly the best team in the world.

United looked for long spells like they could have done with Sheringham in his prime now. Yakubu, lifted by his goals at Nottingham Forest, went close, as did Berger with a shot just over the

Roy Keane is congratulated by his United team-mates after
scoring the second goal in Pompey's 3-0 defeat at Old Trafford.

bar and Yakubu again, dispossessing a hesitant Rio Ferdinand, forced Tim Howard into a decent save. It was half an hour before van Nistelrooy got the better of Stefanovic in the air and hammered the loose ball against the bar. Then the Dutchman was played clear from the half-way line but, with only Hislop to beat, sent his shot over the bar. After 37 minutes, largely belonging to Pompey, it was United who went ahead when Gary Neville's cross from the right was won by Ryan Giggs in the air above Zivkovic and Diego Forlan fired into the corner. Zivkovic should have equalised but his header from no more than six yards from Yakubu's cross failed to trouble Howard. But worse was to follow in terms of missed chances, not least when Berger, clear after Darren Fletcher's error, opted to pass with only Howard in his way and Sheringham and Yakubu could only despair as the ball went behind them. It was a miss reminiscent in importance and wastefulness of Quashie's in the FA Cup ten months earlier, coming at a critical time and with the match delicately poised. United are not the sort of team even now against whom it is advisable to throw away opportunities like that and, with 15 minutes left, Ferguson sent on Roy Keane and Cristiano Ronaldo in an attempt to put the outcome beyond Pompey's reach. Five minutes later van Nistelrooy was fouled and Ronaldo's skidding free kick found its way into the far corner. Two minutes after that and United had scored an undeserved third when Keane scored from the edge of the area.

So 3-0 it was and, while Pompey could moan about the injustice of the score-line, as they did, the facts spoke for themselves. It was their fifth defeat in six matches; Pompey had not scored away since Highbury in September and the table showed them heading south into the bottom half. Redknapp was right when he said: "I thought a point was there to be had. For 80 minutes we were right in the game and there was nothing in it. For the first 30 minutes we were on top. The first goal was poor with Giggs winning a header from Zivkovic. The second was a very bad one to concede although I thought the free kick which led to it was harsh. We had a big chance when Berger was through but he tried to square the ball to Teddy. Yakubu was a handful for them but United are a fantastic team. Just look who they had on the bench - Ronaldo and Keane."

Man Utd (4-4-2): Howard; Gary Neville, O'Shea, Ferdinand, Fortune; Fletcher, Butt, Djemba-Djemba (Keane 76), Giggs (Bellion 81); Forlan (Ronaldo 76), van Nistelrooy.
Subs Not Used: Carroll, Phil Neville.
Goals: Forlan 37, Ronaldo 80, Keane 82.

Portsmouth (4-4-2): Hislop; Zivkovic (Roberts 81), Foxe, Stefanovic, De Zeeuw; Stone, Sherwood (Taylor 69), Quashie, Berger; Sheringham, Yakubu.
Subs Not Used: Wapenaar, Schemmel, O'Neil.
Booked: De Zeeuw, Sherwood, Quashie.

Att: 67,639
Ref: N Barry (N Lincolnshire).

STATS:
Shots on target: Man Utd 4 Pompey 4
Shots off target: Man Utd 8 Pompey 5
Corners: Man Utd 3 Pompey 3
Fouls: Man Utd 13 Pompey 12
Offside: Man Utd 1 Pompey 0

The sooner Redknapp got players out of the Fratton Park door, the sooner they came back. Kevin Harper came from Norwich where he played nine matches in what proved to be a championship-winning side (but was sent off playing against old club Derby) and Deon Burton made no lasting impression at Swindon where one goal in four matches was not enough to lead to a contract offer from Andy King. There was better news on the injury front with Alexei Smertin - still settling in and coming to terms with the pace of the Premiership and a new life in a new country - recovering from a knee injury quicker than anticipated, but a scan on Vincent Pericard's thigh revealed a large tear and, while that need not lead to an operation, it would mean a long spell out of action. Quashie was the latest Pompey player to come off worse in a training collision with the Yak, damaging a knee in the process, but in any case the combative Quashie was due for a suspension after collecting five yellow cards. Todorov was said to be making good progress in the United States but, more immediately, Foxe and De Zeeuw were worries as the visit of Leeds approached. This was going to be an important game.

Leeds were in trouble. Debts were spiralling out of control, top class players had been sold and results on the pitch reflected their sagging share price, gloomy indeed. By any standards, Leeds are a major club and when they were acquiring the likes of Rio Ferdinand in a money-no-object spree, Redknapp was not alone in imagining them to be a dominant club in

Nigel Quashie became another victim of a collision with Yakubu. However, he was due an enforced rest after collecting no fewer than five yellow cards in the opening months of the season.

Europe over the next decade. Their downfall, therefore, was all the more spectacular and against a background of boardroom chaos, incompetence and Middle East buy-outs, Peter Reid was attempting to keep together a squad shorn of the

A TALE OF TWO UNITEDS

bright young stars on whom their future was dependent. Relegation was becoming more than a possibility, even in November, and the thought of Leeds playing in the Nationwide League without television money was already leading to talk among economic experts of closure and bankruptcy. Administration or even receivership loomed on the horizon, and it was not difficult to contemplate extinction if debts of £100m and wages of £65,000 a week in Mark Viduka's case were true. Redknapp instinctively leapt to the defence of Peter Reid, believing him to be caught in the eye of a storm over which he had no control. Not that Leeds fans had quite the same sympathy for

Reid, who had failed to cover himself in glory at Manchester City and Sunderland, but the crisis at Elland Road had began to unravel long before he took over as manager. Redknapp backed Reid to get Leeds out of trouble on the pitch, pleading with the Leeds board to give him time to get it right, but time, as we all knew, was running out and there had to be a fall guy.

Saturday November 8

**PORTSMOUTH (2) 6
LEEDS UNITED (1) 1**

The visit of Leeds proved to be one of the highlights of a tremendous season. The 6-1 score-line was the

Six of the best against Leeds: Stefanovic celebrates the first ...

biggest of the Premiership season, Leeds' biggest top-flight defeat and its repercussions went on for days. Peter Reid was sacked and two beliefs emerged: that Pompey had it about them to escape relegation and that Leeds, from the way their morale was so obviously shot away, would be lucky to survive. Yet for an hour there was precious little in it. If anything, Leeds looked the classier side, equalising a header from Dejan Stefanovic after 17 minutes with a goal two minutes later from Alan Smith. Gary O'Neil, making his Premiership debut, intercepted Gary Kelly's clearance to beat Paul Robinson with a 25-yard volley which took a minor deflection off Dominic Matteo. At 2-1 and with an hour gone of a fascinating affair, Jermaine Pennant had a glorious chance to level when he found himself unmarked at the far post with room and time to score, but a sec-ond's delay, the tiniest hint of hesitancy, allowed Shaka Hislop to leave his line - as Fratton Park held its breath - and block the shot. It was a crucial save, a calamitous miss. Had Pennant's first touch been a little surer, he must surely have scored and at 2-2 who knows what might have transpired? The fact is, he did not.

Pompey grew from that let-off and Leeds collapsed. After 63 minutes, Sheringham's deft cushion header set up Hayden Foxe to fire a third and Leeds simply gave up, disgracefully so. With 19 minutes remaining, the defence was nowhere as O'Neil, never a prolific scorer, got his second of the match, finishing off a superb move involving Sherwood and Berger. Berger added a fifth, running on to Sheringham's pass and rounding the undefended Robinson for his third of the season. Yakubu, criti-

Hayden Foxe fires home the third ...

A TALE OF TWO UNITEDS

**O'Neil is congratulated by his team-mates
for Pompey's fifth and his second ...**

cised for his poor finishing in some quarters, stabbed home Matt Taylor's cross at the second attempt four minutes from the end for goal number six and his first in ten matches. This was Pompey's biggest home win since beating Derby 6-2 in February and made a mockery of a run of only four goals in the previous eight Premiership matches. Yet the match almost never went ahead. A floodlight failure delayed the kick-off and no one was more pleased than Redknapp, who sensed that Leeds were there for the taking. Redknapp said: "At quarter past three I turned to Jim Smith and said I thought there was no chance of the match going ahead. The police said a decision

had to be made by 3.30pm and we didn't have any floodlights. An abandonment was the last thing we wanted because I felt it was a good time to be playing Leeds. They came here bottom of the table and I was very happy when the lights came on again. It was a terrific day for us, a great performance and some top class goals. It's hard to say if it was the best display since I took over but it's a contender. We were just as good against Charlton last month but this time we put away our chances. Gary O'Neil's a great kid who has come through the youth team and has a real future. Yakubu hasn't scored a Premiership goal for a long time so it was great to see him get one at

STAY UP POMPEY!

**The Yak forces his way through for his first
in ten games and Pompey's sixth.**

the end. Who would have thought we would have got six without Teddy getting any? I feel sorry for Leeds." Hero O'Neil admitted that scoring was part of his game that he needed to work on. "To score two on my Premiership debut was fantastic. I didn't expect to play but when Nigel Quashie failed a fitness test I thought it might happen. I'm pleased I scored just before half-time because, after missing a good chance, I was dreading having to face the manager and Jim Smith at the interval."

Portsmouth (4-4-2): Hislop; Schemmel, Foxe, Stefanovic, De Zeeuw; Stone (Taylor 84), Sherwood, O'Neil, Berger; Sheringham, Yakubu.
Subs Not Used: Wapenaar, Zivkovic, Primus, Roberts.
Booked: De Zeeuw.
Goals: Stefanovic 17, O'Neil 45, 71, Foxe 63, Berger 75, Yakubu 86.

Leeds (4-5-1): Robinson; Kelly, Duberry, Matteo, Olembe; Pennant (Sakho 56), Morris, Milner, Roque Junior (Bridges 72), Seth Johnson; Smith.
Subs Not Used: Carson, Harte, Camara.
Booked: Olembe, Seth Johnson, Smith, Matteo.
Goals: Smith 19.

Att: 20,112
Ref: C Foy (Merseyside).

STATS:
Shots on target: Pompey 7 Leeds 6
Shots off target: Pompey 7 Leeds 3
Corners: Pompey 3 Leeds 2
Fouls: Pompey 13 Leeds 13
Offside: Pompey 0 Leeds 1

We all know what happened next. Peter Reid was fired and while Reid had left behind him an army of haters - particularly on Wearside - at other clubs, it was hard not to empathise with his predicament at Elland Road. As Redknapp said: "Peter Reid is a great character and one of my best mates in football.

Cheer up Peter Reid! Reid had the haunted look of an impending scapegoat in the Leeds dugout at Fratton Park. Redknapp was quick to jump to his defence.

He's a fighter but has to work with what he's got. He was telling me about the number of players he's inherited on massive wages. Other clubs can learn lessons from that." Reid described the second half of the Pompey debacle as his worst 45 minutes in football. "Words fail me for the manner in which we were rolled over." Within days Reid had gone, resurfacing six months later at Coventry, but there had to be a scapegoat for such an abject surrender and it had to be the manager. The problem with Leeds was their history. Don Revie's team of the 60s and 70s was superb but they left a legacy of malice which did not dissipate over the years while their supporters had a habit of leaving trails of devastation in their wake, home and abroad. Now they were in all kinds of trouble and sympathy was not generally forthcoming; indeed there were people laughing at their miserable predicament all around the country. As for Reid, there was no cheering him up. When the inevitable sacking came, Redknapp sprang to Reid's defence, blaming overpaid players for failing to play for him but, if there was any comfort to be gained from Pompey's point of view, it was that Leeds were not going to get out of trouble on the pitch easily.

The way that internationals dominated the autumn calendar meant that Pompey had a free week coming up, but Fratton Park was a hubbub of activity. Amdy Faye was back in training, three months ahead of schedule, Nigel Quashie was out for a month with medial ligament damage and Toddy was back from America, his knee on the

The possible acquisition of Lomana Lua-Lua was again on the agenda in November.

mend. Toddy's presence at the training ground for the first time since his accident there in August was a big boost to him and to his team-mates, but there was no disguising, despite optimistic noises to the contrary, the fact that he was unlikely to play much, if any, part in the season ahead. Meanwhile, there were strong rumours of a Pompey interest in Lomana Lua-Lua, the pacy Newcastle forward. The transfer window was still six

weeks away but Redknapp, a keen fan of Lua-Lua from the player's Colchester days, was aware that at Newcastle there were some formidable names ahead of him in the queue for a place in the Premiership team. Lua-Lua was hardly getting a game at St James' Park but Peter Storrie was anxious to play down Pompey's interest: "Harry is interested in him but I don't think we are in a position to buy him." Newcastle paid in excess of £2m for the Congo international and wanted their money back and, since Pompey already had their quota of two loan players from English clubs, a loan deal looked just as unlikely. O'Neil was evidently back in favour at Fratton after his two goals against Leeds - and in demand. England under-20s had made him captain and, as such, wanted him to travel with the rest of the squad to Dubai for the FIFA World Youth Championships, but that would have meant him missing the trip to Fulham and Redknapp was not happy with that. Les Reed, the England manager, did not like making concessions but, after numerous consultations involving the FA, Redknapp won the day and O'Neil was allowed to fly out the day after. Alexei Smertin, as Russia's captain, played a significant part in denying Wales a place in Euro 2004 and needed to avoid Welsh-born kit-man Kev McCormack on his return to Pompey for fear of retribution. Lee Bradbury, at the same time, headed back to Derby to resume a loan interrupted by injury so cruelly within minutes of it starting, aware that time was running out for him at Fratton Park and that he needed to make an impression elsewhere.

Monday November 24

FULHAM (2) 2 PORTSMOUTH (0) 0

After the euphoria of Leeds came the deflation of Fulham. Sixteen days and a world away, Pompey were as poor overall at Fulham's borrowed Loftus Road as they had been outstanding against stricken Leeds. Redknapp was at a loss to understand why, or how it was that his team had now gone 424 minutes since last scoring on an opponent's ground. Of course Pompey had their moments but two goals from Louis Saha honestly reflected the difference and their bad night

got worse when Patrik Berger was sent off for foul and abusive language, the first player to be shown a red card for 20 months since Todorov at Preston in Redknapp's first game in charge. There was concern among travelling fans even before the kick-off when the teams were read out. No Shaka. One of the best-kept secrets had been the big goalkeeper's hernia problem and no amount of treatment could improve it, although the management had hoped he would be able to play through the pain until the end of the season. Shaka did his best to comply but the soreness stopped him training and, when it became clear that rest and treatment were only delaying the inevitable, an operation was the only the answer.

Shaka Hislop's hernia problems meant an extended run in the side for Harald Wapenaar. Wapenaar had the names of his children engraved on his boots.

This meant a severe test for Harald Wapenaar, the flaxen-haired Dutchman who had been brought in by Redknapp in the summer as Hislop's number two and who was preferred on this occasion to Pavel Srnicek. Ever since an unconvincing debut display in the friendly at Bournemouth, there had been doubts about him. He was not without fault, either, in the Carling Cup victory over Northampton but here at Fulham there was not much he could do about the goals; the blame - if there was any - lay at the feet of others. Hislop aside, the team was the same that had taken Leeds apart with such clinical efficiency, which meant O'Neil and Sherwood in midfield and no place for Smertin. Fulham might have won at Old Trafford but they had lost their previous two home games and had a reputation for inconsistency, flirting with a place in the top four one day and spiralling downwards the next. They looked an ordinary side for the first half hour as Pompey ploughed forward on a wave of confidence induced by the Leeds result. Stefanovic had an effort cleared from the line, Foxe headed wide and Yakubu, running clear, was foiled by a poor first touch. But when the first goal came it was at the other end. Jerome Bonnissel's long ball was cleared only as far as Saha who took a touch before drilling a low shot through a crowded area and beyond the dive of Wapenaar. The setback punctured the self-belief and within minutes, as Pompey attempted to come to terms with the goal, another was conceded. Volz and Lee Clark combined on the right and Saha rose above Foxe to meet Clark's cross with an emphatic header. Fulham had hardly been in the game but now they were two goals up and coasting. Not quite coasting, because Pompey staged a determined rally only to be denied two penalty appeals by Alan Wiley, the referee at the centre of the Pires dive controversy. Sheringham seemed to be tripped by Volz while Zat Knight held back Yakubu eight minutes from time. The last incident was clearly too much for Berger, who gave the referee a volley of abuse in his acquired Scouse accent to earn his needless red card.

What Mr Wiley, a respected and able referee, appeared to hold against Pompey we can only surmise. Perhaps he'd had a bad holiday in Southsea. However, the perceived injustices disguised an unconvincing Pompey second half performance and, since the draw at Highbury, the away record read: ten goals against and none for. Redknapp acknowledged an opportunity lost. "Fulham were devoid of confidence and not playing well. For half an hour they couldn't put two passes together and we were dominating the game. But suddenly they get two goals in three minutes and it gives them a massive lift. We couldn't believe what was happening and nor could Fulham. We have not been scoring enough away goals. We make chances but don't take them. It was poor, poor defending. For the second goal Foxe was waiting for the ball to come to him and should have gone for it. That's basic defending and it's a disappointing result." Redknapp was less sympathetic for red-carded

A TALE OF TWO UNITEDS

Berger. "People do swear at referees. I'm not condoning it, but some do. Some get sent off, some don't."

Fulham (4-4-2): Van der Sar; Volz, Melville, Knight, Bonnissel; Legwinski, Clark, Sean Davis, Malbranque; Saha (Sava 70), Hayles (Inamoto 68).
Subs Not Used: Crossley, Djetou, Pratley.
Goals: Saha 30, 33.

Portsmouth (4-4-2): Wapenaar; Schemmel, Foxe (Taylor 60), Stefanovic, De Zeeuw; Stone (Burton 73), Sherwood, O'Neil (Smertin 60), Berger; Sheringham, Yakubu.
Subs Not Used: Srnicek, Zivkovic.
Sent Off: Berger (82).
Booked: Stone, Schemmel, Sherwood.

Att: 15,624
Ref: A Wiley (Staffordshire).

STATS:
Shots on target: Fulham 3 Pompey 6
Shots off target: Fulham 5 Pompey 6
Corners: Fulham 2 Pompey 10
Fouls: Fulham 10 Pompey 16
Offside: Fulham 2 Pompey 1

Latvia's shock victory over Turkey enabled them to qualify for the European Championships for the first time and the hero of the hour in Riga was the man who scored the winning goal, Maris Verpakovskis. So it was something of a pleasant surprise for Pompey fans, unsure that Yakubu would ever become a consistent goal-scorer, to discover that he was having a trial. Wolves

Fabian Caballero of Argentina and Georgi Nemsadze of Georgia both arrived at Fratton Park on trial following the financial collapse of Dundee. Redknapp, however, did not think they would improve his squad.

were also said to be interested but talk of a £2.5m transfer fee was a bit off-putting and, sadly, nothing came of it. Verpakovskis, a name that would have tested even a skilled linguist like Fratton Park public address announcer Steve Pearson had he signed, went to the championships as a Dynamo Kiev player instead. But it showed the level at which Pompey were now expecting to recruit, namely international-quality players with proven backgrounds. This was further exemplified when Georgi Nemsadze of Georgia and Fabian Caballero, the Argentinian, showed up at training HQ at Eastleigh in the fall-out over the financial collapse of Dundee. Redknapp decided that they were no better than those he already possessed, or expected to possess, once the curtains were pulled back on the transfer window.

From Latvia to Gunwharf Quay, it was all in a week's work at Fratton Park. Gunwharf, built on a 35-acre site around Portsmouth harbour, had raised the profile of the city once it had been completed at great cost in 2001. Flats were expensive but enjoyed wonderful sea views, shopping was extensive and, in terms of clubs and bars, it was the place to be seen. Now the city's football club were intending to create Pompey Village, a £90m property development around the new stadium. The big, unasked question at the press conference to announce the new stadium a month earlier was how it would be paid for. This was the answer: luxury flats, restaurants and a sports hall built on what is now the car park. Chairman Mandaric was

enthusiastic about a project which did not directly involve him getting out his cheque book if it all fell into place and investment came from elsewhere, as he hoped it would. "We wanted to create a development that was modern, stylish and impressive to complement the new stadium and this is what we have achieved. The Pompey Village will stand out as a distinctive piece of architecture and will be another milestone for Portsmouth. This will be a project which I and all of the people of this city can be justly proud."

Saturday November 29

PORTSMOUTH (0) 0
LEICESTER CITY (1) 2

Forget Arsenal, Manchester United and even Southampton, it was Leicester whose very name sent a tingle of fear through Pompey ranks. What was it about them? After all, no other club felt that way about the Foxes, not even other teams in the Midlands. Perhaps it goes back to 1993 when the spindly Ian Ormondroyd helped knock Pompey out of the First Division play-off semi-final with a goal so blatantly offside that even those Leicester fans with a conscience are embarrassed to talk about it. Leicester got through 3-2 on aggregate and the sense of grievance has lingered to this day. Then, of course, there was the fiasco of last season. It rained and rained and rained. But would the referee call it off? No, he would not. Physically overrun in farcical conditions, Pompey slumped to what proved to be a rare home defeat, a defeat which almost proved to be costly near the end of the campaign when it looked as if Leicester might pip Pompey to the title. It didn't help that Leicester manager Micky Adams was proudly an ex-Southampton player. Saturday, November 28 was therefore not a day to which Pompey fans were looking forward and, almost on cue, it rained for the first time in weeks. There was a curious feeling of foreboding in the air before the start and the crowd was strangely muted except for a small section which chose the occasion to barrack Tim Sherwood. Redknapp recalled Zivkovic and Smertin and left out O'Neil and Schemmel but the man-

ager might just as well have included them all because this was yet another Leicester catastrophe.

Leicester won and won easily and not even the rain, so crucial a year before, could be excused for the poorest home performance so far. The passion, pace and power which had overwhelmed and crushed Leeds was never in evidence and there was an inevitability about the result when Pompey target Les Ferdinand put Leicester ahead in the 31st minute. Muzzy Izzet rolled a free kick to Ferdinand whose powerful shot took a deflection to leave Wapenaar stranded and rooted to his line. Mike Dean turned down appeals for a penalty when Yakubu appeared to be

Whatever Pompey threw at Leicester was easily rebuffed.

brought down by Ian Walker and Marcus Bent put the game out of reach in the 59th minute when he headed a free kick from Izzet past the unprotected Wapenaar. Pompey, to their credit, battled away with Walker denying Yakubu brilliantly, substitute Taylor hitting the bar and pressure incessant but unavailing. Yakubu was booked for diving and Sheringham for protesting at that decision too vigorously. It was Pompey's seventh defeat in nine Premiership matches and, by an unfortunate coincidence, it was the first time Pompey had failed to score at home since the infamous, sodden clash of the previous year. Leicester went above Pompey into 14th place and it was hardly the best preparation for the upcoming Carling Cup clash with Saints, now only a matter of days away. Redknapp said: "Leicester are a difficult side to play against. They proved that in beating Manchester City 3-0 away. I thought we would get back into the game at 1-0 because we were right on top but we paid for letting in goals at two free kicks. Les Ferdinand is still a threat. I wanted to sign him last year."

Former Southampton man and Leicester manager Micky Adams was smiling after his team's victory, but, as Harry Redknapp (below) knew, football is a funny old game.

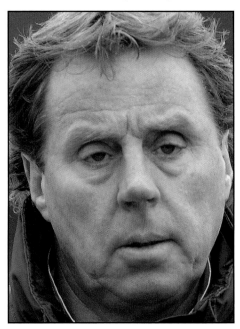

Portsmouth (4-4-2): Wapenaar; Zivkovic, Foxe (Taylor 65), Stefanovic, De Zeeuw; Stone, Sherwood, Smertin, Berger; Sheringham, Yakubu.
Subs Not Used: Srnicek, Primus, Schemmel, Burton.
Booked: De Zeeuw, Smertin, Berger, Yakubu, Sheringham.

Leicester (4-4-2): Walker; Curtis, Howey, Scimeca, Thatcher; Stewart, McKinlay, Izzet, Scowcroft; Ferdinand (Davidson 81), Bent (Hignett 90).
Subs Not Used: Coyne, Elliott, Gillespie.
Booked: McKinlay.
Goals: Ferdinand 31, Bent 59.

A TALE OF TWO UNITEDS

Att: 20,061
Ref: M Dean (Wirral).

STATS:
Shots on target: Pompey 3 Leicester 3
Shots off target: Pompey 4 Leicester 4
Corners: Pompey 11 Leicester 4
Fouls: Pompey 14 Leicester 16
Offside: Pompey 2 Leicester 1

Earlier, Redknapp had rowed with a fan who wanted the struggling Sherwood substituted and was unhappy with those who continued to boo the former England player. Redknapp was quick to remind the perpetrators that Pompey had come a long way quickly. "In the past 18 months the fans here have seen the greatest miracle ever at a football club. It was only two years ago they were getting smashed 4-1 by Leyton Orient in the FA Cup. People have short memories. Things go a bit boss-eyed and suddenly the fans turn on Sherwood. It's not as if the fans had been brought up on good football for six years before I took over. I'm sure what they were watching was the biggest load of rubbish they'd seen in their lives. Tim Sherwood has been there and done it and he's not going to hide from anyone. If you're going to have a scrap, he's a man you want in there fighting for you. It's easy for fans to sing when we are beating Leeds 6-1 but it's when things are going badly that you need support. The players have to keep believing in me, I have to keep believing in them and the fans have to keep believing in all of us. But we'll be okay, we won't go down."

All this and Southampton to come. With fears about rival fans clashing outside or even inside St Mary's, Mandaric and Saints chairman Rupert Lowe joined forces to plea for peace. They told fans: "You can be rivals, but friendly rivals." It was the first meeting in eight years and was being televised, just to add spice to an already over-hyped occasion. Mandaric said: "We want football to be the winner. Rupert and I have a professional and friendly relationship and we want supporters to have the same. The nation will be watching and this will be a big stage for both clubs. It would be a crying shame if it was spoiled by anything untoward." Saints legend Ted Bates had just died and a minute's silence was planned for the Pompey match, the first available occasion on which it could be held. Bates was the club's president and had done perhaps more than most to establish Southampton's pre-eminence over Pompey in recent years. The fear was that even a minute might seem like an hour.

The Premiership
BOTTOM 10 AT END OF NOVEMBER 2003

	P	W	D	L	F	A	Pts
Bolton Wanderers	14	4	6	4	13	19	18
Southampton	14	4	5	5	10	9	17
Leicester City	14	4	3	7	22	22	15
PORTSMOUTH	**14**	**4**	**3**	**7**	**17**	**20**	**15**
Tottenham Hotspur	14	4	3	7	13	18	15
Blackburn Rovers	14	4	2	8	19	24	14
Aston Villa	14	3	5	6	11	17	14
Everton	14	3	4	7	15	19	13
Wolverhampton Wdrs	14	2	5	7	9	27	11
Leeds United	14	3	2	9	12	33	11

8.

Scummers and Skates

SCUMMERS AND SKATES. THE dictionaries define 'scum' as foam or froth: matter rising to, and floating on, the surface: anything superfluous or worthless. 'Skate' is either a sole or sandal mounted on a blade or one of several species of large flat fish of the ray order. Anywhere other than southern Hampshire, to call someone you disliked superfluous foam or a sandal on a blade would hardly be regarded as the most hurtful of insults but, in Southampton and Portsmouth, football fans were either scummers or skates.

Once the fixtures were known, December was the month most eagerly anticipated by fans of both clubs with so much local pride and prestige at stake. It was also dreaded. Defeat by the old enemy would be just too awful to bear, just too near Christmas to be comfortably swept aside and forgotten. What made it worse, for Pompey fans (skates) at least, was that the Carling Cup draw had also paired them together which meant two trips in a matter of days to the gleaming new home of Southampton (scummers). All this after eight years of not crossing one another's paths. For the foam and the roller blades/large wet fish this was going to be one hell of a month. Nerves were becoming frayed long before

December 2, the date of the Carling Cup fourth round match, but Pompey's would have jangled even more on their way to St Mary's when the team coach was involved in a major crash on the M27 at Hamble, the mythical boundary, coincidentally, between those who support Southampton and those who back Pompey. Here, it needed the skills of driver Mick Pullen to negotiate his way through three separate accidents involving 14 cars on the westbound carriageway. Pullen wove and swerved his way through the debris and Redknapp, who sat behind him, was convinced they would join the mayhem. "The driver performed a miracle. How he managed to avoid other cars, I don't know. Cars started smashing into each other and we were going to plough right through them. We went into the hard shoulder and on for about 80 yards before we stopped."

Tuesday December 2

SOUTHAMPTON (1) 2
PORTSMOUTH (0) 0
(CARLING CUP 4TH ROUND)

There was plenty of hype in the local media; after all, they had been waiting for this for the best part of a decade, but all the passion and commitment of the occasion was generated off the pitch on radio, television and in newspapers and, of course, by the fans. On the pitch, the match was strangely low-key and a blood-and-thunder local derby it was not. It will probably not be remembered in the long term for anything other than the minute's silence that was supposed to have been observed for Ted Bates. There were plenty of Pompey supporters inside St Mary's and most of them behaved as they should have done, with dignity and pride in their club and respect for a top football man. But there was inevitably a sizeable minority who used the silence, called for by referee Graham Poll, to shout meaningless and infantile abuse at their rivals. This provoked a huge round of booing from home fans and the whole sombre silence disintegrated into a shambles, forcing the disgusted Poll to abandon the tribute. Pompey fans are rightly recognised as being among the very best in the country and their generous and sporting performance in the FA Cup when Arsenal annihilated their team was one of the talking points of the season. There is, however, a not inconsiderable yob element who come close to ruining the club's name and that of the city they proclaim to be their home and who appear intent only on looking for trouble. If they only realised the damage they did to themselves, the reputation of the club they say they support and to the image of the whole area.

As to the match itself, Gordon Strachan said the result was everything and, once Saints had nosed in front, Pompey did not have it about

Srnicek - a chance in goal for the Carling Cup game with Southampton.

them to respond. Redknapp gave a chance to Srnicek in goal, Taylor replaced Foxe and Faye returned after five weeks out with a knee injury. Sherwood was rested. Pompey were bright enough at the start, Jason Dodd escaped a penalty appeal when he sent Sheringham crashing and Yakubu failed to make the best of a great opportunity when left with Antti Niemi to beat. Then, after 33 minutes, the moment Pompey fans most feared. Zivkovic was robbed by Brett Ormerod, Marsden collected his pass down the left and his low centre was met by James Beattie, gliding in between Zivkovic and Stefanovic. Pompey fans were less than pleased to see his over-elaborate celebrations right in front of them. It was a shock to the system

STAY UP POMPEY!

De Zeeuw - debatable sending off in the final minute which led to Beattie's second goal.

and, although De Zeeuw wasted an opening to equalise, Pompey could find no way past the formidable Claus Lundekvam-Michael Svensson central defensive barrier. Saints sat back in the second half and the game never sparked to life. Srnicek made up for another Zivkovic blunder by saving from David Prutton. Then, in the 89th minute, Pompey almost levelled when Berger split the defence, but Taylor could not get a decent touch and, within seconds, Pompey were being punished. Deep into stoppage time, Beattie was adjudged to

have been tripped by De Zeeuw and, though television replays cast doubts on that decision, the luckless Dutchman got a red card as the last man in defence and Beattie despatched the spot-kick. With a ban for five bookings just around the corner, De Zeeuw now had this to be added and an appeal to the FA fell on deaf ears. Redknapp, acknowledging the subdued atmosphere, gave his players a blasting in the sanctity of the dressing room but showed public disapproval for the part Zivkovic played in helping Saints score their first goal. "Zivkovic made a silly mistake and they scored. Until then we were the better side. In the second half we ran out of legs and it showed. I've got a thin squad and Faye and Taylor were tired after being out for so long. We had a blatant penalty when Dodd pulled back Sheringham but the ref did not see it. I thought the sending-off was harsh. If a forward comes across you like Beattie did to De Zeeuw it's very difficult for a defender. To send him off was scandalous. Arjan is the most honest defender I've seen in my life."

Southampton (4-4-2): Niemi; Dodd, Lundekvam, Michael Svensson, Higginbotham; Fernandes, Delap, Telfer, Marsden (Prutton 75); Beattie, Ormerod (Delgado 84).
Subs Not Used: Blayney, Anders Svensson, Pahars.
Goals: Beattie 33, 90 pen.

Portsmouth (4-4-2): Srnicek; Zivkovic (Foxe 83), De Zeeuw, Stefanovic, Taylor; Stone, Smertin, Faye (Sherwood 75), Berger; Sheringham, Yakubu.
Subs Not Used: Wapenaar, Primus, Schemmel.
Sent Off: De Zeeuw (90).
Booked: Smertin.

SCUMMERS AND SKATES

Att: 29,201
Ref: G Poll (Hertfordshire).

STATS:
Shots on target: Saints 4 Pompey 5
Shots off target: Saints 3 Pompey 3
Corners: Saints 6 Pompey 3
Fouls: Saints 14 Pompey 10
Offside: Saints 2 Pompey 3

The Pompey boss had hoped the Bates' silence would have held over to the next, less-potentially volatile match. His only consolation was that this had not been a league match and the points were still to be contested. Redknapp called those who had broken the silence a 'disgrace', but it was Hampshire police, in a major pre-publicised operation, who came up with the real statistics. More than 40 arrests were made despite the presence of some 300 police. Sixteen were arrested at the ground, five more were ejected during the game and 20 more were detained and charged after attempting to goad opposition fans into a fight.

Adrian Ilie, the Romanian international, arrived at Eastleigh for trials. The Ilie of his prime would have been a huge asset by any standards and Pompey hoped there might just be a hint of the great player still to be found. But that's all there was. A hint. Ilie was being touted around by his agent and Wolves also had a look only to come to the same conclusion that here was a player with a bigger past than future. The transfer window was about to be flung open and Redknapp knew, by the recent run of poor results, that he needed to be busy in the four short weeks of its existence. That sequence of setbacks could well worsen at Middlesbrough where Steve McClaren's side were always a tricky proposition.

Saturday December 6

MIDDLESBROUGH (0) 0
PORTSMOUTH (0) 0

As it happens, the sequence did not get worse. The outcome was a goalless draw in a match of not many incidents, not the sort of game to live long in the memories of the 1,000 fans who made the journey to the north east. Steve Stone will remember it, though, for all the wrong reasons. Booked for a foul on Bolo Zenden, a regulation trip later on Massimo Maccarone, the sort seen in every game, earned a second yellow card and, with it, a red. Redknapp was astonished at referee Steve Bennett's decision but it meant suspensions in quick succession for Berger, De Zeeuw and now Stone and, with the size of Pompey's first team squad, they were not going to be replaced easily. "Stone's sending-off was harsh. When's Stoney ever hurt anyone? He runs up and down and works his socks off. But then I've had Berger and De Zeeuw go the same way." McClaren was sympathetic and said that if it had been one of his players dismissed in such a fashion he too would have felt aggrieved. Redknapp reckoned his team had 70 per cent of the possession, and it's true that Taylor, Yakubu, Berger and Sheringham all had bright attacking moments. But at the other end, Danny Mills shot against the underside of the bar with the goal at his mercy and

STAY UP POMPEY!

Steve Stone - became the second Pompey player to be sent off harshly in a week at Middlesbrough

Middlesbrough (4-4-1-1): Schwarzer; Mills, Cooper, Southgate, Queudrue; Mendieta, Greening, Boateng, Zenden; Juninho (Nemeth 68), Ricketts (Maccarone 67).
Subs Not Used: Nash, Riggott, Davies.
Booked: Greening, Nemeth.

Portsmouth (4-4-1-1): Srnicek; Zivkovic, Foxe, De Zeeuw, Taylor; Stone, Smertin, Faye (Quashie 66), Berger (Sherwood 90); Sheringham (Primus 81); Yakubu.
Subs Not Used: Wapenaar, Burton.
Sent Off: Stone (78).
Booked: Foxe, Stone, Berger.

Att: 28,031
Ref: S Bennett (Kent).

STATS:
Shots on target: Middlesbrough 3 Pompey 1
Shots off target: Middlesbrough 5 Pompey 5
Corners: Middlesbrough 6 Pompey 5
Fouls: Middlesbrough 19 Pompey 19
Offside: Middlesbrough 4 Pompey 0

Srnicek's nervousness was enough to remind travelling fans how good Hislop was. A point was about right, all things considered, and at least it ended a run of four successive away defeats. On the other hand, it was now 514 minutes since Pompey last scored an away goal. Redknapp thought the real heroes were the fans, foresaking Christmas shopping for the long haul north. "They deserve applauding," he said. "But then they've had great football for the last 15 months since I took over."

Was Harry Redknapp's achievement in bringing the first division title to Portsmouth greater than Gordon Strachan taking Saints to the FA Cup final, or Sean O'Driscoll leading Bournemouth into the second division without ever having had the luxury of buying any more than one player (for £12,000)? BBC South thought so. At their annual sports personality ceremony at the De Vere Grand Harbour Hotel, Redknapp was named manager of the year. Redknapp dedicated the award to his chairman and Mandaric responded with a tear-jerking: "Harry did what no other manager could do for me by turning the fortunes of this football club fully around and taking us to the Premier League. I put my faith in Harry and he did not let me down, producing an unbelievable season season that was beyond my wildest dreams. This is a thoroughly deserved award."

For further manager/chairman back-slapping, fast forward to May 2004. Gossip columns in tabloid newspapers are among the most eagerly read sections of the paper. Some of it is inspired by agents trying to move on their clients or get them a better deal, some of it is actually true and some of it is, well, inspired. But that does not stop fans raking through the most trivial of tittle-tattle to discover if their team might be involved. It is compulsive stuff. For Pompey fans, certainly since Redknapp took over, it was a rare day indeed if their club did not get a mention somewhere,

often being linked with a name only stattos would know. Who, for instance, had ever heard of Sebastian Olszar? Tall Macedonian defender Igor Mitrevski of Spartak Moscow was rumoured to be joining Pompey via the Chelsea-Smertin route on a long loan. But it never happened, though some reference sites on the internet insisted it had. One to catch Redknapp's eye was Dada Prso of Monaco but he was way out of Pompey's financial league and the spotlight settled instead on 18-year-old Richard Duffy, a right-back of great promise at Swansea. Swansea were unhappy to receive Pompey's £100,000 bid by fax rather than speak to any

Milan Mandaric had no hesitation in declaring that Harry Redknapp's award as BBC South's manager of the year was a deserved accolade.

It was in December that Sebastian Olszar was first muted as a possible transfer target.

Also in December a bid was made for Richard Duffy, the Swansea right-back.

of the managerial staff. Chairman Huw Jenkins said: "It is a very underhand way of doing things and we feel it's an attempt to unsettle the player." Swansea felt Duffy was worth £500,000 even after a handful of appearances and a poor disciplinary record. Clearly there was room for negotiation.

Saturday December 13

PORTSMOUTH (1) 1 EVERTON (2) 2

Nigel Quashie was still a key member of the first team squad although he had his terrace critics. Twisting a knee in training, medial ligament damage was diagnosed, as was a long spell on the sidelines but at least Jason Roberts was playing in the reserves and was none the worse for his injury problems.

SCUMMERS AND SKATES

Declaring himself fit again, Roberts was the surprise inclusion for his Premiership debut in the home game with an Everton side going nowhere much. De Zeeuw and Berger were suspended and Redknapp opted for a formation which had Sheringham playing behind Roberts and Yakubu. O'Neil was on the bench after coming back from England under-20 international duty. This gave a more attacking emphasis to the line-up and, after 15 minutes, Sheringham opened up a gap which Roberts exploited with a crisp shot past Nigel Martyn for his first Premiership goal and Pompey's first in an agonising 379 minutes. The turning point came in the 24th minute when an injury to Steve Watson led to the prodigy Wayne Rooney entering the action earlier than expected. Within three minutes, Kevin Kilbane sprinted on to a Gary Naysmith pass, eluded Zivkovic and pulled the ball back for Lee Carsley to fire home from 12 yards. Three minutes before half-time, Srnicek flapped at a Kilbane cross and Rooney pounced for what proved to be the winner.

Yakubu was denied an equaliser by a strong tackle from Alan Stubbs but the main talking point of the afternoon came when Rooney pushed over Steve Stone.

Believing he was destined for an early bath, Rooney started to make his way to the touchline, only to be hauled back by referee Uriah Rennie. To the astonishment of all, including the teenager, Rooney collected a yellow card. "Premier ref, you're having a laugh," sang the disgruntled home fans but even the golden boy of English football must have been having a quiet chortle to himself. Pericard, on as a replacement for Sheringham, tested Martyn but Everton held on for their first away win since April. For Pompey, it was the eighth defeat in eleven Premiership matches and next up was Southampton again at

Jason Roberts is congratulated by Hayden Foxe after scoring his first Premiership goal for Pompey.

121

STAY UP POMPEY!

Wayne Rooney not only scored the winning goal for Everton at Fratton Park, but also decided to send himself off.

St Mary's. This was turning into a very depressing run. Redknapp blamed schoolboy defending for the latest downturn. "For the first goal the ball was played inside our right-back in a way you wouldn't see in an under-12s game. A ten-year-old kid doesn't make mistakes like that. I really got the needle about that. If you give away goals like that you're going to get punished." The manager admitted the loss of De Zeeuw proved costly and said he felt it had got to the time when he needed to give crowd favourite Linvoy Primus a chance to play in the Premiership. "I need Berger, De Zeeuw and Hislop back," he groaned. As for Rooney, Harry was

keeping most of his feelings to himself. "I don't think the ref knew what he was doing. Rooney's got to learn to control himself. But I'm not worried about Rooney, I've got more important things to worry about."

Portsmouth (4-3-1-2): Srnicek; Zivkovic, Foxe, Stefanovic, Taylor; Stone, Faye, Smertin; Sheringham (Pericard 79); Roberts, Yakubu.
Subs Not Used: Wapenaar, Primus, Sherwood, O'Neil.
Booked: Taylor.
Goals: Roberts 15.

Everton (4-4-2): Martyn; Pistone, Unsworth, Stubbs, Naysmith; Watson (Rooney 24), Gravesen, Carsley, Kilbane; Campbell, Radzinski (McFadden 84).
Subs Not Used: Simonsen, Jeffers, Li Tie.
Booked: Rooney.
Goals: Carsley 27, Rooney 42.

SCUMMERS AND SKATES

Att: 20,101
Ref: U Rennie (S Yorkshire)

STATS:
Shots on target: Pompey 5 Everton 3
Shots off target: Pompey 2 Everton 4
Corners: Pompey 7 Everton 10
Fouls: Pompey 16 Everton 13
Offside: Pompey 2 Everton 2

Sebastien Schemmel. A Redknapp signing if ever there was one. Fast and skilled going forward, Redknapp went back to his old club West Ham to take him off their payroll on a free transfer just before the season started. It looked a good signing but then the relationship between player and manager started to fall apart. Frenchman Schemmel had too much of the spontaneous Gallic temperament about him for Redknapp's liking and his heart was at home in France, not at Fratton Park. Schemmel's mother-in-law was diagnosed with cancer and his wife fled home to nurse her. Schemmel started commuting from France so that he could be with his wife and hoped to maintain some level of match fitness by a weekly visit to England to go training on Thursdays. Pompey found this unacceptable. Schemmel was one of the higher wage-earners and Redknapp had every right to expect him to be available for selection, even in these exceptional circumstances. Chief executive Peter Storrie struggled to find a solution acceptable to both parties. "The club could be heavily criticised for not supporting the player in difficult personal times but we can't agree to demands from the player which we consider to be unfair."

Sadly, it was not a problem that was ever properly resolved, Redknapp blasting him publically for unsettling the rest of the team at a time of crisis. Both sides dug in and Schemmel's part in Pompey's battle for survival became smaller by the day.

Carl Robinson was one of Pompey's more curious signings. Brought in from Wolves on a three-month trial, Robinson impressed enough to earn a three-year con-

Despite being a favourite of Redknapp's from his West Ham days, Sebastien Schemmel fell out with his boss when his mother-in-law became ill at home in France.

tract but was almost immediately farmed out on a succession of loans so that he hardly ever played for the club. If Pompey rated him highly enough to grant him a long-term agreement, why did they then let him go out at every available opportunity? Rotherham were the latest club to use him and Ronnie Moore, their manager, liked him but any chance of a deal foundered on the thorny question of his wages, even though a substantial proportion of those were being paid by Pompey. There was talk of him going to the burgeoning American league on his latest return to Fratton Park but nothing ever came of that avenue of escape. Youth defender Gary Silk got some grown-up action at Martin Allen's Barnet while the size of his wage packet also precluded any

chance of Jamie Vincent, another drain on precious resources, joining Walsall when his loan there ended. Darren Huckerby, a great success on loan at Norwich, was thought to be a Pompey target as whispers grew louder, the transfer window already beginning to creak open.

The only real topic of conversation, though, was the next Saints game four days before Christmas. The perfect present for any Pompey fan would have been revenge for defeat at St Mary's earlier in the month. Surely Pompey could not play so indecisively a second time against the old enemy? Defeat is always hard to take but when it's Southampton who inflict it, there is an air of mourning and despair among those who support the blue and whites which is hard to shake

In the multitude of comings and goings from Fratton Park, Carl Robinson was one of the strangest.

off. The thought of it happening again, and so soon, could lead to a very unhappy Yuletide. There is no doubt Redknapp felt the full impact of that Carling Cup defeat, not that there was ever any animosity between himself and Gordon Strachan, but he knew that the greater impact was felt by the club's supporters for whom the games against Saints were the biggest of big days. For a variety of social, economic and historical reasons the two communities, 20 or so miles apart, do not get on and football rivalry is its hostile expression. To the outsider, this mutual hatred is hard to understand but it exists and it is as intense as it has ever been. Another defeat, therefore, was just too much to contemplate. With Amdy Faye injured against Middlesbrough, the club he almost joined, and O'Neil suffering from tendonitis in an ankle, it was time to find a big man looking for a challenge. Step forward Linvoy Primus.

Linvoy Primus is an object lesson to all lower division players not to lose hope. At the age of 30 he was about to make his Premiership debut after, it must be said, a career that was for the most part undistinguished. Bombed out by Charlton as a lad, there followed years of efficient but unspectacular defending at Barnet and Reading while he worked his way back up the divisions, never attracting any special attention. The highlight of his professional life was the award of Player of the Year by fans in Pompey's promotion year, but even Redknapp was not convinced Primus had it about him to perform in the Premiership. The hugely pop-

Harry Redknapp and Gordon Strachan: Best of enemies, best of friends.

ular Linvoy was ready for the toughest of baptisms. "I have always said I have got to be ready when the opportunity comes along and now I'm ready to take my chance." Primus duly lined up in place of Zivkovic but Stone joined Berger and De Zeeuw on the unavailable list and there was a place for the troubled Schemmel on the right in a 5-3-2 formation, behind which Wapenaar returned in goal in place of the erratic Srnicek. Yakubu was rested, Sherwood replaced Faye and there was a surprise starting chance for Richard Hughes.

Linvoy Primus was about to step forward and make his Premiership debut, going on to play a leading role in Pompey's Premiership survival battle.

Sunday December 21

**SOUTHAMPTON (1) 3
PORTSMOUTH (0) 0**

For 34 largely uneventful minutes, Pompey were just about the better side, the decision to play five at the back confounding and smothering Saints' attacking plans. But then, as so often before, an error in defence undermined all the best intentions. Dodd's inswinging corner eluded the flat-footed Wapenaar and was nudged over the line by the top of Schemmel's head as he guarded the far post. The goal was given to Dodd, his first in two years, only for it to be later credited, if that is the right word, to Schemmel by the Dubious Goals Committee. Roberts caused a few problems to Saints on his own in attack and it was no surprise when Yakubu came on for Hughes on the hour and Zivkovic took over from Schemmel. Eight minutes later, the match as a contest was over. Zivkovic, having been warned of the propensity of Marian Pahars to cut in from the left on to his favoured right foot, allowed the Latvian to do just that. Wapenaar was beaten from 20 yards for 2-0. No one could blame the typically solid Primus for the deficit; it was fellow central defender Foxe who lost possession for Dodd to whip in a centre which James Beattie glanced past the goalkeeper for a third.

SCUMMERS AND SKATES

Southampton (4-4-2): Niemi; Dodd, Lundekvam, Michael Svensson, Higginbotham; Pahars (McCann 80), Telfer, Prutton, Marsden (Baird 90); Beattie, Ormerod (Phillips 81).
Subs Not Used: Jones, Anders Svensson.
Goals: Schemmel 34 o.g, Pahars 67, Beattie 90.

Portsmouth (5-3-2): Wapenaar; Schemmel (Zivkovic 56), Primus, Foxe, Stefanovic, Taylor; Hughes (Yakubu 59), Sherwood, Smertin; Sheringham, Roberts.
Subs Not Used: Srnicek, Robinson, Burton.
Booked: Schemmel, Sherwood, Foxe.

Att: 31,697
Ref: J Winter (Cleveland).

STATS:
Shots on target: Saints 4 Pompey 2
Shots off target: Saints 6 Pompey 4
Corners: Saints 7 Pompey 5
Fouls: Saints 9 Pompey 22
Offside: Saints 2 Pompey 2

The defeat hurt Redknapp badly. Redknapp decided to cancel his Christmas, bad news for family and friends, but there was absolutely nothing to celebrate in his view. "I'm not bothering about Christmas this year. I won't eat my Christmas dinner. I'm going to be the most miserable person you've ever seen in your life, I swear to God. My wife's Christmas isn't even worth bothering about. The first goal was poor. I've got to get springs in the goalie's boots. Then I brought a sub on and the first thing he did was let Pahars turn inside him on to his

James Beattie scored his third goal in two games against Pompey - and his second in the final minute.

right foot. I asked him: 'Were you watching the first half? Were you doing something else?' I came here with no team but I came in at half-time wondering how we were 1-0 down." Redknapp pointed out how he was missing six players. "Take six out of Gordon Strachan's team, take out the goalkeeper, one of the centre halves, all of his midfield and one of his strikers and see how they cope." It's fair to say that Boris Zivkovic would not have been on the Redknapp Christmas card list and a terminal bust-up was on the way. As for Christmas, *The Sun* newspaper, for whom Harry wrote a weekly betting column, sent round a hamper of goodies to lighten the mood in the Sandbanks mansion.

Pompey's lack of goals was becoming a chronic problem and many fans could not understand why Mark Burchill was being ignored. Some supporters held up placards demanding the former Celtic striker be given a chance to solve the scoring crisis but there was never any chance of it happening. Instead, he was shunted off to Sheffield Wednesday on Christmas Eve on yet another loan, leaving those who rated him as a born goalscorer mystified by his continued absence from the first team squad. Courtney Pitt, meanwhile, headed for Coventry and Redknapp ruled out a move for Mitrevski. One of the good things about Christmas, good enough even to cheer the manager, is that matches come round thick and fast and, after the morale-crushing setback at Southampton, there was another match five days later on Boxing Day at home to Tottenham.

Friday December 26

PORTSMOUTH (0) 2
TOTTENHAM HOTSPUR (0) 0

Tottenham were not short of talent but they were short of consistency and were just the sort of fickle opponents Pompey needed in order to expunge the memory of St Mary's. Redknapp must have used his short Christmas break to mull over his line-up because there were five changes which saw Stone, Berger and De Zeeuw coming back from suspension while Yakubu replaced Roberts in attack and Zivkovic was given another chance. Pompey were much brighter, Sherwood having a header cleared off the line by Robbie Keane, Yakubu firing over from six yards and Kasey Keller turning over a 30-yard screamer from Smertin. When Spurs attacked, Wapenaar kept out Keane's shot with his left leg but the decisive moment came in the 52nd minute. Yakubu was brought down by Anthony Gardner 35 yards out and Berger stepped up to unleash a 35-yard thunderbolt into the corner of the net past a startled Keller. Yakubu's pace earned Pompey a second after 68 minutes, when he was fouled on the edge of the area by Dean Richards, and Berger's deflected free kick found its way into the net.

Pompey's richly-deserved win was marred by a tragic injury to Sherwood, playing against his old club. Sherwood had been a dominant force throughout but a collision with Mauricio Taricco in the 77th minute left him with a broken shin. It was the

SCUMMERS AND SKATES

Berger fires home one of his brace against Spurs.

end of his season. Yakubu should have added a third near the end but it was the old defensive pairing of De Zeeuw and Primus which brought a new stability at the back and was responsible for Pompey's second clean sheet of the season. Redknapp admitted Sherwood would be a major loss. "We showed a fighting spirit and Sherwood epitomised that. He's the sort of player you need in your team and his injury looks to be a bad one. I heard a crack when he went in for the challenge but was hoping it was boot on boot. De Zeeuw was magnificent, Primus as well. De Zeeuw outshone Kanoute, Keane and Postiga and didn't put a foot wrong." But it was Berger's audacious free kick which was the talking point, stunning the Pompey bench with its speed, power and placement. When they saw Berger pacing his run-up, Smith turned to Redknapp and said: "What's he doing? He can't shoot from there." But when it thundered past Keller, Redknapp looked at his sidekick and responded: "Oh yes he can."

Portsmouth (4-4-2): Wapenaar; Primus, De Zeeuw, Stefanovic, Zivkovic; Stone, Sherwood (Hughes 78), Smertin (Taylor 90), Berger; Sheringham, Yakubu (Roberts 84).
Subs Not Used: Srnicek, Schemmel.
Booked: Sherwood.
Goals: Berger 52, 68.

Tottenham (4-4-2): Keller; Carr, Gardner, Richards, Taricco; Jackson, Poyet (Postiga 61), King, Dalmat (Ricketts 69); Kanoute (Zamora 85), Keane.
Subs Not Used: Burch, Doherty.
Booked: Taricco.

STAY UP POMPEY!

Tim Sherwood is stretchered off with a broken shin after a collision with Mauricio Taricco.

Att: 20,078
Ref: S Dunn (Gloucestershire).

STATS:
Shots on target: Pompey 6 Spurs 3
Shots off target: Pompey 1 Spurs 2
Corners: Pompey 3 Spurs 5
Fouls: Pompey 11 Spurs 10
Offside: Pompey 8 Spurs 1

Pompey made one last attempt to broker a peace deal with Schemmel. Schemmel was still an integral part of the first team squad but a reluctant one. Redknapp decided to give him one final chance to commit himself to the Pompey cause but did not expect to succeed. "He played well for the first few match-es but when I replaced him for the Manchester United game he spat out his dummy and behaved like a 10-year-old. What am I supposed to do?"

Sunday December 28

CHELSEA (0) 3 PORTSMOUTH (0) 0

In the meantime, there were more pressing matters at hand, the most important of which was a trip to Chelsea's Stamford Bridge two days after the heartening win over Spurs. Until the last 17 minutes, Pompey were in with a great chance of springing a surprise. That win over Tottenham had done them good. They were more confident, less tentative and more ready to attack even without the rapidly improving Smertin, who was left out as part of the deal by which Chelsea allowed him to join on loan at the start of the season. It was a small price to pay for having at Pompey's disposal a world-class midfield operator. Whether or not he would have made any difference is hard to say but Pompey gave a decent account of themselves in a 3-0 defeat, the scoreline not fully reflecting

Alexei Smertin was left out of the team for the visit to Stamford Bridge as part of the deal that brokered his arrival at Fratton Park.

Pompey's contribution to an entertaining encounter.

Yakubu shot at Neil Sullivan from close range, Sullivan saved superbly from Stone and Frank Lampard hit a post for Chelsea. It was brewing up into a proper contest only for Stone, who had given Wayne Bridge plenty to think about, to limp off with a hamstring injury after 53 minutes. Bridge came in for some fierce abuse from Pompey fans because of his Saints links so imagine his delight when, with 25 minutes remaining, he burst down the left, outpaced Schemmel and angled a shot past Wapenaar. What happened then was more than a little controversial. Bridge hurtled off towards his tormentors in the crowd behind the goal to begin long and poignant celebrations. The England full-back was lucky to escape official retribution. There was no way back for Pompey after this and Lampard fired home from the edge of the area after Zivkovic had been robbed by Adrian Mutu in the 73rd minute. Geremi added a third with a dipping volley from 25 yards that somehow went over Wapenaar. Redknapp tipped Chelsea to finish in the top three and did not rule them out for the championship. He added: "We lost our way near the end because people didn't do the jobs I wanted them to do. When Schemmel came on, he was playing deeper and deeper and inviting Bridge to come forward. That's where their first goal came from. Schemmel was on Linvoy's toes and allowed them to push forward, which I didn't want."

STAY UP POMPEY!

Chelsea (4-4-2): Sullivan; Melchiot, Terry, Gallas, Bridge; Geremi, Makelele, Lampard, Gronkjaer; Mutu, Gudjohnsen.
Subs Not Used: Johnson, Desailly, Hasselbaink, Cole, Ambrosio.
Goals: Bridge 65, Lampard 73, Geremi 82.

Portsmouth (4-5-1): Wapenaar; Primus, De Zeeuw, Stefanovic, Zivkovic; Stone (Schemmel 54), Hughes, Berger, O'Neil (Robinson 85), Yakubu (Taylor 85); Roberts.
Subs Not Used: Sheringham, Srnicek.

Att: 41,552
Ref: G Barber (Hertfordshire).

STATS:
Shots on target: Chelsea 6 Pompey 3
Shots off target: Chelsea 12 Pompey 4
Corners: Chelsea 7 Pompey 1
Fouls: Chelsea 7 Pompey 15
Offside: Chelsea 2 Pompey 2

"To do more washing up", and, as people around the world saw out the old year with drink-fuelled renditions of 'Auld Lang Syne', Harry was probably on his mobile. The washing up could wait.

The Premiership
BOTTOM 10 AT END OF DECEMBER 2003

	P	W	D	L	F	A	Pts
Everton	19	6	5	8	23	25	23
Bolton Wanderers	19	5	8	6	20	28	23
Manchester City	19	5	6	8	27	27	21
Blackburn Rovers	19	6	3	10	26	29	21
Middlesbrough	18	5	6	7	14	18	21
PORTSMOUTH	**19**	**5**	**4**	**10**	**20**	**28**	**19**
Leicester City	19	4	6	9	28	31	18
Tottenham Hotspur	19	5	3	11	19	29	18
Leeds United	19	4	5	10	18	40	17
Wolverhampton Wdrs	18	3	5	10	16	39	14

Not a very good December then, but it was the end of the year now, the halfway point. Pompey were being linked with all kinds of players: Andy Reid of Nottingham Forest, Nigel Reo-Coker (again) of Wimbledon, Millwall's Tim Cahill, Saints keeper Paul Jones and Eyal Berkovic (again). Pompey were also in negotiation with Swansea, much to the Welsh club's disappointment, over Richard Duffy. Mandaric agreed that another three or four were needed to make sure relegation was avoided since it was now becoming a reality after a promising start. In the dark days of late December, the sheer delight at topping the table back in sun-baked August seemed a million miles away. It had been an incredible calendar year for the old club and there was much more to look forward to with the transfer window open for business. Asked for his New Year resolution, Harry joked,

9.

The January Sales

NEW YEAR, NEW RESOLUTION. On the first day of 2004, Mandaric was saying all the right things at a time when the club in which he had invested not just money, but huge heaps of emotion, was at something of a low ebb in terms of results. "I'm going to be here for the next three years at least," he assured fans who were already becoming concerned that he might in due course jump a sinking ship. "I'm on a mission and I want to continue building the club by giving it a stadium to be proud of. I'm totally committed to the fans and the city of Portsmouth. Of course we want to stay in the Premiership but whatever should happen I will be here for three more years and nothing will change my mind. We have tasted life at the top of the division and at the bottom. I'd gladly settle for a place in the middle."

Redknapp had more pressing matters to consider, like new signings and getting a team together to face second division Blackpool in the FA Cup third round at Fratton Park. Top of his worry-list was the African Cup of Nations which was about to deprive him, or so he thought, of Amdy Faye and Yakubu Ayegbeni for as much as five weeks. As it happened, Faye never went because of injury while curfew-buster Yakubu was sent home after playing (poorly) in only one match for Nigeria. As for new signings, Redknapp had 31 precious days to prevent Pompey's slide into trouble becoming an uncontrollable spiral. Gustavo Lopez, a Paraguayan striker at Maccabi Haifa, was a confirmed Redknapp target while the Finnish international defender Petri Pasanen, who had lost his place at Ajax, was more than just a target. Pasanen agreed to join Pompey on loan for the remainder of the sea-

Luckily for Pompey, Amdy Faye was ruled out of the African Nations Cup through injury.

Petri Pasanen, the Finnish international defender, became Redknapp's first acquisition in the January transfer window.

Berkovic since he was first spotted by Graeme Souness and brought to Southampton, but he would not have won any popularity contests in subsequent moves to Redknapp's West Ham (remember the John Hartson incident?), Celtic, Blackburn or Manchester City, who, incidentally, were now very much relegation rivals of Pompey's. The drawback, as always, was the spectacular size of his wage packet but Redknapp was not put off. Of all the managers for whom he had played, Berkovic appeared happiest with Redknapp because he understood his moods, his temperament and his need to be appreciated. Above all, Redknapp loved the way Berkovic played his football; his close control, his vision, his passing ability and his zest for the beautiful game.

Saturday January 3

**PORTSMOUTH (1) 2
BLACKPOOL (1) 1
(FA Cup 3rd Round)**

son, starting with the trip to Villa, but the name which wagged most tongues was that of the mercurial Israeli international Eyal Berkovic.

Manchester City wanted to get rid of him and were not even worried about asking for a fee. Kevin Keegan appeared to be positively encouraging his departure when he said: "Pompey have made an initial inquiry but, if it works out, Eyal needs to go and play football and I need to reduce the numbers in my squad." There was never any doubting the tremendous ability of

How seriously should Premiership clubs take the FA Cup, or any other cup for that matter, when the only aim for the vast majority in the top echelon is to stay there? Manchester United made it clear one year that the FA Cup was an irrelevance by not entering the competition, while others no longer appeared to fear the proverbial giant-killing acts which had once been an irresistible feature of the country's footballing landscape. In Pompey's case, there had been a long and interesting run in the Carling Cup but, here at the turn of the year, the league was getting a bit tense and a match at home to Steve McMahon's uncompromising Blackpool, the team with everything to gain, was one they could have done without in the circumstances. How the Pompey hierarchy must have wished for glorious failure at somewhere like Manchester United again, as had happened the previous year. They would have remembered how long and creditable runs in both cup competitions to the semi-finals ultimately drained Sheffield United so that they did not even get promoted through the play-offs. For fans at least, here was a match to be enjoyed on its own merits, free from the anxiety of losing league points and caring what rivals might be doing. Redknapp might have liked to rest some of his bigger names but injuries, of whom Hayden Foxe was the latest, meant that it was a question of dipping deep into reserve resources to fill the substitute positions.

As it happened, it needed an injury-time goal from the Yak to prevent a replay, which would have been the worst possible outcome, after Blackpool had predictably made life difficult for a Pompey side which, in reality, was down to the bare bones. So bare that Redknapp resembled a Sunday morning parks manager scratching around for players as kick-off loomed. Unlike them, at least hangovers were not to blame but Redknapp had to change his line-up three times between 10.30am and 1pm. He explained: "At around 10.30 I got a call to say Patrik Berger had 'flu, then another to say Linvoy Primus had gone down with a bug. Then,

when I arrived at the ground, Foxe's ankle had swollen up like a balloon. That left me with 13 players including two goalkeepers so I went into the bootroom and found two kids, Anthony Pulis and Warren Hunt, having a cup of tea. Then I found Shaun Cooper, who was having a meat pie or something, and told them: 'You're on the bench'." It was then that depressing memories of the Manny Omoyinmi incident came flooding back. Redknapp had loaned out Omoyinmi from West

Schemmel celebrates his opening goal for Pompey.

STAY UP POMPEY!

Ham to Gillingham and the little winger had appeared in the League Cup for both clubs in the same year, a registration blunder which cost two Hammers executives their jobs and forced West Ham to replay a cup tie which they had already won but which they subsequently lost. The damage on all fronts was incalculable. Cooper had been on loan at Leyton Orient and had been on the bench, like Omoyinmi, and the question was: "Are you cup-tied?". Redknapp added: "I needed to know for sure. I said to him 'Don't do a Manny Omoyinmi on me'. I asked him 55 times to be certain but in the end I didn't have to put him on anyway."

Deon Burton made his first full appearance in place of Roberts among five changes made from the Chelsea match and Blackpool made light of the two-division gap. Taylor and Yakubu went close for Pompey and Wapenaar needed to be alert to tip over a Gareth Evans cross-shot. Revelling in his old left wing-back slot, Matt Taylor looked more like his old self and, after 36 minutes, it was he who crossed for Schemmel to head past Lee Jones for his first Pompey goal. Blackpool showed no signs of buckling and, two minutes before the break, the prolific Scott Taylor turned away from De Zeeuw on to Martin Bullock's pass to level. The second half was all Pompey. Yakubu appeared to be brought down only to be shown a yellow card for diving and shots rained in from all angles but, just as Blackpool began to look forward to a replay pay-day, Pompey won in stoppage time, Yakubu forcing home a close-range shot after Sheringham's header had been blocked by Jones on the line. "With

The Yak spares Pompey's blushes - and a replay - with the injury-time winner in the FA Cup against Blackpool.

a couple of minutes to go, we were thinking of having to go to Blackpool," said Redknapp. "It would have been a day out; we could have got some rock or something." Goal-scorer Schemmel said he feared for his mother-in-law's life but then gave a valuable insight to the Redknapp management style. "Harry was angry at half-time. Even if you play well he is not happy because he is a perfectionist. When he talks we all listen and when he is angry he talks for all of the half-time and no-one else can speak but everything he says is right."

Portsmouth (3-4-1-2): Wapenaar; Zivkovic, De Zeeuw, Stefanovic; Schemmel, Hughes, Smertin, Taylor; Sheringham; Burton, Yakubu (Robinson 90).
Subs Not Used: Srnicek, Cooper, Pulis, Hunt.
Booked: Hughes, Yakubu.
Goals: Schemmel 36, Yakubu 90.

Blackpool (4-4-2): Jones; Grayson, Flynn, Davis, Evans; Bullock, Wellens (Clarke 79), Coid, Hilton; Murphy, Taylor (Johnson 90).
Subs Not Used: Barnes, Sheron, McMahon.
Sent Off: Evans (90).
Booked: Taylor, Evans.
Goals: Taylor 43.

Att: 13,479
Ref: S Dunn (Gloucestershire).

STATS:
Shots on target: Pompey 7 Blackpool 3
Shots off target: Pompey 13 Blackpool 2
Corners: Pompey 7 Blackpool 3
Fouls: Pompey 11 Blackpool 10
Offside: Pompey 2 Blackpool 3

What Redknapp feared above all was injuries and, true to form, he got them. Wapenaar had damaged his back and, with Hislop out of action, it was a question of finding a back-up keeper for the trip to Villa. Fourth choice was Chris Tardif and Craig Bradshaw was

With Wapenaar having damaged his back and Hislop out long-term, it was only half in jest that Redknapp suggested that it might be time for the recall of the 42-year old Alan Knight.

also on the professional staff but neither of those were going to get in ahead of Alan Knight, the legend of Fratton Park who, at 42, was the club's goalkeeping coach. Redknapp was only half-joking when he said: "If the keeper's back has gone, he'll be on the bench. Alan's only 42 so we'll stick the youngster in and give him a chance." The record-breaking Knight last played in

STAY UP POMPEY!

January 2000. Replacements were urgently sought and the loan signing of Pasanen was duly completed in time for the Villa match, arriving at Fratton Park with a decent pedigree of six international caps and appearances for Ajax in the Champions' League. "He will be a big help in eradicating the silly goals we are giving away," said the Pompey boss. The search continued. Pompey were reported to have bid £2m for Frederic Piquionne, the Rennes striker, with a suggestion that Schemmel might move in the opposite direction. The French were not keen. The American Landon Donovan was another name hoisted from nowhere but there was no doubt that Berkovic was the man most coveted. "I like Berkovic," said Redknapp. "He was a fantastic player when I had him at West Ham. But whether or not we can afford him I'm not sure. He's not going to be cheap. Mustapha Hadji at Aston Villa has still got ability and could do a job for me. You have to take gambles. I can't afford the likes of Michael Owen but I'd take a chance with Ricardo Fuller at Preston if I had a few million. Trouble is, I haven't got it." In under two years, Redknapp had become a dominant force, assuming the position nationally in the consciousness of the footballing public that he once held in London at West Ham. He was a deity in Portsmouth, so much so that the most popular name registered in the city during 2003 was Harry. Just as well Arsene Wenger was not in charge at Fratton Park.

Tuesday January 6

ASTON VILLA (1) 2
PORTSMOUTH (0) 1

Aston Villa were shocking at Fratton Park on that sultry August afternoon. They missed easy chances, gave away soft ones and left David O' Leary talking in terms of a hard winter ahead dealing with the threat of relegation. It was, therefore, something of a surprise that they should recover to compete for a place in Europe on the back of a strong record at home and on the resurgence of the sulky Juan Pablo Angel. Three days after seeing off Blackpool, Pompey confronted reality again at Villa Park. Another defeat, the seventh away in eight Premiership matches, gave cause for concern but if there was a consolation, it came in the manner of the performance; a competitive display in a 2-1 setback, the match only decided by a deflected shot five minutes from time by Darius Vassell. Alan Knight was on the bench and there were five changes from the team which saw off Blackpool only with difficulty. Srnicek was in goal and Pasanen made his expected debut after arriving from Holland and there were places also for Primus and Berger while Sheringham, willing though he was, recovered his breath on the bench. Roberts took his place in attack.

Villa were the better side in the early part of the match and went ahead after 22 minutes when Zivkovic allowed Gareth Barry to collect a throw from Jloyd Samuel and hit a deep centre from the left

THE JANUARY SALES

With Pompey having serious goalkeeping problems, Thomas Sorensen put in an outstanding performance for the home side at Villa Park.

to the far post when Angel stretched beyond De Zeeuw to head his 14th of the season. Lee Hendrie hit the woodwork as Pompey held on but slowly their recovery began and Taylor had a right-footed inswinger tipped over at full stretch by Thomas Sorensen. Smertin went close and then, four minutes after the break, Hendrie handled on the edge of the Villa area. Berger took the free kick and Yakubu headed in his sixth of the season and Pompey's first away goal in 743 minutes of Premiership football. If any side was going to snatch a winner after the Yak's goal, it was more likely to be Pompey but, with time running out, Villa were handed a bizarre decider. Barry's free kick found Olof Mellberg whose shot was blocked by Primus and, as the Pompey defender attempted to clear, the ball went in off the right hip of the unwitting Vassell. Even then there was almost another equaliser but an effort from the otherwise subdued Roberts was turned away by Sorensen.

Aston Villa (4-4-2): Sorensen; Delaney, Mellberg, Dublin, Samuel; Hendrie, McCann, Whittingham (Hitzlsperger 66), Barry; Angel (Crouch 89), Vassell (Moore 86).
Subs Not Used: Postma, Ridgewell.
Goals: Angel 22, Vassell 85.

Portsmouth (3-5-2): Srnicek; Primus, Pasanen, De Zeeuw; Zivkovic (Harper 89), Berger, Smertin (Sheringham 89), Hughes, Taylor; Yakubu, Roberts.
Subs Not Used: Knight, Robinson, Burton.
Goals: Yakubu 49.

Att: 28,625
Ref: J Winter (Cleveland).

STATS:
Shots on target: Aston Villa 8 Pompey 4
Shots off target: Aston Villa 9 Pompey 9
Corners: Aston Villa 8 Pompey 6
Fouls: Aston Villa 19 Pompey 15
Offside: Aston Villa 4 Pompey 3

STAY UP POMPEY!

The result was a bit of a stunner after Pompey had enjoyed a full share of the possession, but it left Redknapp aware that all was not necessarily lost. "I'm very confident we will stay up," he said. "We gave them problems and lost to a freak goal. It was an awful goal to concede, absolutely farcical. Villa are sixth in the table and we beat them 2-1 at our place and lost 2-1 here, there's nothing between the sides. Pasanen was excellent on his debut, especially as he had only one training session and Yakubu's confidence will be boosted by his goal." The Legend did not get the chance to add to his long list of appearances but joked: "I heard Sven-Goran Eriksson watched me in the warm-up."

There was evidently no love lost between Keegan and Berkovic and it was ironic that Pompey's next fixture should be against Manchester City, the club Berkovic was desperate to leave. Negotiations went on long into the night on one occasion as Mandaric made every effort to complete one of the club's more glamorous signings. The problem is that glamour comes with a price, as chief executive Storrie admitted when a deal was finally agreed after much detailed discussions also involving the Israeli's cigar-chomping agent Pini Zahavi. "Milan had to take some tough decisions to work out how far to go to buy Eyal. It's fair to say there would not have been too many clubs in our position that would have gone to the lengths we went to." This was taken to

Mandaric finally gets his man - Berkovic arrives at Fratton Park.

mean the player's wages. Berkovic instantly became Pompey's highest-paid player and, while Manchester City contributed some £5,000 a week towards the grand total, talk of an annual salary in the £1.2m range was not dismissed. Around the same time in mid-January, there were plenty of other possible transfers; Oyvind Leonhardsen trained at Eastleigh for a few days and the name of Francis Jeffers cropped up more than once but, by bringing in Berkovic, there was suddenly far less cash around for further newcomers.

Saturday January 10

PORTSMOUTH (1) 4
MANCHESTER CITY (2) 2

Berkovic took his place in the Portsmouth midfield when Keegan brought his City side to Fratton Park on January 10 a couple of days after his switch and, if ever there was a grudge match, this was it. Redknapp changed his system to a 4-3-1-2 to accommodate the new man and, while he was by no means the man of the match, Berkovic proved a point with some telling contributions in Pompey's 4-2 win. By doing so, Pompey moved out of the bottom three, overcoming a 2-1 deficit to drag City into the relegation reckoning. It was City's 14th match without a win and, as a collector's item, the last ever in David Seaman's distinguished career. Seaman had played the best part of 1,000 matches but was now 40 and in his final season. Nursing a shoulder injury, Seaman became the latest player to feel the full force

There was no love lost between Berkovic and Kevin Keegan, the Manchester City manager, so it was ironic that his debut would be against his former club.

of a challenge from the Yak and departed from the field 13 minutes after the kick-off, never to be seen in action again. The announcement of his retirement soon afterwards was a formality. In contrast, Hislop was back in goal for Pompey, bringing a whole new stability to the defence with his calm reassurance and reminding fans and management alike what they had been missing in his enforced absence.

Seaman's deputy Kevin Stuhr-Ellegaard had hardly been on the pitch more than five minutes when he was picking a header from Stefanovic from the net, but City had the quality to hit back and they did. Nicolas Anelka equalised and

Antoine Sibierski finished off a move involving Anelka and Joey Barton. Pompey also enjoyed, at last, enormous good fortune because City hit the woodwork no fewer than three times as Pompey struggled to get their game together. That survived, Pompey made the most of it, Yakubu levelling after 52 minutes only for a Joey Barton 'goal' to be disallowed because Anelka was standing in an offside position, a decision which infuriated Keegan. It was clearly not City's day as Sheringham scored his first goal since October with a trade-

Stefanovic opens the scoring for Pompey.

THE JANUARY SALES

Berkovic, who ran the show, congratulates Yakubu after his second goal.

mark header and, after Anelka and Robbie Fowler had missed great chances to equalise, Yakubu make it four with 13 minutes remaining. Home fans hummed the theme from 'The Great Escape' as the Yak outpaced Sylvain Distin for his second and their irony was justified.

If he had not been outstanding on the pitch, the celebrating Berkovic was far and away the star of the post-match press conference, using the opportunity to blast Keegan for ignoring him for so long and advising him to quit while he was still ahead. Grown reporters wept with joy as Berkovic launched into a bitter tirade at his old boss. "Everyone knows how I feel about Kevin Keegan. I don't see any reason why he didn't play me. I was the best player in City training for

six months. Everyone knew that and 45,000 City fans knew I should be playing. But Kevin Keegan was behaving like a big baby. I think at the end of the day he deserves the sack." Keegan tried to retain his dignity in the face of such a personal onslaught, although he had encountered far worse as England coach. "Eyal is entitled to his opinion. Sadly, people will print what he says but he should learn to keep his counsel more. I sold him and he might be a bit bitter. I wished him good luck and made it all easy for him to leave. His comments don't bother me because I've had worse things said about me." Redknapp tried to be diplomatic, knowing that the temperamental Berkovic had overstepped the mark. "I'm disappointed at Eyal saying what he has.

STAY UP POMPEY!

I love Eyal but Kevin felt he could not fit him into his team. Football's a game of opinions and Kevin Keegan had to do what he thought was right."

Portsmouth (4-3-1-2): Hislop; Primus, Pasanen, De Zeeuw, Stefanovic; Hughes, Smertin, Berger; Berkovic (Harper 74); Sheringham, Yakubu.
Subs Not Used: Wapenaar, Taylor, Schemmel, Roberts.
Booked: Smertin.
Goals: Stefanovic 19, Yakubu 52, 77 Sheringham 58.

Man City (4-4-2): Seaman (Stuhr-Ellegaard 13); Sommeil, Dunne, Distin, Tarnat; Sinclair, Bosvelt, Barton, Sibierski; Fowler, Anelka.
Subs Not Used: Wiekens, Macken, McManaman, Tiatto.
Booked: Dunne, Fowler.
Goals: Anelka 21, Sibierski 45.

Att: 20,120
Ref: M Messias (N Yorkshire).

STATS:
Shots on target: Pompey 10 Man City 5
Shots off target: Pompey 4 Man City 10
Corners: Pompey 2 Man City 8
Fouls: Pompey 8 Man City 9
Offside: Pompey 5 Man City 1

Boris Zivkovic was something of a star signing in the summer. A Croatian international and his country's captain, Zivkovic had played Champions' League football for Bayer Leverkusen and was still in the prime of his career. No wonder Pompey were pleased to have lured him to their unfashionable, newly-promoted club on a free transfer, although wages of £13,000 a week reflected his background. But as the season progressed it became clear that he was struggling to justify extravagant claims about his pedigree. Short of the pace required to play in the hectic atmosphere of the Premiership, bungling Boris was also making some crucial errors, not least at Southampton before Christmas. Zivkovic felt he was not being seen at his best because he was not playing in his preferred central defensive role, but he did not take too kindly to being blasted in public by the manager for making mistakes. "When the manager starts telling the papers that I've played badly, enough is enough. He has totally ruined my confidence. He thinks everything is my mistake and is always saying that things are my fault in front of the other players. He never spoke to me, the only players he spoke to were Sheringham and De Zeeuw. He doesn't have a relationship with the others." After the technical proficiency of continental coaching methods, Zivkovic was surprised by Redknapp's easy-going approach to training sessions. "Training was always the same, we just played eight-a-side all the time and he spent more time on the phone than he did coaching us."

Redknapp was not the sort of person to accept those comments without making a few of his own. Laid back he might be, but he was not going to take them lying down. As Zivkovic negotiated a move to stately Stuttgart, feeling he might be better appreciated in Germany where he was still held in higher regard than in England, Redknapp gave his own version of the breakdown of the relationship. "I don't think he wanted to be here from day one. I got that feeling when we were in Scotland on our pre-season tour. We're talking about a sour player. He was a horror and I'm

"Bungling" Boris Zivkovic, or, as Redknapp liked to call him, "Boris The Terrible", left Fratton Park for Stuttgart after a series of error-strewn displays and re-emerged in the Germans' Champions' League side that played Chelsea and also for Croatia in the European Championships.

glad he's gone. His attitude stank the place out. He said he didn't enjoy the training sessions. I dropped him against Manchester City and it was a better dressing room without him. If you ask the other lads, they'll be pleased to see the back of him. I try to build a team with terrific spirit but there's always one bad apple in the barrel and he was the one. He said I was on the phone the whole time. Well, I was on the phone trying to find someone to replace him. Boris the Terrible I call him. I could make a video out of all the rickets he made, he cost us so many goals. He's got to be the worst defender in the history of the Premiership. He reckons he should have been playing centre-half but every time he went to head the ball he was found wanting." Redknapp then reeled off his errors against Manchester United, Southampton, Everton and finally Villa, all of them leading to goals. "He said I crushed him; well, he crushed me with the goals he kept giving away. This is what happens when you take gambles. We signed him on a free transfer and we've not had to pay him to leave. The only damage he's done is in goals cost and points lost." So Zivkovic departed unlamented, re-emerging in the Stuttgart side which played against Chelsea in the Champions' League and in the European

Was Steve Claridge a victim of a cruel hoax when he was offered the services of the former Pompey striker and record buy Rory Allen for his current club Weymouth?

Championships, playing with the sort of confidence and authority which had eluded him at Fratton Park. He was the right player for Stuttgart and the wrong player for Pompey, simple as that.

If Redknapp thought he had problems, former Pompey boss (briefly) Steve Claridge, now pioneering at Weymouth, got a call from a man claiming to be Rory Allen, the talented but injury-decimated striker who was once Pompey's record signing at more than £1m. Allen got fed up and fled, mid-championship-winning season, to Australia where it was thought he had joined the Barmy Army watching the Ashes tour, turning his back on the sort of wage packet which would have had most people drooling with envy. Claridge was not sure. Was this a cruel wind-up? A fit and motivated Allen would have been a huge asset in the Doc Martens League, not to say at a much higher level, but Claridge asked him to phone back to confirm his identity and to fix up a trial. The call never came. And still the names poured forward. The famous Guatemalan Carlos Ruiz stopped off for a trial, Kevin Campbell looked as if he might come down on loan but, as for Frederic Piquionne, he was staying at Rennes despite an improved Pompey bid. You can never have enough Milans and Pompey tried to get Baros of Liverpool on loan, but that failed and Paul Smith, the highly-rated Brentford goalkeeper, came on trial before pitching up at St Mary's as number two to Antti Niemi.

But it was not all one way, far from it. Jason Roberts, having cost Pompey £200,000 for half a year on loan, took himself off to Wigan and greater first team opportunities for £2m from parent club West Bromwich without ever having seriously suggested he was a Premiership player. Then there was Jamie Vincent. One of the forgotten men of Fratton Park, Vincent had been a Claridge signing but once Redknapp had brought in Matt Taylor he was doomed. Doomed to spend the remainder of a substantial contract either on loan (Walsall most recently) or in the reserves. When Pompey were promoted, Vincent got a hefty pay rise without having started a single match in the promotion side, but it was a contractual obligation and the former Huddersfield left-back partied hard with players who had not, in the main, been his team-mates. Derby stepped in during January to end some 18 months surplus to requirements and to reduce the wage bill by the best part of £8,000 a week. No doubt the experienced Vincent would rather have played some part in the Pompey success story, as most footballers would, and it was not his fault that he was not wanted. While no club wanted to sign him he was forced to become part of a large group of players at training, like Burchill, Pitt, Tardif and Bradbury, who were never going to play in the Premiership even when the manager was talking about being down to the bare bones. Pompey were linked with a move for Carl Cort, another player not wanted by his club but too expensive for most potential buyers, who was available at Newcastle. Newcastle had paid £7m for him and now

STAY UP POMPEY!

wanted £2m just to get him off the payroll, a familiar scenario all around the country in hard times for football clubs. Wolves won that battle, but still went down.

Saturday January 17

BOLTON WANDERERS (0) 1
PORTSMOUTH (0) 0

Yakubu delayed his departure to the African Cup of Nations so that he could play at Bolton and, talking of bare bones, Redknapp was justified in making such a claim after the Reebok Stadium visit. Out were Foxe, Howe, Quashie, Faye, Sherwood, O'Neil, Stone, Todorov, Burton, Pericard and Bradbury (all injured) while Stefanovic and Harper were about to be suspended and the Yak was expected to be away for a few weeks. There were only eleven fit outfield players and at Bolton, Robinson and Anthony Pulis were on the bench. Bolton's home record (two wins) was something Pompey had hoped to exploit during a turgid first 53 minutes before Kevin Davies, the ex-Saints' striker, half-hit a shot which bobbled under Hislop. The keeper, who made few mistakes over the season, beat the ground in rage. Yakubu had a shot deflected on to a post by defender Emerson Thome, Smertin was denied by a great save and Berger went close with a powerful left-foot drive. But, as Pompey pressed desperately for an equaliser, deep into stoppage time Stefanovic swore at referee Phil Dowd and became the club's fourth red card of the season. Dowd said he had been sworn at once and then again as he

sent him off. Redknapp said Stefanovic had spent too long in the company of Jim Smith and was trying out the words he had learned but, more seriously, said a club fine would accompany the inevitable suspension. "This is the last thing I need with all the injuries. I haven't got a team to face Wolves in a couple of weeks; it's scary. I don't blame the ref, Dejan will be suspended for being stupid." It did not help to discover that Roberts had scored after 34 seconds of his Wigan debut.

Having recovered from injury, Shaka Hislop made one of only a handful of mistakes in the season which saw Bolton score their only goal at the Reebok Stadium.

Bolton (4-3-2-1): Jaaskelainen; Hunt, N'Gotty, Thome, Barness; Okocha (Giannakopoulos 90), Campo, Nolan; Djorkaeff (Pedersen 84), Javi Moreno (Ba 62); Davies.

Subs Not Used: Poole, Charlton.
Booked: Okocha.
Goals: Davies 53.

Portsmouth (4-3-2-1): Hislop; Primus (Harper 77), Pasanen, De Zeeuw, Stefanovic; Smertin, Hughes (Taylor 77), Berger; Berkovic, Sheringham; Yakubu.
Subs Not Used: Wapenaar, Robinson, Pulis.
Sent Off: Stefanovic (90).
Booked: Hughes.

Att: 26,558
Ref: P Dowd (Staffordshire).

STATS:
Shots on target: Bolton 5 Pompey 2
Shots off target: Bolton 6 Pompey 5
Corners: Bolton 2 Pompey 2
Fouls: Bolton 9 Pompey 16
Offside: Bolton 2 Pompey 3

The Wolves match was going to be important and at least there was the FA Cup fourth round match at home to third division Scunthorpe as a distraction in between. Two weeks also in which to initiate and finalise the many transfer deals still bubbling away under the surface at Fratton Park. The Landon Donovan deal, complicated by the involvement of San Jose Earthquakes and Bayer Leverkusen, spluttered into oblivion, strangled by red tape while Redknapp headed for Spain to watch Ivan Alonso of Alaves just as Attila the Hungarian invaded the training ground for a trial. Attila Tokoli of Ferencvaros, that is. He did well, but not well enough, and that avenue closed as time began to run out. Mark Burchill came back from yet another loan, this time at Sheffield Wednesday, while another of Fratton's Legion of the Forgotten, Neil Barrett, followed Graham Rix to Dundee where Jim Duffy was boss. If all that was not enough, along come Scunthorpe. Redknapp

used the opportunity to rest De Zeeuw and gave a rare chance to Harper.

SATURDAY JANUARY 24

PORTSMOUTH (1) 2
SCUNTHORPE UNITED (0) 1
(FA Cup 4th Round)

For a ground rightly famous for its atmosphere, there was precious little excitement as Scunthorpe kept out Pompey without much trouble until the 35th minute, when Tom Evans failed to hold a stinging effort from Berkovic and Matt Taylor gratefully snaffled the rebound. Peter Beagrie may have been 38 but his tremendous, some would say unfulfilled, talent was still in evidence at free kicks even if his legs could no longer get him about the pitch with quite the same alacrity of

Matt Taylor celebrates his brace of goals against Scunthorpe.

old. There were chances at either end before Taylor put an end to some growing anxiety with a right-foot shot after Harper and Berkovic had combined. Stefanovic failed to deal with a long throw for Andy Parton to make it 2-1 and Pompey had to survive some difficult moments before earning a place in the fifth round draw. It was all getting a bit serious.

Portsmouth (3-4-2-1): Hislop; Primus, Pasanen, Stefanovic; Harper (Robinson 88), Smertin (Schemmel 58), Hughes, Taylor; Berkovic, Berger (Faye 58); Sheringham.
Subs Not Used: Wapenaar, De Zeeuw.
Booked: Stefanovic.
Goals: Taylor 35, 66.

Scunthorpe (4-4-2): Evans; Graves (Lee Ridley 30), Byrne, Stanton, Sharp; Sparrow, Barwick, Kilford, Beagrie; Hayes (Parton 75), Torpey.
Subs Not Used: Capp, Kell, Featherstone.
Booked: Byrne, Hayes.
Goals: Parton 89.

Att: 17,508
Ref: G Barber (Hertfordshire)

STATS:
Shots on target: Pompey 3 Scunthorpe 5
Shots off target: Pompey 5 Scunthorpe 5
Corners: Pompey 3 Scunthorpe 4
Fouls: Pompey 15 Scunthorpe 14
Offside: Pompey 3 Scunthorpe 1

Redknapp knew Pompey had been stretched but expected nothing less with a depleted squad and instead gave an insight into life on the scouting road. "I was in Italy last week and only got back from Spain at 4am Friday morning. I flew all the way out there to look at a striker who ended up on the bench and only came on for the last 20 minutes on the left wing. Nobody wants

Ivica Mornar signed in time to make his debut against Wolves.

to give you their best players for nothing." Who can forget Bartholomew Ogbeche of Paris St Germain or Dimitri Bulykin, the Russian striker? Both of them were Pompey targets, we understand, and who, in time, will remember Sebastian Olszar, the Polish under-21 international striker 'spotted' by Pompey playing for the Austrian League side Admira Wacker Modling? Olszar looked as if he might have something about him and was signed for the remainder of the season, but Redknapp was still looking for someone more experienced and more capable of stepping straight into the Premiership cauldron. That man was Ivica Mornar, a 29-year-old Croatian international playing for Anderlecht in Belgium. Mornar had played in eight countries and was strong and aggressive, just the sort of qualities required more and more in the English top flight. Mandaric played a key role in the negotiations, bypassing an army of agents all eager for some reason to play a part in the deal by speaking to Mornar's father in his native tongue. Anderlecht wanted to keep him and offered him a new contract but Mornar had made up his mind and a fee of around £400,000 was reluctantly agreed by the Belgians. There was the little problem of completing the formalities and, with icy weather playing havoc with airports, the bald-pated Mornar fled to England on the Eurostar. Arriving at Woking for a medical, Mornar duly signed in time to play against Wolves.

January 2004 will go down as the most cyclonic month of the Redknapp era and still the activity

When Yakubu was ejected from the Nigerian squad at the African Nations Cup, Redknapp saw the opportunity to get him in the side for the Wolves game. A mad dash and a police escort saw him take his place on the subs' bench at 3.17pm.

showed no signs of abating. For instance, Yakubu was accused with team-mates of breaking a curfew, set for 10.30pm, by 25 minutes and was sent home by the Nigerian FA. Lurid bedroom tales were denied by the genial Yak but his tournament was over and the beneficiaries of it all were Pompey. Spotting the possibilities of getting him back in time to face Wolves at Fratton Park, the race was on. Leaving Tunisia on the Saturday morning, Yakubu got as far as Belgium before catching a connection to Heathrow. The plane was delayed until 1pm, two hours before kick-off, and it was a further

40 minutes before he got through customs. A car was waiting for him outside and as the turnstiles clicked away at Fratton Park and Redknapp checked motorway progress via his infamous mobile, a police car waited at junction 11 of the M27 to provide an escort over the remaining few miles to the stadium. By now it was 3.02pm, the match was under way and Yakubu had been listed as a substitute, while the police red-lighted him through the dense Portsmouth traffic. Peter Storrie said: "I met him outside and we rushed him in to get changed. We made sure he got lots of fluids after the flight, he sluiced himself down with water and at 3.19 he ran up the tunnel to take his place on the bench. The police were fantastic, I cannot praise them enough." Not everyone saw the police generosity in the spirit it was intended. The squad car driver was a Pompey fan and top brass were not happy, after a torrent of complaining letters that proper use had not been made of the vehicle.

The Swansea full-back Richard Duffy at last completed his move to Pompey on a four-year contract, the one transfer with tomorrow in mind, but Redknapp realised that there were more pressing matters at hand demanding more experienced personnel. Stern John, Christian Dailly and Chris Powell were all possibles as the countdown continued to the end of the month. Actually, the deadline was not, as many thought, the last day of January but Monday, February 2 and that gave Redknapp vital space in which to manoeuvre in his quest for last-minute signings. Carl

Robinson was off on his travels around the first division again, this time to Sheffield United and Schemmel came within a nod of joining the French club Bastia. With it all apparently agreed, Schemmel pulled back from the brink. Redknapp said: "It doesn't look like he wants to go. If he wants to stay I hope he knuckles down and gets on with it."

Saturday January 31

PORTSMOUTH (0) 0
WOLVERHAMPTON WANDERERS (0) 0

Schemmel was nowhere to be seen when it came to team selection for the Wolves match on January 31. Wolves had predictably found the Premiership hard going after sneaking in via the play-offs but were doggedly hanging on and, having beaten Manchester United, were not being underestimated. Even so, here were three points for the taking, on paper at least three of the easiest points of the season. But it never works out the way it should, otherwise we would all be Pools millionaires. The match ended goalless, Pompey being unable to find a way past ex-Saints goalkeeper Paul Jones (once, like many, a Pompey target) or avoid the woodwork which they hit four times. In gale-force winds, Wolves did not contribute much in attacking terms but Berkovic, Sheringham (with the goal at his mercy), Primus and De Zeeuw all hit the post or bar and Jones made some stunning stops. Pompey gave Mornar a debut after his hectic race across the Channel but the biggest cheer came when

THE JANUARY SALES

Carl Cort, who had been a Pompey target in January, forced a fine save from Hislop in Wolves' only attack of note.

Yakubu got off the bench, bringing the save of the match from Jones with his first touch. Hislop made a great save from Cort to prevent an undeserved away win but a point had to be enough and it looked all the better when news came through of heavy home defeats for Leeds and Leicester.

Portsmouth (4-3-1-2): Hislop; Primus, Pasanen, De Zeeuw, Taylor; Smertin (Quashie 88), Faye, Berger; Berkovic (Stone 75); Sheringham, Mornar (Yakubu 46).
Subs Not Used: Wapenaar, Hughes.

Wolverhampton (4-4-2): Jones; Irwin, Craddock, Butler, Naylor; Cameron, Ince, Rae, Kennedy; Cort (Iversen 67), Miller (Ganea 90).

Subs Not Used: Oakes, Silas, Clyde.
Booked: Naylor.

Att: 20,112
Ref: H Webb (S Yorkshire)

STATS:
Shots on target: Pompey 8 Wolves 3
Shots off target: Pompey 7 Wolves 5
Corners: Pompey 6 Wolves 7
Fouls: Pompey 14 Wolves 11
Offside: Pompey 3 Wolves 0

Redknapp was pleased he had gambled on naming Yakubu as a sub even though he was closer to Heathrow than Portsmouth when the team sheets were handed to the referee. "Mornar tweaked a hamstring so we weren't prepared to take a chance with him. He could have done serious damage and been out for six weeks. So it was lucky we had Yakubu there. Paul Jones was outstanding. I was going to sign him a couple of weeks ago and he was keen to come. But he goes back a long way with Dave Jones." Meanwhile, Redknapp found it difficult to equate the mild-mannered, shy and amiable Yakubu with the trouble-maker the Nigerians made him out to be. "Yakubu was sitting in the hotel having a coffee when he was told he should have been in his room. I couldn't imagine him causing a problem. The boy's an absolute gentleman. You couldn't meet a nicer man, he's not even a drinker." As for Dave Jones, he laughed off chants of 'Jones is a scummer'. "I'm not sure which one the crowd meant," he said.

But still the month was not over, or at least the transfer part of it was not. With time ticking away, Pompey made a £1.5m bid for Andy

Griffin and Lomana Lua-Lua of Newcastle, but Sir Bobby Robson had no problems fending that off. Robson felt the pair were worth £2.25m so the deal looked to have died, at least until the summer and perhaps for ever. But Redknapp loves transfer deadlines and, feeling that his squad was still not quite strong enough to cope with the second half of the season, he launched into a spot of last-minute shopping. On Monday February 2, Pompey had until 5pm to add to their squad. By the time the clock struck five, Pompey had brought John Curtis, the Leicester full-back, in on a free transfer on an 18-month contract and Lua-Lua, spurning Leeds, arrived on loan for the rest of the season. One month, seven signings. Phew.

The Premiership
BOTTOM 10 AT END OF JANUARY 2004

	P	W	D	L	F	A	Pts
Aston Villa	23	8	6	9	26	27	30
Middlesbrough	22	7	7	8	23	26	28
Tottenham Hotspur	23	8	3	12	23	33	27
Everton	23	6	7	10	25	29	25
Manchester City	22	5	8	9	31	33	23
Blackburn Rovers	22	6	5	11	32	36	23
PORTSMOUTH	**23**	**6**	**5**	**12**	**25**	**33**	**23**
Leicester City	23	4	8	11	31	43	20
Wolverhampton Wdrs	23	4	8	11	20	44	20
Leeds United	23	4	5	14	19	47	17

10.

Cup Fever

WITH SEVEN SIGNINGS ABOARD, the drawbridge was pulled up ready for the siege ahead. Only time would tell if they could all make a contribution to the second half of a season which was already boiling up into a colossal battle for survival. By the start of February it was already clear that Wolves, Leicester and Leeds were all in the mire with Pompey but it was perhaps more surprising to see Manchester City and Blackburn, both of whom might have expected to be chasing honours, struggling along with them. City and Blackburn had spent envious amounts of money on players but had only consistent failure to show for it, Kevin Keegan and Graeme Souness appearing to keep their managerial jobs only on the reputations of the outstanding players they had once been.

Pompey received a piece of good news after the dust settled at Fratton Park as the Yak had spurned the chance to rejoin the Nigerian squad. In his absence, Nigeria had reached the quarter-finals of the African Cup of Nations and were due to take on favourites Cameroon. It was at this juncture that the Super Eagles coach Christian Chukwu decided he might have acted a little hastily in sending him home and now wanted him back. He said: "The players made mistakes. They asked the country to forgive them and the country has forgiven them. If they want to come back, they can." Yakubu wanted to play for his country again but what still hurt him was allegations that he had arranged for a woman to stay in the team hotel, an accusation which had appeared in Nigerian papers and which he had always strenuously denied. Redknapp was a worried man. "I don't think Yak will be going back. He is not one for breaking curfews and he has been very disappointed at what has been said. I don't know if he has got to go back, but he's not keen." Luckily for Pompey, Yakubu did not take long to make up his mind: Nigeria could manage without him. "I very much love playing for Nigeria but I felt very let down by the circumstances of my dismissal from the squad last week. I felt I was harshly treated for being 20 minutes late through taking coffee in the hotel. It is unreasonable for them now to ask me to return and I will not be returning."

Lomana Lua-Lua had been a fringe player at Newcastle behind some top class strikers and when he did get first-team opportunities it was often only as a substitute and, in his anxiety to show what he could do, he often failed to justify

Lomana Lua-Lua had had a difficult time at Newcastle and jumped at the chance to join Pompey during the transfer window, but he must have wondered what he had let himself in for when he witnessed a mock fight between Sheringham and Smertin on his first day at training.

himself. Arriving at Fratton Park, Lua-Lua was keen to make up for what he perceived as lost time. "He's strong and quick and can turn games," said an enthusiastic Redknapp. As something of an initiation ceremony, Lua-Lua watched in horror on the training pitch as Sheringham and Smertin staged a mock fight in front of him, Sheringham grabbing Smertin by the neck and threatening all kinds

of things before the joke was explained to the startled newcomer. Lua-Lua was lined up as a substitute at Tottenham where the presence of Mornar was thought to place in doubt Sheringham's return to White Hart Lane, where he had spent many happy years. As it happened, Yakubu replaced Mornar, Curtis made his debut in place of Pasanen and Quashie started his first game for three months in place of Berger. Sheringham need not have worried; he was in the starting line-up.

Saturday February 7

TOTTENHAM HOTSPUR (2) 4
PORTSMOUTH (1) 3

Three days before Pompey headed to Tottenham, White Hart Lane had witnessed an extraordinary match in which Manchester City, reduced to ten men by a sending-off, had overturned a three-goal deficit to win 4-3. Much as Spurs fans would have hated it, it was a match to rank with the finest in terms of drama ever seen at the famous old ground. They very nearly saw a repeat, but this time Tottenham scraped home 4-3 in a pulsating finish which had everyone on the edge of their seats. Pompey had managed only three goals in their previous 12 Premiership away games so, while it was pleasing to see the tally doubled in the space of 90 hectic minutes, it was just as pointless. Three times Pompey equalised without ever looking as if they had it about them to hold on even for a draw, not that Spurs looked any stronger in defence. There were chances at both ends before Jermain Defoe, a £7m signing and protege of Redknapp's at West Ham, opened the scoring after 13 minutes, shooting in from the edge of the area through the legs of De Zeeuw. But Pompey looked progressive going forward and when, after 39 minutes, Stephen Carr sliced Yakubu's cross, Berkovic headed in his first Pompey goal.

Pompey needed to get to half-time on level terms but, within three minutes, defensive inadequacies were exposed again when Carr and Defoe combined for Robbie Keane to turn sharply and beat Hislop from 25 yards. Sheringham, as he had done at Old Trafford, got a heartfelt reception from Spurs fans but he had made little impression by the time a hamstring injury defeated his attempts to return for

Berkovic - equalised first for Pompey at White Hart Lane.

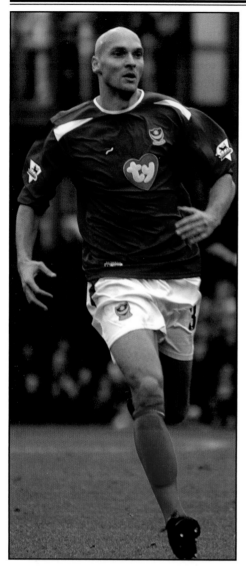

Mornar - scored his first goal for Pompey and was roundly praised by Redknapp.

the left before striking a right-footed shot into the net off the inside of a post. As Pompey fans exploded in joy, Lua-Lua took off in what became a celebratory trademark triple somersault which would have won him an Olympic gymnastic gold in other circumstances. But the cheers had hardly died down before Pompey were trailing again. There were only eleven minutes remaining when Keane was allowed to wriggle his way into the penalty area before clipping a shot past Hislop with the aid of a Smertin deflection. Not that Spurs looked any more capable of holding a lead than Portsmouth and, with six minutes left, Taylor and Yakubu worked together down the left and Mornar turned in a cross for his first Pompey goal. So a draw it was... or was it? In the last minute, Simon Davies took a corner which was headed back across goal by Dean Richards for Gus Poyet to score the winner off his knee.

Tottenham (4-4-2): Keller; Carr, Gardner, Richards, Jackson; Dalmat (Ricketts 73), Brown, King, Davies; Defoe (Poyet 82), Keane.
Subs Not Used: Burch, Doherty, Yeates.
Booked: Dalmat.
Goals: Defoe 13, Keane 42, 79, Poyet 89.

Portsmouth (4-3-1-2): Hislop; Curtis, Primus, De Zeeuw, Taylor; Smertin, Faye (Lua-Lua 64), Quashie; Berkovic (Stone 85); Sheringham (Mornar 45), Yakubu.
Subs Not Used: Wapenaar, Berger.
Booked: Faye.
Goals: Berkovic 39, Lua-Lua 73, Mornar 84.

Att: 36,107
Ref: P Walton (Northamptonshire).

the second half, Mornar replacing him. Mornar, Yakubu and Berkovic were all close to an equaliser before Lua-Lua was introduced at last in place of the toiling Faye. Lua-Lua had only been on the pitch nine minutes when he beat two men on

CUP FEVER

STATS:
Shots on target: Spurs 8 Pompey 7
Shots off target: Spurs 3 Pompey 7
Corners: Spurs 6 Pompey 5
Fouls: Spurs 16 Pompey 14
Offside: Spurs 0 Pompey 7

Pompey were devastated. Redknapp was never very good at hiding his feelings and he was in no mood to keep them to himself afterwards. "I'm bitterly disappointed because I could not see us getting beaten today. In the end I would have settled for a point when we deserved three. That would have given us a four-point gap over the bottom three." Redknapp praised Mornar, his energy, strength and attitude and his superb touch. The manager was delighted Mornar had chosen Pompey over Rangers and hoped that his goal might be the first of many between now and the end of the season. "We paid £200,000 for him with another £100,000 if we stay up and he is a good signing. I can't afford to pay £7m for Defoe but we have got good players. The players are very low after this result but the fans should be proud of them. I am." The one setback, apart from the loss of three points, was the injury sustained by Sheringham. Nursing a torn hamstring, he did not expect to play again for a few weeks at a time when Pompey needed his cunning, his knowledge and his international class. "I've got more chance of playing next week," moaned Redknapp.

Meanwhile, although the transfer window had closed on Premiership clubs, those in the lower divisions could continue trading until the end of March. Carl Pettefer, one start in five years at Pompey, went to Southend on loan and O'Neil went back to Walsall to complete the loan truncated earlier in the season by the emergency call to join Pompey's squad at Nottingham. Lua-Lua, still basking in the glory of his fine debut goal, took the opportunity for a blast at genial old patriarch Sir Bobby Robson for ignoring him. He said he had come to Portsmouth to show Robson he had been wrong and to prove to his three-year-old son Keenan that he could be a star. "My son thinks I'm just a Premiership substitute. I want him to see I'm more than that." Tear-jerking stuff.

Wednesday February 11

PORTSMOUTH (0) 0 CHELSEA (1) 2

Chelsea were hardly the sort of opponents to be recommended after letting in four the previous week. Backed by the incredible, mind-blowing wealth of Roman Abramovich, they were pursuing Arsenal at the top of the Premiership and moving through the later rounds of the Champions' League. Chelsea were full of goals. Redknapp attempted to counter this threat by restoring Stefanovic after suspension while Smertin was again obliged to sit out the match under the terms of his loan agreement. Sheringham was out and Mornar's strength was preferred to Lua-Lua. Then, in the warm-up, Stone went down injured with a suspected stress fracture of a leg. It was not the best way to start such a daunting occasion against a Chelsea side conservatively estimated to have cost £120m. For 20 minutes,

STAY UP POMPEY!

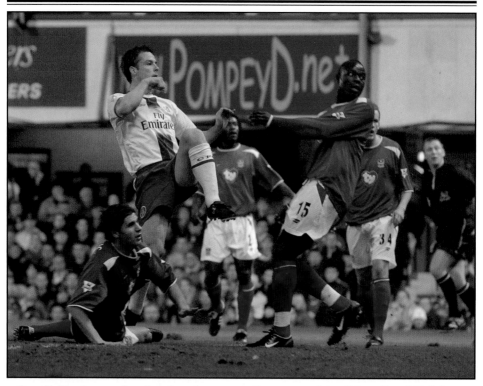

Scott Parker, who had only recently moved to Stamford Bridge, finishes a move that he started for Chelsea's opening goal.

Chelsea revealed a huge gap in expectation and took the lead they warranted in the 17th minute when Scott Parker, in his second appearance, started a move which he finished from six yards after getting a return pass from Adrian Mutu. At this point Pompey, who had not beaten Chelsea in the league since 1957, began to regain their senses and should have equalised seven minutes later. Neil Sullivan's poor clearance let in Yakubu but the Yak's nerve let him down as he burst into the area with the goal seemingly at his mercy, blazing miles wide when a touch would have done it. Then Berger curled in a left-foot shot from 30 yards which struck a post, Sullivan well beaten. Pompey were

the dominant side but found no way past the impressive John Terry and then, as Chelsea were obliged to dig in, Berger collided with Sullivan and took no part in the rest of the season. Lua-Lua came on and bothered Chelsea with his pace and determination, twice missing when well placed. It was while Pompey were pressing in search of an equaliser that, with eleven minutes left, Jimmy Floyd Hasselbaink broke down the right and lobbed against the bar for Hernan Crespo to chest the rebound into the vacant net. It was a dreadful blow. There was no coming back from this and Chelsea ended as they had started, firmly in control. It was the fifth home defeat of the season and, while for the most part they had been outplayed, it proved to be the last home defeat of the season.

Portsmouth (4-3-1-2): Hislop; Primus, Pasanen, De Zeeuw, Stefanovic; Quashie, Faye, Berger (LuaLua 56); Berkovic (Taylor 84); Mornar, Yakubu.
Subs Not Used: Wapenaar, Curtis, Hughes.
Booked: Stefanovic.

Chelsea (4-4-2): Sullivan; Melchiot, Terry, Gallas, Bridge; Parker (Cole 74), Makelele, Lampard, Gronkjaer; Mutu (Crespo 62), Gudjohnsen (Hasselbaink 71).
Subs Not Used: Ambrosio, Huth.
Booked: Parker, Crespo.
Goals: Parker 17, Crespo 79.

Att: 20,140
Ref: G Poll (Hertfordshire)

STATS:
Shots on target: Pompey 2 Chelsea 4
Shots off target: Pompey 10 Chelsea 7
Corners: Pompey 9 Chelsea 10
Fouls: Pompey 10 Chelsea 5
Offside: Pompey 2 Chelsea 1

Redknapp felt it had been even until the second goal. "I told my players after the game that I would be worried if I looked around the dressing room and didn't see good players and good characters. Patrik is going to be missed if, as we think, he will be out for a long time. He's been important this season." Berger was a man of very few words. Claiming to have been misquoted in his youth, he gave journalists a wide berth and did not give inter-

Roman Abramovich - came to Fratton Park with his £120 million team and was satisfied with the outcome.

Patrik Berger's impressive first season at Fratton Park was ruined by a knee injury caused by a collision with Chelsea goalkeeper Neil Sullivan. It meant that he missed another opportunity to put one over his former club Liverpool.

views. So it was something of an exclusive when he spoke to the club's official magazine, *Pompey Monthly*, edited by Rob Treloar. Berger had hoped for a nostalgic return to Anfield for the FA Cup tie but his knee injury put paid to that. It was the same knee that had kept him out for a year at Liverpool and, in effect, ruined his career there. He re-lived his match-winning goal for Pompey nearer the start of the season, which had been the perfect way of showing the Liverpool management that he was by no means finished. "It was a strange feeling facing Liverpool because I had played for them for seven years and I knew all the players and staff. I just wanted to get the best result for Portsmouth and scoring the goal was just a bonus. I think everyone enjoyed it, not just me. It was a great day for us." Berger's injury led to a trip to Dr Richard Steadman in the United States to evaluate the problem, but it also provided an unexpected lifeline for Richard Hughes, who had been on the verge of a temporary move to Rotherham when the midfield vacancy cropped up. Hughes had had his own injury problems and his Pompey career had been in danger of ending before it had really started until this sudden, belated opportunity.

It was going to be a big match at Liverpool for whom the FA Cup was a real chance of bringing a trophy to Merseyside. The league had long since slipped from their grasp. What sort of side Pompey would put out was anyone's guess. While Smertin was available again, Sheringham, Stone and Berger were all injured and newcomers

Curtis and Lua-Lua were cup-tied. Even as little as a year ago, Liverpool would have expected a comfortable afternoon against upstarts like Pompey. They still regarded themselves as footballing aristocrats and Anfield as something of a citadel. The defeat at Fratton Park had been a big blow to their pride, not least because the only goal had been scored by a player they regarded as no longer up to the Premiership. The problem for Liverpool was that the setback against Pompey had proved already to be worse than a temporary blip. Teams they would have considered as inferior as Pompey had also beaten them and complacency had given way to anger and disquiet at the managerial record of Gerard Houllier. Houllier, a much-respected and liked man, had delivered over five years half a dozen trophies, it is true, but at a high cost in terms of transfer fees and Liverpool had fallen far behind traditional rivals like Arsenal and Manchester United. This was a big cup tie for Liverpool and for Houllier while Pompey, their minds still on the league, could afford to be relaxed about the outcome.

Sunday February 15

LIVERPOOL (1) 1
PORTSMOUTH (0) 1
(FA Cup 5th Round)

Smertin replaced Berger as the only change from the side beaten by Chelsea and, as purposeful Liverpool roared into action, Pompey found themselves a goal down after two minutes. Berkovic lost possession, Steven Gerrard exchanged passes with Bruno Cheyrou and Michael Owen made no mistake. Liverpool poured forward in search of the goals to make the match safe. Owen skimmed the bar and Hislop made a great save from Emile Heskey, who then fired wide with only the keeper to beat. Redknapp fiddled with the formation, bringing Primus into the middle in a bid to frustrate Liverpool but how Pompey survived that early barrage will remain a mystery. But survive it, they did. Liverpool could not find a way through again, Jamie Carragher and Gerrard going close, but there was always a chance for Pompey while they were only a goal behind. Taylor came on for the tiring Berkovic and Olszar for the injured Mornar. Then, almost unbelievably in the context of what had happened in the first 77 minutes, Pompey drew level. Smertin crossed for Yakubu to head down for Taylor who, relishing his attacking opportunities, smashed in from ten yards in front of a silent and distinctly unimpressed Kop. Realising that there was not much point in celebrating down at that end of the pitch, Taylor showed world class pace for a man with his arms raised in going down to the other end where 3,000 Pompey fans were already celebrating. "No one was going to stop me," he said. "I was on my way to the fans and that was it. You could see from the jubilation on my face that I was just happy to get on and get the goal." Liverpool gathered their senses and re-doubled their efforts for a winner but it never looked like coming. As away fans leapt for joy at the final whistle, punchless Liverpool were booed by their supporters. Portsmouth were not the sort of team who should leave Anfield with a draw, they reckoned. Redknapp welcomed the replay. "Wait until we get Liverpool at our place. It looked like we were on for a beating at one point but we showed great character and didn't give up. I'd be a liar if I told you I didn't fear the worse when they went in front but we gave it everything. As for Matt Taylor, he's got a great left foot but his right isn't too bad either."

Liverpool (4-4-2): Dudek; Finnan, Henchoz, Hyypia, Carragher; Kewell (Le Tallec 84), Hamann, Gerrard, Cheyrou (Sinama-Pongolle 82); Owen, Heskey.
Subs Not Used: Kirkland, Murphy, Biscan.
Booked: Sinama-Pongolle.
Goals: Owen 2.

Portsmouth (4-3-1-2): Hislop; Primus, Pasanen, De Zeeuw, Stefanovic; Smertin, Faye, Quashie; Berkovic (Taylor 70); Mornar (Olszar 56), Yakubu.
Subs Not Used: Wapenaar, Schemmel, Hughes.
Booked: Smertin, Pasanen.
Goals: Taylor 77.

Att: 34,669
Ref: M Halsey (Lancashire).

STATS:
Shots on target: Liverpool 8 Pompey 5
Shots off target: Liverpool 9 Pompey 6
Corners: Liverpool 12 Pompey 4
Fouls: Liverpool 5 Pompey 9
Offside: Liverpool 0 Pompey 2

With Liverpool still involved in the UEFA Cup, the fifth round replay was a mere seven days away and over the first three of those, home fans queued for tickets. Ticket office manager Elaine Giles and her staff were constantly busy, Peter Storrie deflecting criticism of a price-hike by pointing out that tickets had been reduced in cost for previous cup ties with Blackpool and Scunthorpe. As pleasing to the Pompey management as long lines of people proferring handfuls of cash was the sight of the popular Todorov coming on as a substitute in a reserve match against Charlton. A crowd of 600 at West Leigh Park gave him a rousing reception and he was even involved in one of Pompey's goals in a 3-1 win. It was his first match of any kind since he damaged cruciate knee ligaments in August and here he was playing in the middle of February, the best part of four months ahead of schedule. The shame was that Toddy was not quite ready to play in the first team because Redknapp was already tut-tutting about the replay. Mornar's groin injury looked like keeping him out and the Pompey boss was talking in terms of damage limitation. "I'm not joking when I say that there might even be a couple of kids involved in the replay." The prize for eliminating Liverpool was a home quarter-final with Arsenal, then still pursuing the treble. It was a massive incentive.

Meanwhile, Srnicek was on his way to West Ham on loan, a move to sign golden oldie Sasa Curcic collapsed at an early stage and Pompey denied any interest in Scott Taylor, the free-scoring Blackpool forward who had played well against Pompey in the third round. It was never quiet at Fratton Park for long even when the transfer window was supposed to be tight shut.

There was, however, a spot of local difficulty when Mandaric, with

CUP FEVER

Svetoslav Todorov - despite the growing injury list, some good news was the re-appearance of last season's top goalscorer on the training pitch four months earlier than schedule.

the best of intentions for the welfare of his club, decided to call off a women's international between England and Denmark which was scheduled to take place at Fratton Park on the Thursday, three days before the replay. Mandaric wanted to preserve the state of the pitch but calling off the match was no longer his prerogative once he had signed a legal document handing over the stadium to the control of the Football Association. The FA threatened to sue for breach of contract, bearing in mind that the best part of 10,000 tickets had been sold, and Mandaric was forced into a hasty U-turn. Not even that appeased Hope Powell, the England women's coach, who thought she detected some old-fashioned chauvinism. "To hear Portsmouth were prepared to call off the game is very disappointing. We were beginning to think the perception of women's football was changing, then this happens." Pompey and the FA were at loggerheads again when Redknapp and Storrie were summoned to explain the club's poor disciplinary record. The FA wanted to know why Pompey had had four players sent off and many yellow cards, the second highest number of cautions in the Premiership. Storrie pleaded Pompey's case when he said: "Only one red card was for a violent foul." The FA were not massively impressed and demanded an improvement over the remainder of the season.

Sunday February 22

PORTSMOUTH (0) 1
LIVERPOOL (0) 0
(FA Cup 5th Round Replay)

Anyone who attended the FA Cup replay will remember it for ever. It was an extraordinary match for so many reasons and yet for the first

STAY UP POMPEY!

45 minutes it was almost entirely devoid of incident. Michael Owen could not get the better of the perservering Primus and De Zeeuw was no less resolute alongside him in the heart of a 4-4-1-1 formation in which Harper and Taylor were restored as wing-backs. Mornar was injured and Faye suspended and Redknapp was not wrong when he made his gloomy forecast about having to use youngsters. Cooper, Olszar and O'Neil were on the bench. But nothing happened in a barren first half apart from a Heskey shot striking Hislop's legs. The crowd were hardly buzzing as the players made their way out for what was about to become a sensa-

tional second half. There was no sign of Stefanovic; he had damaged ankle ligaments. Richard Hughes came on as his replacement and then, suddenly, the whole complexion of the match changed with the first of two astonishing decisions by the experienced Yorkshire referee Matt Messias.

Messias has a reputation as a sound referee, his dependability reflected in his rise through the league ranks, but what happened to him that day will forever remain a baffling mystery. In the 49th minute, he awarded a penalty when he judged that Primus had handled a centre. Clearly, the culprit was Liverpool's Milan Baros but, in the

It was an astonishing second half in the FA Cup replay with Liverpool as referee Matt Messias gave two hotly-disputed penalty decisions.

CUP FEVER

The referee changed his mind about the first decision but gave the second. Michael Owen, much to the delight of the Fratton Park crowd, missed from the spot.

absence of any admission of guilt, a penalty it was. Berkovic led the protests and, to his credit, the referee was persuaded to speak to his assistant Guy Beale who had not flagged. Beale was not in the best position to see what had happened but, in fairness to the referee, he was big enough to change his decision. A penalty became a free kick to Pompey and it emerged later that Messias had not been influenced in any way by his assistant. The reaction of both sets of players was enough to inform him he had got it wrong. Full marks to the ref for bravery, but nought out of ten for

what happened 12 minutes later. A superb, last-ditch tackle by Taylor on Baros was not seen as such by the official. He saw it instead as a penalty - and this time he was not changing his decision or even discussing it. Up stepped Owen, the deadliest present-day English finisher bar Alan Shearer, and not the sort to spurn an opportunity like this, surely. But Owen had not been playing well and his success rate with recent penalties had been distinctly average. His kick was a weak one, poorly struck to the goalkeeper's left but not far enough. Hislop did not even need to make

STAY UP POMPEY!

Robert Pires-lookalike Richard Hughes, whose career at Fratton Park had been plagued by injury, benefitted from the injury to Berger and stepped up to score the winning goal.

much of a dive, only to make the right decision about which way to tumble. It was all so pathetically simple. Owen was crestfallen, the Liverpool fans behind Hislop's goal at the Milton End staggered at the ineptitude of his failure. Better penalties have been taken by fans in the half-time kickabout.

As for Pompey, it was just the spur they needed and after 72 minutes they were ahead. Richard Hughes had figured so little in Pompey's 18-month surge to glory that only a remarkable resemblance to Robert Pires kept him in the public consciousness. But here he was, unmarked, on the edge of the area, receiving a pass from Yakubu. Fratton Park froze. The Liverpool defence was all over the place but

none of it anywhere near the Italian-raised Scot. For a terrible moment, as Hughes took what seemed an age to get the ball under control, it looked as if the chance had gone, but a low left-foot shot angled across Chris Kirkland and into the corner of the net. It was Hughes's first goal for Pompey and he will never score one more precious. Liverpool were stirred into retribution and Hislop, ever outstanding, turned away a goalbound header from Gerrard, who was again the one opponent to play to his reputation as one of the world's best midfielders. With the minutes passing desperately slowly, Owen got away from Primus but again Hislop was out to block his shot and at the final whistle there was massive jubilation. Liverpool players slumped to the floor and Redknapp punched the air with delight.

Portsmouth (4-4-1-1): Hislop; Primus, Pasanen, De Zeeuw, Stefanovic (Hughes 45); Harper, Smertin, Quashie, Taylor; Berkovic; Yakubu.
Subs Not Used: Wapenaar, Cooper, O'Neil, Olszar.
Booked: Quashie, Hughes, Smertin, Yakubu.
Goals: Hughes 72.

Liverpool (4-4-2): Kirkland; Finnan, Henchoz, Hyypia, Carragher; Hamann, Gerrard, Le Tallec (Murphy 59), Cheyrou (Sinama-Pongolle 82); Heskey (Baros 45), Owen.
Subs Not Used: Dudek, Biscan.

Att: 19,529
Ref: M Messias (N Yorkshire)

STATS:
Shots on target: Pompey 5 Liverpool 3
Shots off target: Pompey 4 Liverpool 8
Corners: Pompey 3 Liverpool 8
Fouls: Pompey 13 Liverpool 9
Offside: Pompey 6 Liverpool 2

The ghosts of the 1992 semi-final had been well and truly laid. As for Hislop, the Pompey star, it was a great way to celebrate his 35th birthday and he was last seen heading away from Fratton Park nursing the man-of-the-match champagne. What we did not know was that the giant Trindadian was also nursing a broken finger. The words tumbled from Redknapp. "When you have characters like Primus and De Zeeuw defending for their lives, you've got a chance. This is a great achievement. We have a fantastic team spirit here and I don't think we realise how good a result this is. We had 16 players out but it's incredible, a great day for this club. The referee had a nightmare. The first penalty was handball by their player. Then Matt Taylor makes the best tackle of the match and he gives another penalty. They were two diabolical decisions." Calm down, Harry. Hislop, in his mellifluous Caribbean tones and from his imposing 6ft 6 inches, revealed that in more than a decade of professional football this had been his first penalty save. "I never seem to guess right. I have saved a few in shoot-outs but not in ordinary play. I don't know how many have gone past me but I never fancy myself with penalties and Michael Owen is a top-class finisher. Luckily his shot came a lot closer to me than I expected and, for once, I guessed right. I didn't think it was a penalty in the first place because I thought it was a good tackle by Matt Taylor. As for the first penalty decision, the referee showed great courage in changing his mind. You never see that happen." Hughes, his thunder stolen a little by Hislop, described his goal as the highlight of his career. That night, they were both Pompey heroes. Later, Messias admitted what everyone knew already thanks to the wonders of video replays, that he had got both major decisions wrong and it was as well for him that the result had been unaffected by his strange lapses.

Had Hislop broken his finger making any one of a number of outstanding saves against Liverpool it would have been understandable. But it transpired that the digit had been damaged in the warm-up and he had played the whole of the 90 minutes in great pain, not that anyone would have known from the manner or the authority of his per-

STAY UP POMPEY!

Shaka Hislop had performed heroics against Liverpool playing with a damaged finger. A special glove was constructed for him so he could play against his former club, Newcastle.

formance. The possibility that Hislop might be missing, even for a match or two, sent a shiver of panic through the Pompey ranks and prompted the search for some way to keep him active. His last enforced absence had coincided with a poor run of results and, while it would be easy and unfair to blame his replacements, there is no doubt the defence as a whole was much the better for his presence behind it. The solution was to construct a special glove which would allow him to strap two fingers of his left hand together to protect the injury. It sounded simple, but the medical men were not happy; they wanted him to rest it but, when it was clear Hislop was happy with the glove, they recommended he used it for the next four matches. Newcastle's visit to Fratton Park was a big match anyway for Hislop as a former Newcastle player but, coming as it did a week after the Liverpool match, here was an immediate test of his protective glove and of Pompey's resolve.

Sunday February 29

PORTSMOUTH (0) 1
NEWCASTLE UNITED (1) 1

It was an even bigger match for Lua-Lua who had been allowed by Newcastle to join Pompey on loan in exchange for £100,000 for a half season. The Magpies, either by mistake or deliberately, did not insert a clause in the temporary transfer precluding Pompey from playing him against them. Peter Storrie, who handled the negotiations, could not believe the omission. "We thought there might be a ban on Lua-Lua. But there wasn't, so I got my pen out quickly and signed the agreement." It had to happen, of course. With a minute left, the lithe little Congo international, a childhood refugee from famine and persecution, tucked in an equaliser, thereby depriving his employers of two much-needed points in their quest for European qualification. Sir Bobby Robson has a sad, hangdog face when things go wrong and he can make you feel injustice only ever happens to him. All of this was in evidence afterwards. "It means one of our players has taken points off us. But I'm not making any comment about him being allowed to play. It's a club issue and I have got to accept it." It was clear, however, that some strong talking would be done once the team had returned to the sanctuary of Tyneside and the locked doors of St James' Park.

Lua-Lua was everywhere during the previous 89 minutes, twisting and teasing team-mates with the relish of a man with a score to settle. Twice Shay Given denied him early in the match, leaving Newcastle fans to wonder whether or not this was the same man who so often flattered to deceive in the black and white stripes. They had something to cheer in the 34th

Craig Bellamy runs on to the ball to score Newcastle's goal.

minute when Kieron Dyer got past De Zeeuw and Craig Bellamy used his pace to nudge in front of Primus before scoring his fourth goal in as many games. Not that De Zeeuw and Primus were often beaten; in fact neither Shearer nor Bellamy could get away from them for long and, when Shearer kicked at thin air to miss a chance from six yards, it summed up his, and Newcastle's, afternoon. Smertin missed a good chance to equalise and, with time running out, Redknapp sent on Mornar to pep the attack. It worked. With seconds remaining, Lua-Lua drilled a shot through a packed penalty area for the equalis-

STAY UP POMPEY!

Lomana Lua-Lua was a constant thorn in the side of Newcastle at Fratton Park and fully deserved his 89th minute goal which gave Pompey a share of the points.

er Pompey had deserved. A shot from Jermaine Jenas apart, Newcastle offered little as an attacking force and the point gained by Pompey took them out of the bottom three.

Lua-Lua had no doubts where his loyalties lay, even temporarily. "I am so happy. Portsmouth are a team who fight and work and it paid off. When I was told I would be allowed to play in this game that said something to me. I wanted to show what I could do. I apologise to Newcastle fans for scoring but they don't know what I have been through. Football is a well-paid sport but I'm not happy if people don't want me. I saw some Newcastle players before the game and they said they were going to win and that I would not score. So

CUP FEVER

that fired me up. I have got three months to impress and that's what I intend to do. There is a great team, great manager and great training staff here at Portsmouth and they are good enough to stay up." Shaka Hislop was happy with his glove, not that Newcastle tested its durability. "The finger feels okay. I had no real pain from it. I'm glad I got through the match without real incident. The glove takes some getting used to, but it stood up well. I'm going to have to put up with it for the next three or four weeks." As for Redknapp, he expressed his astonishment at Lua-Lua's availability and was delighted with his goal.

Portsmouth (4-3-1-2): Hislop; Pasanen, Primus, De Zeeuw, Taylor; Smertin, Faye (Mornar 71), Quashie; Berkovic (Harper 90); Lua-Lua, Yakubu.
Subs Not Used: Wapenaar, Curtis, Hughes.
Booked: Berkovic, Faye.
Goals: Lua-Lua 89.

Newcastle (4-4-2): Given; Hughes, Bramble, O'Brien, Bernard; Bowyer (Bridges 82), Speed, Dyer (Jenas 40), Robert (Viana 78); Shearer, Bellamy.
Subs Not Used: Harper, Woodgate.
Booked: Bernard, Bramble.
Goals: Bellamy 34.

Att: 20,140
Ref: A D'Urso (Essex).

STATS:
Shots on target: Pompey 6 Newcastle 3
Shots off target: Pompey 12 Newcastle 3
Corners: Pompey 7 Newcastle 6
Fouls: Pompey 11 Newcastle 11
Offside: Pompey 6 Newcastle 0

Of more concern was the future of Primus and De Zeeuw, the twin pillars of the Portsmouth defence. Neither was in the first flush of youth and were running out of con-tract in the summer. On one thing manager and chairman were agreed: They must be retained at all costs. Redknapp said: "We need to get them sorted out. The pair have done really well and we want to offer them each another two years." Mandaric went even further in his praise. "They are two of the best characters I have met in football and I want them to finish their careers at Portsmouth." It had not escaped the attention of Pompey fans that 2004 was a leap year. Was it too much of a leap in faith to expect them to survive? In February, all 29 days of it, they had taken giant strides to secure their future.

The Premiership
BOTTOM 10 AT END OF FEBRUARY 2004

	P	W	D	L	F	A	Pts
Bolton Wanderers	26	8	10	8	32	40	34
Southampton	27	8	9	10	27	27	33
Middlesbrough	25	8	7	10	27	31	31
Everton	27	7	8	12	33	39	29
Blackburn Rovers	27	7	7	13	39	44	28
Manchester City	27	6	9	12	36	39	27
PORTSMOUTH	**26**	**6**	**6**	**14**	**29**	**40**	**24**
Wolverhampton Wdrs	27	5	9	13	24	52	24
Leicester City	27	4	11	12	37	51	23
Leeds United	27	5	7	15	26	53	22

11.

41 years of hurt

FOOTBALL CAN SERIOUSLY DAMage your health. Perhaps there should be cigarette-style warnings on managerial contracts and, as for chairmen, it's all self-inflicted. Harry Redknapp admitted nearer the end of the season how he could never get any sleep for worrying about results. Milan Mandaric tossed and turned through the night at his flat in Port Solent as he considered the financial implications of relegation. As March began, the evenings lengthened and a hint of green appeared in the hedgerows but relegation was still the major topic at Fratton Park. Not even the impending prospect of an FA Cup quarter-final with Arsenal could conceal the fear of failure. "It keeps me awake at night," the chairman admitted. "But I want to continue with building the new stadium. If I don't build a stadium, it might never happen. So I have got to be bullish."

More immediately, there was a warning to his manager that relegation would mean higher-paid players would have to go. There was no future in £20,000 a week footballers in the first division. More than most chairmen, Mandaric was acutely aware of just how much a football club means to its fans and, in Portsmouth's case, acknowledged the sheer fanaticism of its supporters. How many chairmen, for instance, have fans chant their name from the terraces every match as Mandaric does? And it is heartfelt because Pompey fans realise that, without him, they would still have been competing with Grimsby and Walsall for a first division relegation place, the Premiership a distant, unattainable dream. Mandaric liked the fervour of the Pompey fans and their commitment to a cause that had been through, in recent years, far more thin than thick.

One such fan was Gary Lammas, who died aged 38 from cancer on March 1. For fouteen pain-racked months, Lammas followed his beloved Pompey home and away while undergoing draining chemotherapy. His last visit to Fratton Park was to see Pompey defeat Liverpool but it was only the previous month that Mandaric had presented him with the Supporter of the Year award, paying tribute to his courage and his devotion. It was with deep shock that he discovered Lammas had died. "Not only was he a wonderful supporter but a wonderful person also. Now and then when you look at other people you gain inspiration and when I met Gary at the awards night this was a feeling I came away with. I am so glad the last match he saw had the right result." Mandaric was among many

Pompey mourners at the funeral.

Arsenal were chasing the treble when they were scheduled for Fratton Park in the FA Cup quarter-final and such was the breathtaking quality of their football that it would have taken a brave man to bet against them doing it. We now know it was never achieved, undermined over a long season in a matter of days with defeats by Chelsea in the Champions' League and Manchester United in the FA Cup, but in the build-up to March 6, they were beginning to look invincible. Not that Pompey felt any sense of inferiority; Fratton Park

Redknapp and Mandaric contemplate the possibility of failure.

was proving a difficult place for opponents and every team had an off day or two. There was (wild) talk of Todorov making a shock return to the side, of Eddie Howe springing an even bigger surprise by coming into the squad and the deeply religious Primus admitted to praying for celestial help in stopping Thierry Henry. It was certainly beyond a mere mortal to do so. Redknapp was an Arsenal supporter as a boy though born and bred in West Ham territory but, in the best part of half a century as a Gooner, he had never seen an Arsenal side as good as the one now assembled by Arsene Wenger. "If we beat Liverpool and Arsenal in successive rounds, they ought to give us the cup there and then." Mornar came in for the cup-tied Lua-Lua in an attacking formation designed to pressure Arsenal into making mistakes and crushing their midfield creativity. So much for plans. What happened next will live long in the memories of all who were lucky and privileged enough to see it at Fratton Park and on television. It is a match, a mismatch, that will be talked about forever all the while there are pubs in Portsmouth and people to drink in them.

STAY UP POMPEY!

Saturday March 6

**PORTSMOUTH (0) 1 ARSENAL (3) 5
(FA Cup 6th Round)**

But it wasn't just the result, a 5-1 win for superb, exhilarating Arsenal. The Pompey supporters produced a result of their own with a spontaneous, genuine show of appreciation for the victors, applauding off Henry and Patrick Vieira when they were substituted and rising as one at the final whistle to salute a world-class performance. Arsenal were simply awesome, sweeping aside Pompey with a glorious exhibition of the footballing arts which made a mockery of the valiant attempts of their game but overwhelmed opponents. Pompey never gave up and nor did their fans who sang, chanted and roared through the rain on a damp and chill Saturday evening. For 20 minutes, maybe a little more, Pompey gave as good as they got but Arsenal began to exploit gaps down the flanks where Pasanen and Stefanovic found themselves outnumbered.

Jose Antonio Reyes had already hit the bar by the time, in the 25th minute, Henry seized on Pasanen's attempted clearance to lash in the first. The rest was processional as Edu had a shot blocked by Hislop's legs and Vieira headed wide. Pompey were within two minutes of hearing the half-time whistle when Edu, collecting 40 yards out, nonchalantly exchanged passes with Vieira before threading a pass through for the overlapping Freddie Ljungberg, who curled his shot over Hislop.

Pompey were still reeling when Kolo Toure turned in a half-cleared Henry corner in first half injury-time for the third. The interval at least gave Redknapp the chance

Freddie Ljungberg - scored the second and added the fifth.

to reorganise, Stone replacing Berkovic in a 4-4-2 system aimed at stopping Arsenal rampaging down the flanks at will. But it made little or no difference and within five minutes Henry had side-footed past Hislop's outstretched hand for the fourth from the best part of 25 yards and struck with such impudence that many people inside the ground were not sure the ball had gone in. Ljungberg hustled in the fifth, aided by a deflection in the 57th minute and there was still plenty of time for more, many more. It was at this stage that Redknapp turned to the equally bemused Jim Smith and said: "This could be anything." And still the crowd refused to give up, refused to bow to the inevitable. With a big European match coming up, Wenger took off Vieira and Henry and it was

Thierry Henry celebrates his brace.

then that armchair viewers, perhaps waiting for 'Casualty', witnessed what must be a unique moment; vanquished fans rising to praise their executioners. Arsenal visibly relaxed as Yakubu and Taylor hit the woodwork, Gunners reject Hughes had a shot cleared from the line and, deep into stoppage time, substitute Sheringham finished off a Stone cross. As a former Tottenham player with an

STAY UP POMPEY!

ingrained dislike for Arsenal, the consolation goal gave him obvious pleasure.

Portsmouth (4-3-1-2): Hislop; Pasanen, Primus, De Zeeuw, Taylor; Smertin, Faye, Quashie (Hughes 70); Berkovic (Stone 45); Mornar (Sheringham 77), Yakubu.
Subs Not Used: Wapenaar, Harper.
Goals: Sheringham 90.

Arsenal (4-4-2): Lehmann; Lauren, Campbell, Toure, Cole; Ljungberg (Bentley 72), Vieira (Clichy 72), Edu, Silva; Reyes, Henry (Kanu 72).
Subs Not Used: Taylor, Cygan.
Goals: Henry 25, Ljungberg 43, 57, Toure 45, Henry 50.

Att: 20,137
Ref: J Winter (Cleveland).

STATS:
Shots on target: Pompey 4 Arsenal 9
Shots off target: Pompey 10 Arsenal 6
Corners: Pompey 5 Arsenal 10
Fouls: Pompey 12 Arsenal 17
Offside: Pompey 3 Arsenal 1

The post-match comments were as much about the behaviour of the Portsmouth supporters as about the result, but Redknapp gave credit where it was due. "They are the best in Europe and probably the best in the world. I think they could win everything put in front of them. I think I could pick six of them to win the Boat Race. The only trouble is you would struggle to find anyone small enough to be the cox." Wenger thought there was room for improvement and then admitted his worldwide travels had provided him with nothing to compare with Pompey's support. "They were fantastic. It's enjoyable to see the opposing fans cheer your team so you have to take your hat off to them. I can't say I have seen anything like that before from supporters." Thierry Henry, brought up on the funereal atmosphere of half-

In the aftermath of the heavy defeat by Arsenal in the FA Cup, it was the Pompey fans who received all the plaudits.

filled French stadia, joined Vieira and Edu in reciprocating the applause from the centre circle. "I have never seen anything like that. Even when they were four or five down they kept singing. I hope Portsmouth don't get relegated. They deserve to stay in the Premiership with fans like that. The way they gave me that ovation when I came off was something special." Fred Dinenage said veteran television commentator Barry Davies, another man to have seen it all, found the fans to be extraordinary. "If there was a Premier League for supporters we'd be European champions, world champions," said Dinenage. Mandaric summed it all up perfectly. "We had the best team in the world in front of the best supporters in the world."

Rowan Vine, a product of the youth system at Fratton Park, had some significant success while out on loan and was rewarded with a two-year extension to his contract.

Rowan Vine had been continuing an elongated form of apprenticeship with a year on loan at Colchester, having spent the whole of the previous season at Brentford. Vine, a promising young striker from Basingstoke and a product of the youth system, had enjoyed a few moments of national glory when he scored a hat-trick for Colchester in knocking Coventry out of the FA Cup and then dedicating it to his imprisoned brother. Like Lewis Buxton at Bournemouth, Pompey were happier for Vine to further his education in the lower divisions than play in the less competitive environment of the reserve league. Far from being forgotten, Vine was given a two-year extension to his contract by Redknapp who felt he might still have a future at Fratton Park. It was a timely boost for the player who must have felt he was

STAY UP POMPEY!

doomed to spend his Pompey career permanently playing for other teams. But while Vine could rejoice in the vote of confidence, it was being made clear, as the Football League transfer deadline approached, that peripheral figures like Pitt, Burton, Pettefer, Burchill, Bradbury and Tardif could go. If Vine turned out to be half as good as Sheringham, then the faith in him would have been justified. Sheringham, meanwhile, unsure of a starting place, said he was committed to playing until beyond his 39th birthday as his 38th approached. But for whom?

Saturday March 13

EVERTON (0) 1 PORTSMOUTH (0) 0

Not many years ago Everton were every bit as glamorous as Arsenal and certainly as big. But over the years a gulf had emerged between them and the major Premiership clubs and, like Tottenham, they could no longer count themselves among the elite. Everton were like a rump of sides in the Premiership that Pompey encountered in their first season: good enough to retain their status but not good enough to win anything worthwhile. In fact, Everton had become one of the dullest sides in the division, hard-working, honest and difficult to beat at Goodison Park and it was to Goodison that Pompey went on March 13, anxious to avoid becoming victims of a league double. The big question among Pompey fans concerned the amount of damage done by the Arsenal defeat. It was all very well praising Arsenal but

Pompey had been hopelessly out-classed and it was not unreasonable to assume that morale could have been affected. Redknapp attempted to tighten his defence with Curtis taking over from Taylor and Stone and Hughes drafted into midfield. Lua-Lua came in on the left side of midfield and there was a place on the bench for the rehabilitated Todorov, fresh from scoring two goals in the reserves. This left Yakubu on his own up front and the first 45 minutes was forgettable stuff.

Pompey began to look better only when Taylor came on at the start of the second half in place of Lua-Lua but, in territorial terms, Everton were the dominant side without ever making the best of it. It began to look as if Pompey might hold on for a draw but, with 12 minutes remaining, Wayne Rooney beat Curtis and then Hislop from 20 yards. The talented but temperamental youngster then raced to the other end of the pitch to taunt Pompey fans who had jeered him through the afternoon. Rooney had three good chances after that as Pompey went in search of an equaliser but missed them all while Mornar, on as a substitute, headed over at the other end. Three more points gone. Redknapp realised it had been an opportunity lost and lamented the lack of a natural scorer. "We make one mistake and we lose, it can't be right." Mandaric said he was enjoying the way Pompey played but not the results. "We have got to grind out the points even when we are not playing well." Alarm bells? Not quite.

41 YEARS OF HURT

Everton (4-4-2): Martyn; Hibbert, Stubbs, Yobo, Naysmith; Watson, Linderoth, Nyarko, Kilbane; Ferguson (Radzinski 32), Rooney.
Subs Not Used: Wright, Unsworth, McFadden, Carsley.
Goals: Rooney 78.

Portsmouth (4-4-1-1): Hislop; Pasanen, Primus, De Zeeuw, Curtis; Stone (Sheringham 80), Faye, Hughes, Lua-Lua (Taylor 45); Berkovic (Mornar 68); Yakubu.
Subs Not Used: Wapenaar, Todorov.
Booked: Berkovic, Pasanen.

Att: 40,105
Ref: N Barry (N Lincolnshire)

STATS:
Shots on target: Everton 5 Pompey 1
Shots off target: Everton 10 Pompey 2
Corners: Everton 6 Pompey 4
Fouls: Everton 10 Pompey 12
Offside: Everton 1 Pompey 4

March was the month of Redknapp's birthday. At 57, he was one of the more senior managers in English football, the pressures of which increasingly demanded that younger men should be in charge of teams. Football had been good to Harry. He admitted in an interview that, after quitting as a player at Bournemouth, he was close to buying a yellow taxi as a means of making a living but here he was 25 years down the line a rich man, rich enough not to need to work again. After West Ham had unceremoniously dumped him, it looked as if he might retire to his seashore home, his golf and his racing. A year overseeing Graham Rix as director of football had renewed his appetite but it is questionable that, had his old friend from America, Milan Mandaric, not pursued him, if he would ever have returned to the all-consuming passions of football. No one exemplified the highs and lows of football more than Redknapp; he loved it and hated it all at the same time. We were still two months away from May's Big Row and all was well between manager and chairman.

Mandaric was aware of Redknapp's value and, even with the prospect of relegation in the background, offered him a year's extension of his contract, taking him through to the summer of 2006. Mandaric said: "This is a tricky, pressurised time for the club and I felt it right that at this time I show my support and encouragement. Though we dropped into the bottom three after losing at Everton, I want to remain positive and look to the future." Redknapp revealed that the contract offer had been on the table for him to sign for some weeks. "I agreed it with the chairman a while ago but only got round to signing it at the weekend. We've got great supporters and I could not have enjoyed two years more than I have done here. It's been absolutely brilliant. When I took over, the club was fourth or fifth from bottom of the first division and had been for much of the previous six years, so I think I've earned anything I get. While I'm enjoying it, I'll continue doing it. I enjoy working and enjoy the people I work with and work for."

Brave words, bearing in mind what was to happen two months down the line, and brave words had been Mike Neasom's stock-in-trade as the journalist responsible for covering Pompey for The News, Portsmouth, for more than 20 years. Neasom lost a seven-year battle against illness on March 15

181

aged 69 and his loss was deeply mourned within the reporting and local sporting communities. For many Pompey fans Neasom had a dream job, but it was never easy attempting to discover the truth in the Deacon and Gregory eras and to make sense of what information came his way for those, in pre-internet and Teletext days, who hung on to his every word. His honesty did not always endear him to Pompey management but his integrity was recognised by supporters when he got a moving ovation as he stood on the pitch at Fratton Park after covering his last match in 1996. Jim Smith and Frank Burrows, two managers he much admired, were among hundreds of mourners at St Thomas's,

Mike Neasom, the long-standing Portsmouth FC correspondent of The News, who died on March 15.

Bedhampton, while Lawrie McMenemy, John Mortimore and a large contingent of Southampton representatives also paid their genuine respects. Hampshire County Cricket Club and Havant Hockey Club, on whom he also reported, joined family and supporters in marking Neasom's passing. Over the best part of three decades he had seen some remarkable events in the history of the famous old football club and, while he came to like and respect many of those at Pompey's helm, there were others he regarded as charlatans and self-seekers and for whom he had no time. Alan Knight, whose career had been chronicled by Neasom from the moment he made his debut as a 16-year-old, said: "He was a great man, a real gentleman. Mike upset one or two managers with his honesty which probably showed he was doing his job."

Not even Neasom was covering Portsmouth when Bert Barlow was in his pomp. It was hard to believe for modern generations, as Pompey battled for survival in the Premiership, that in the past they had won the league and the FA Cup. Barlow had done both. Barlow was the only player ever to win a league championship and FA Cup winners' medal while a Pompey player so it was with a measure of sadness when it was reported that he, too, had died after a short illness at his home in Colchester, aged 87. In terms of what he achieved, Barlow could claim with some justification to be Pompey's most successful player. Arriving from Wolves for £8,500 in February 1939, Barlow had the distinction of

41 YEARS OF HURT

Bert Barlow, who died in March, was the only person ever to win both the FA Cup and league championship in a Pompey shirt. He is pictured here being introduced to the Fratton Park crowd and (inset) as he looked in the post-war years.

playing in the team which beat Wolves in the FA Cup final, scoring against his old club in a shock 4-1 win. While World War II sliced through his productive years, he was still a key player in 1948-49 when Pompey again surprised the football world by winning the first division championship. Barlow scored 32 goals in 105 league appearances and made frequent trips to Fratton Park in later years.

Wednesday March 17

**LIVERPOOL (2) 3
PORTSMOUTH (0) 0**

Pompey were back on Merseyside days after losing at Everton to take on a Liverpool side which had failed in three previous attempts to beat them. Among four changes, Todorov made a starting return after some promising performances in reserve matches and seven months after damaging his knee so severely that no one expected him back for a year. Mornar and Lua-Lua partnered him in attack and Yakubu and Berkovic were rested with Southampton's visit in mind. This time Liverpool made no mistake, roaring into a two-goal lead and winning so comprehensively that statistics showed that Pompey failed to muster a single shot on target. Only Hislop, still nursing his broken finger, stood between Liverpool and double figures. Not that even Hislop could do anything to stop Dietmar Hamann putting Liverpool ahead in the sixth minute with a 20-yard scorcher before the

STAY UP POMPEY!

Michael Owen put the disappointment of his penalty miss at Fratton Park in the Cup behind him to score two goals against Pompey at Anfield, combining with Steven Gerrard for the second.

predatory Michael Owen added another in the 28th. Todorov's appearance had been a gamble and it was one which had not paid off by the time he failed to reappear after the break. Lacking sharpness and predictably off the pace, Toddy was replaced by Taylor while Stone took over from the labouring Smertin. Pompey were better in the second half, Stefanovic hitting the bar, but Owen headed in Gerrard's cross and it was all over. Murphy and Heskey hit the woodwork and Hislop made seven top-class saves. It was the eleventh time Pompey had failed to score in an away game so it was not hard to see where the problems lay.

Liverpool (4-4-2): Dudek; Carragher, Biscan, Hyypia, Riise; Murphy, Hamann, Gerrard (Cheyrou 74), Kewell (Diouf 80); Owen, Heskey.
Subs Not Used: Luzi Bernardi, Henchoz, Baros.
Goals: Hamann 6, Owen 28, 58.

Portsmouth (4-4-2): Hislop; Primus, De Zeeuw, Stefanovic, Curtis; Smertin (Stone 45), Faye, Hughes, Lua-Lua; Todorov (Taylor 46), Mornar.
Subs Not Used: Wapenaar, Sheringham, Pasanen.
Booked: Stefanovic.

Att: 34,663
Ref: B Knight (Kent).

STATS:
Shots on target: Liverpool 10 Pompey 0
Shots off target: Liverpool 8 Pompey 4
Corners: Liverpool 10 Pompey 8
Fouls: Liverpool 9 Pompey 23
Offside: Liverpool 0 Pompey 6

Redknapp thought Liverpool were a bit edgy until Owen got the second. "We have been in most away games without scoring so I switched it to three up front but it still didn't make any difference." It was almost as if, to the casual observer, Pompey were going through the motions at Anfield because of a far bigger match four days later, in local terms at least, when Southampton came to Fratton Park. After defeats at St Mary's, Pompey needed to win to satisfy their honour and erase from the memory two poor performances. A third setback could well have had a deep psychological affect and it was lucky for Pompey that Saints, after a typically chaotic change of manager, had begun to doze in the Premiership's comfort zone. Like a fox in a hen-house, Southampton's short trip along the coast caused a lot of squawking and ruffled feathers. Matt Taylor had to go on the record to say his friendship with James Beattie meant nothing when it came to playing against him and the chairman, mindful of a violent fringe of fans, warned the yobs and thugs to stay away. Extra police were being drafted in to make sure the only activity was on the pitch. Southampton's new manager Paul Sturrock caused further consternation on both sides of the great divide when he said he hoped Pompey would stay up. He really was new. Historically, the omens were not good either. You needed a good memory to recall Brian Lewis and Ron Saunders scoring the goals on September 28, 1963, when Saints were last vanquished at Fratton Park. Pompey were last successful at the Dell in January 1988 so 16 long, nagging years of Saints supremacy had bitten into the Pompey psyche.

Sunday March 21

PORTSMOUTH (0) 1
SOUTHAMPTON (0) 0

As with many long-awaited events, the reality is often a let down. It was for some 2,000 Saints fans who got a pre-match soaking at the open Milton End when a hailstorm descended with some venom. It was for Michael Svensson, who was injured in the warm-up and it was for Berkovic, who missed the chance to play against his old club because of a virus. The luckless Toddy stood down. The match itself was also something of a non-event. Pompey's players gave everything and three sides of the ground reverberated in a wall of sound but the opposition failed to materialise. Taunted by incessant 'scummers' chants, Saints plodded through the match as if it was a pre-season friendly, riding their luck as the wasteful Yakubu snatched at enough chances to have scored five or six. Antti Niemi made a couple of saves while, at the other end, Hislop had nothing to do. But, at last, the tension was broken midway through the second half. Smertin set Stone racing down the right and his low cross eluded the Saints defence for Yakubu, gloriously, to score from four yards. Three parts of the ground erupted in joy so uncontrollable that two fans defied tenacious stewards to leap from the Fratton End to join in the celebrations. Yakubu was an instant hero for life. Would Saints now respond? Kevin Phillips smashed a shot against an upright for Primus to clear the rebound

STAY UP POMPEY!

The Yak became an instant Pompey legend when he scored the goal that beat Saints at Fratton Park.

and, deep into stoppage time, Hislop excelled in keeping out another Phillips shot and a header, somehow, from Claus Lundekvam. It was far too late for Saints and, in any case, any equaliser would have been undeserved because, without ever needing to be excellent, Pompey had been by some distance the better side.

Portsmouth (4-4-2): Hislop; Pasanen, Primus, De Zeeuw, Stefanovic; Stone, Faye, Smertin, Taylor; Sheringham, Yakubu (Lua-Lua 83).
Subs Not Used: Wapenaar, Curtis, Hughes, Mornar.
Goals: Yakubu 68.

Southampton (4-4-2): Niemi; Dodd, Lundekvam, Higginbotham, Crainey (Fernandes 80); Telfer, Delap, Anders Svensson (Prutton 60), McCann (Pahars 73); Beattie, Phillips.
Subs Not Used: Smith, Hall.
Booked: Higginbotham, Prutton.

Att: 20,140
Ref: M Halsey (Lancashire).

STATS:
Shots on target: Pompey 7 Saints 6
Shots off target: Pompey 8 Saints 4
Corners: Pompey 6 Saints 3
Fouls: Pompey 16 Saints 15
Offside: Pompey 7 Saints 0

The scenes at the final whistle as players and fans hugged each other would surely have provoked a nod of recognition from medal-winning Bert Barlow had he survived a few extra days. It was like a cup final and, in many respects, the parallels for Pompey were not too far-fetched. For them, this was a big, big match. So, as the city of Portsmouth broke into days of celebrations, the fox slunk back to Southampton, tail between legs. Sadly, that was not the end of it. There was fighting (not involving opposition fans) down Goldsmith Avenue and into the Fratton Centre, many arrests then and later after troublemakers had been snared by CCTV and much damage was done to shops and property. But the operation involving some 400 police had been a good one, efficiently planned and executed and a major incident had been averted. Pompey were still in the bottom three, on goal difference from Leicester, but the lift given to the club and the city by that single, largely uneventful win was almost tangible.

In far-away Trinidad, Barmy Army member Steve Harman, a taxi driver by trade, kept the Pompey flag flying in his replica shirt and ginger wig (was Rory Allen there?). Leaving the Queens Park Oval early, Harman and half a dozen fellow Pompey fans headed for Trotters beach bar where an equal number of Saints fans kept their counsel at the other end of it to watch the match on satellite television. They were joined just before kick-off by Saints' holidaying chairman Rupert Lowe, who watched in increasing desperation as Pompey took the lead and then went on to

Milan Mandaric gets to grips with his Southampton opposite number Rupert Lowe. Lowe was in Trinidad at the time of the Fratton Park derby, watching the cricket and looking for a large slice of humble pie!

win. Harman and his pals turned Trotters into a faraway piece of Fratton Park with celebrations every bit as wild as those in murky England and Lowe was forced to eat a large helping of humble pie with his hot roti. As least he had the decency to congratulate the Pompey fans, adding his best wishes for the future to those of his manager. "I hope you stay up," he said. "We need more derbies." He even posed for pictures with them, trying hard to smile, before heading to the cricket.

Back at Fratton Park, Sturrock said he was sorry for his fans because only one team was trying to win the game and Fred Dinenage, working among a hotbed of Saints fans, knew he could walk into Meridian's television newsroom on Monday, his head held high. No one at Pompey was underplaying the significance of the three points. Primus said: "The result means so much to everyone. There was a lot of pride at stake and to beat them is an achievement that everyone wanted. This was the biggest fixture in everyone's calendar really." Redknapp also realised just how big a win it had been. "If we had lost this one, it could have ruined it for us this season. If we can win three more home games and one away we should be okay, but who knows what it will take to stay up this season?"

Carl Pettefer spent five years as a professional, clocking up more managers than first team appearances so that his move on loan to Southend hardly warranted a mention. But, as Pompey were beating Saints, Pettefer was enjoying his day in the sun as Southend went down to Blackpool at the Millennium Stadium in the final of the LDV Vans Trophy, a magnificent stadium, a large crowd and a far cry from the handful of fans who had watched him in Pompey's reserves. Pettefer, a neat and skilled midfield player, earned a Southend contract with some sound performances despite breaking a leg as his loan came close to expiring. There were other outgoings as the Nationwide League's transfer deadline approached. Courtney Pitt followed Graham Rix to Oxford (only to be freed at the end of the season), Olszar went to Coventry, Bradbury to Walsall, Robinson to Sunderland, Hunt and Cooper to Leyton Orient - many of those on loan - while Srnicek made his move to West Ham permanent. Poor old Eddie Howe, his knee improving by the day, went to Swindon on loan but failed to play in a match for them because of an ankle injury and returned to Fratton Park, his morale crushed again. Hands up all those who had heard of Mark Casey? Almost three years after Rix had brought him down from Celtic, Casey was not even a regular in the reserves but St Patrick's Athletic liked the look of him and lured him across the Irish Sea. Pompey did not stand in his way.

As ever with crowd problems, there is always the fear that the Football Association might get involved. The police were none too happy either. But the referee's report did not contain mention of a plastic bottle aimed at Beattie or coins thrown at Hislop. What happened outside the ground was not

Pompey's immediate concern and no blame could be attached. But Peter Storrie was determined that problem fans should be rooted out, among them those who had run on to the pitch when Yakubu scored. Two season ticket holders were later banned and, from CCTV footage, a steady trickle of miscreants were arrested in the weeks that followed.

Luther Blissett was known as Luther Missit in his 80s heyday for the easy chances he failed to put away but more than 200 goals suggested he found the net more often than not, earning him a lucrative season with AC Milan and getting him into the England side briefly. Redknapp knew Blissett from the couple of years he spent at Bournemouth and it was to him the Pompey manager turned when it became clear Yakubu was not making the most of his many attributes. In particular, the hefty Nigerian struggled to come to terms with the offside law. Only Ruud van Nistelrooy, with 59 offences, had been flagged more times than his 56. Lua-Lua was another frequent culprit so Blissett was hired to improve that and other aspects of their forward play. Blissett watched the Yak on video and could see that he needed to bend his runs instead of moving in a straight line and quickly set about the task of rectifying the problem. Redknapp said: "All season away we have had an equal share of games but haven't been scoring. Luther is an excellent coach and will be here two days a week to work with our strikers. We need one or two players to get into double figures."

Luther Blissett, the former Watford and AC Milan target man, was hired by Redknapp to coach Yakubu and Lua-Lua into staying onside as often as possible.

Saturday March 27

**BLACKBURN ROVERS (1) 1
PORTSMOUTH (1) 2**

What Portsmouth needed above all else was an away win. Blackburn may have won at Fratton Park but

Teddy Sheringham had been used sparingly by Redknapp in the second half of the season but it was his free kick which gave Pompey the lead at Ewood Park.

trip to Ewood on March 27 was a fixture, therefore, between a team who could not win at home against a team who could not win away. Pompey had to prove that the victory over Saints had not been a local fluke, but there was a discernible air of relief on the training ground in the few days between beating Saints and heading north to Blackburn. The immediate pressure was off. As a result, Pompey played with a great sense of freedom and vigour at Blackburn, tearing them apart with some sharp, incisive forward play. Some 2,500 Pompey fans, heartened by the derby win, were in full voice and cheering again after 17 minutes when Sheringham curled in a 25-yard free kick after Yakubu had been fouled. It was the first time Pompey had led away since Arsenal in September. Both sides missed chances, Taylor, Sheringham and Stone for Pompey and Jon Stead for Blackburn. Fresh from a good win at Aston Villa, Blackburn did not look any happier at home but they were level after 37 minutes through a Matt Taylor own goal, a deflection from a shot by Tugay. Garry Flitcroft and Andy Cole should have done better with clear openings and for a time it looked as if Pompey might cave in. But Rovers, who had not won at home since November 29, did not have the killer instinct and Pompey were able to survive and counter attack as time whittled down. With eight minutes remaining, Lua-Lua's pace took him away from three defenders and, after Lucas Neill had dispossessed him, the ball ran free for Yakubu to beat Brad Friedel from the edge. "We are

they were extremely vulnerable at Ewood Park and had already lost there more than they had won, a curious fact which had been threatening to send them spiralling into the first division's nether world. The staying up," chanted the Pompey fans but right at the death, the normally lethal Cole, unmarked at the far post, missed from six yards. On such incidents are entire campaigns won and lost. It was Rovers' ninth home defeat and, with Wolves and Leeds losing and Leicester gaining only a point the next day, Pompey were out of the bottom three again.

Blackburn (4-4-2): Friedel; Neill, Short, Todd, Gray (Gallagher 83); Andresen (Yorke 71), Flitcroft, Tugay, Emerton; Stead (Reid 78), Cole.
Subs Not Used: Enckelman, Amoruso.
Goals: Taylor 37 o.g.

Portsmouth (4-4-2): Hislop; Pasanen, Primus, De Zeeuw, Stefanovic; Stone, Smertin, Faye, Taylor (Hughes 88); Sheringham (Lua-Lua 71), Yakubu.
Subs Not Used: Wapenaar, Berkovic, Mornar.
Goals: Sheringham 17, Yakubu 82.

Att: 22,855
Ref: P Durkin (Dorset).

STATS:
Shots on target: Blackburn 4 Pompey 4
Shots off target: Blackburn 7 Pompey 4
Corners: Blackburn 5 Pompey 3
Fouls: Blackburn 11 Pompey 10
Offside: Blackburn 1 Pompey 1

Redknapp was pleased the jinx had been beaten and hoped it might lead to other away wins. "I don't know if Luther Blissett made the difference. Yakubu played well last week and scored but he has not got as many as he should have done. Two in two games will have been great for his confidence." Mandaric saw it as a massive win. "We have got six points in seven days and it's a sweet feeling. Confidence is riding high." What a month March had been. Defeats by Arsenal, Everton and Liverpool had largely been for-

gotten in the wake of wins over Southampton and Blackburn and the talk now was of staying up, not of going down. There were now six weeks left of an emotion-charged season, plenty of time for Pompey to save themselves but time also for rivals to get their acts together. It promised to be a magnificent April and a nervous May.

The Premiership
BOTTOM 10 AT END OF MARCH 2004

	P	W	D	L	F	A	Pts
Middlesbrough	30	10	8	12	35	39	38
Tottenham Hotspur	30	11	4	15	40	47	37
Bolton Wanderers	30	9	10	11	34	46	37
Everton	30	8	10	12	36	41	34
Manchester City	30	7	10	13	41	42	31
Blackburn Rovers	30	8	7	15	42	48	31
PORTSMOUTH	**30**	**8**	**6**	**16**	**32**	**45**	**30**
Leicester City	30	5	13	12	39	52	28
Leeds United	30	6	7	17	29	60	25
Wolverhampton Wdrs	30	5	9	16	26	62	24

12.

The Great Escape

Braveheart Jock McQuashie throws his lot in with Scotland.

APRIL FOOL'S JOKES ARE COMmon in newspapers, some more sophisticated than others, and all the funnier if readers fail to spot them and believe them to be true. There is always someone who really does believe martians have landed at Buckingham Palace so, when Nigel Quashie announced to Sam Matterface on Quay FM that he was now a Scotsman, there was a fair amount of healthy cynicism in the Portsmouth area.

Braveheart Jock Quashie did not seem to be very likely. For a start, the London-born midfielder had played four times for England under-21s and for England B while his father hailed from the Caribbean island of St Vincent, so the Scottish link would have to be tenuous - and it was. His Rangers-supporting grandfather, Andrew McFarlane, came from Glasgow and although he lived most of his life in London, he had never lost his accent or a misty-eyed love of the old country. Quashie later explained: "After I had mentioned it to Kevin Harper, my agent got a call saying Scotland were interested in me. I have been asked to get my grandfather's birth certificate and I have got to go to London to pick up the paperwork. If I play for Scotland I will give it every-thing. I want to be able to look back at my career and say I have achieved things. A good CV is more important to me than money and playing international football would be a great a c h i e v e m e n t ." Luckily for Quashie, all his appearances for England were non-competitive so the transition to McQuashie was smooth and, above all, not a hoax. Richard Hughes, whose mother flew home from Italy where the family were domiciled to make sure he was born in Scotland, had no such qualification problems and both he and Quashie were selected by Berti Vogts for the squad

to face Romania. Sadly there were no happy ending. Hughes, seeking his first cap, was an unused substitute and Quashie, proudly clutching the birth certificate of his dead grandad, was ruled out by injury.

Eyal Berkovic had something of a 'reputation' when Pompey signed him. There was a famous incident at West Ham where he had so riled team-mate John Hartson during a training session that Hartson was pictured attempting to kick Berkovic in the head. But Redknapp enjoyed a rapport with

Eyal Berkovic had come to Pompey carrying with him something of a reputation for divisive behaviour. However, his relationship with Redknapp was so good that he soon fitted into the set-up.

STAY UP POMPEY!

Berkovic where others did not and was happy to bring him to Fratton Park. Perhaps Berkovic was becoming more of a team man, mellowing with age (he was 32 on April 2), because Redknapp wondered how he would take to being dropped at Blackburn. He need not have worried. "Eyal took it fine. He's been terrific. It was not his fault he was not playing at Blackburn. He was ill before the Southampton game and then we kept the same team. He was as happy as anyone we won at Blackburn. After Yakubu got the winning goal, Eyal was the first to put his arms around him in the dressing room. Eyal's had his ups and downs with people but he's a very clever guy and a terrific player." Sheringham shared Berkovic's birthdate but at six years older was inevitably beginning to feel the strain and, with a rush of fixtures coming up over Easter, Redknapp was wary of playing him twice in three days.

Pompey had no game in the week before Easter but the absence of any match involvement only meant a fretful weekend for sleep-deprived Redknapp, who admitted whiling away the early hours working out result permutations for Pompey and their relegation rivals. "I'm wondering who's going to beat who and I keep looking at the run-in everyone has got. Waiting for the results and watching them come through is a nightmare after every game. It's so nerve-wracking. Until you're there, you can never appreciate what it's like. I wish we were playing as I want to keep going after two terrific results." What Redknapp would have made of that

weekend's results is anyone's guess. Some were good from Pompey's point of view, some were disappointing and, overall, it was as inconclusive as expected from a set of scores with so much of the season still to run. Wolves lost at home to Saints, Blackburn were trounced at Liverpool, Everton lost at Newcastle and Manchester City drew with Villa. But the big one was at Elland Road where Leeds came back from two goals down to beat Leicester. These results left Pompey fourth from bottom, six points clear of Wolves at the bottom and two points ahead of Leeds and Leicester. Manchester City, Everton and Blackburn were still in deep trouble and Pompey had this precious game in hand. The bad news was that it was against Arsenal.

For Vincent Pericard and Svetoslav Todorov, the season looked to be over. Toddy had come back too soon and he was now injured again, nursing a left knee injury sustained in a closed-door friendly against Brentford. A scan did not look promising and Pompey were prepared for the worse. As for Pericard, the season had been a wash-out. Signed permanently from Juventus, the striker had managed a paltry 58 minutes of Premiership football and now had a thigh injury which showed no signs of improvement. "It's been an empty season," he said. "You have to be strong because you don't have a choice. I try to smile and be positive. I was looking forward to playing in the Premiership and improving myself but it has not happened. It has been very frustrating." Pericard started only against Northampton

don't know, the other players don't know, nobody knows. I did not start the season until a month after everyone else because I only signed in mid-July and that didn't help. We don't know exactly what the problem is. I may have come back too early and I can't tell when I will be back in training. It changes every day. Sometimes I will be back in a couple of days, sometimes it's weeks, sometimes it is longer."

The craving for Pompey football memorabilia inspired Southsea auctioneers DM Nesbit & Co to hold four football sales every year and the latest saw 111 lots raise £25,000. For one lucky Gosport pensioner, there was a windfall of more than £11,000. A Pompey fan from the 1930s, his collection of hundreds of home programmes up to the early 50s, each with a match ticket and a newspaper report of the game was snapped up eagerly by enthusiasts. Club historian Richard Owen drooled: "His collection was as good as it gets." Auctioneer John Cameron noted a strange trend. "The vendors with the best and most valuable collections seem to come from Gosport. The star lot was nine Pompey home programmes from the 1939/40 war league season which went for £2,250."

Vincent Pericard, who had played just 58 minutes of football during the season, picked up yet another injury and now his position at Fratton Park was in a state of limbo.

and, with the likes of Mornar coming in, had fallen down the striker pecking order. "The gaffer doesn't know where I stand in the team, I

STAY UP POMPEY!

Redknapp and Mandaric were already looking ahead to next season and recruitment but the problem was knowing which division Pompey might be in. There was talk of former Pompey icon Darren Anderton returning in the summer once his Spurs contract was completed but that was quickly scotched. Jamie Redknapp was another possibility but his dad remained frustrated. "I think we've got the nucleus of what we want, so I don't see much change. But it's hard to decide what to do until we know where we are going. It depends on which division we find ourselves. People ring me about players but I've got to tell them we are not looking at the moment because we don't know what's happening. It's difficult." This left fans wondering what Harry meant by 'much change'. Did that mean one new player or five? Clearly there was room for negotiation between himself and the chairman as to the exact number. That should have been straightforward enough, shouldn't it?

One player who was sure to be part of next season's Pompey was the ever-popular Linvoy Primus. His retention was thoroughly deserved for a season of solid accomplishment after being overlooked for selection for the first few months. If Redknapp had any doubts about Primus's Premiership credentials, they had long since vanished and the proof was the offer, gratefully accepted, of a new

One player who had proved he was good enough for the Premiership against all predictions was Linvoy Primus, pictured here giving the Saints a difficult time.

two-year contract. As Linvoy put pen to paper, he said: "It's a great honour and the peak of my footballing career. I did not know what the future held 18 months ago but things have worked out and it just proves you should never lose heart. My faith was important in keeping me going but also on my part I had to continue to train, work hard and have the right attitude. At the end of this latest contract I would have been here well over five years and this is the most stable part of my football career. I could never have thought of leaving here and it's great that I can continue where I feel at home."

Andy Awford's young reserves, containing only Schemmel and O'Neil who could be described as experienced, brought more smiles to Pompey faces with a 2-1 win over Saints at Fratton Park. In contrast, Southampton had put out a strong side which included Brett Ormerod, Neil McCann and others on the fringes of the first team. Chris Clark and Liam Horstead, capping an impressive display, drove the red and white invaders back across the River Hamble empty-handed.

Saturday April 10

CHARLTON ATHLETIC (1) 1
PORTSMOUTH (0) 1

Easter is a time for reflection but for Pompey and the other clubs around the foot of the Premiership it was a time for collecting points, not chocolate eggs. Pompey were away to Charlton and home to Birmingham. They were just the sort of teams they would have cho-

sen to face: going nowhere in mid-table despite grandiose talk of Europe. Charlton had been lucky to win at Fratton Park earlier in the season. Sloppiness in defence had cost Pompey two late goals and was a slap in the face after a promising start to Premiership life. Here at the Valley, after a brave second-half fightback in which they were undisputably the dominant side, Pompey had to settle for a draw - and a valuable one in context because Leeds won at Blackburn and Wolves drew 3-3 with Manchester City. Paolo Di Canio warmly embraced Redknapp before the start in a show of mutual respect and admiration, inevitably sparking terrace rumours of a summer signing, but there was no starting place for the great Italian. Shaun Bartlett, who had been preferred to him by Alan Curbishley, put Charlton ahead in the eighth minute, getting between Primus and Pasanen for his first goal since getting the winner at Fratton Park in October. Hislop denied Johansson and Konchesky while Jason Euell missed with an overhead kick as Charlton threatened more in a one-sided first half. Redknapp brought on Berkovic for Pasanen for the second and Pompey were immediately a different side.

After 65 minutes, they were level when Taylor swapped passes with Berkovic on the halfway line and strode on to cross for Yakubu to sidefoot his eleventh goal of the season. Lua-Lua, replacing Sheringham, almost added another but the sight of Di Canio coming on caused consternation among travelling fans who remembered the havoc he

STAY UP POMPEY!

wrought after being sent on at a similar stage at Fratton Park. This time he wasn't able to work his magic, although he did have a goal ruled out by an offside flag. While home players were booed off by their fans, Pompey supporters gave a rendition of 'The Great Escape', a tune becoming more familiar with every result. Redknapp, as usual, saw the positive aspects. "I thought we were going on to win. The crowd got a bit edgy and I thought it would go our way after we had scored. We made a bad start but we were excellent in the second half. When we get hold of the ball we are a decent team. Three weeks ago I thought the bottom three would come from four teams - us, Wolves, Leeds and Leicester. Now Blackburn have dropped into it and Manchester City are also in the picture because it's not happening for them at the moment."

Charlton (4-4-2): Kiely; Young, Fortune, Hreidarsson, Powell; Holland, Euell, Jensen, Konchesky; Johansson (Di Canio 78), Bartlett (Cole 71).
Subs Not Used: Royce, Thomas, Turner.
Booked: Euell.
Goals: Bartlett 8.

Portsmouth (4-4-2): Hislop, Pasanen (Berkovic 45), Primus, De Zeeuw, Stefanovic; Stone, Smertin, Faye, Taylor; Sheringham (Lua-Lua 57), Yakubu.
Subs Not Used: Wapenaar, Curtis, Quashie.
Booked: De Zeeuw.
Goals: Yakubu 65.

Att: 26,385
Ref: A D'Urso (Essex).

STATS:
Shots on target: Charlton 2 Pompey 6
Shots off target: Charlton 6 Pompey 3
Corners: Charlton 6 Pompey 2
Fouls: Charlton 15 Pompey 12
Offside: Charlton 2 Pompey 3

Barry Knight has never been a stranger to controversy. The Kent referee needed a police escort to get off the pitch and his Range Rover had its windows smashed when he fled the car park at that infamous trouble spot called Dean Court. This after he had sent off two Bournemouth players in a 4-0 Crewe win. Having reduced that match to a fiasco, it was something of a surprise to chronicle his subsequent eight-year rise to the Premiership. Short of hair and short of common sense appeared to be the general consensus of opinion and now here he was in charge of Portsmouth versus Birmingham, a game Pompey badly needed to win. True to form, Mr Knight made his mark but, luckily for the sake of his Range Rover, at Birmingham's expense and not Pompey's. Redknapp decided to keep Berkovic and Lua-Lua in his starting line-up in place of Pasanen and Sheringham.

Monday April 12

PORTSMOUTH (1) 3
BIRMINGHAM CITY (0) 1

For all but the last few seconds, the first half failed to spark. Then the match exploded. A long ball out of defence by Primus provoked confusion in the Birmingham defence as the Yak gave chase. Maik Taylor, the goalkeeper, and Martin Taylor, the defender, got into a tangle on the edge of the area and the goalkeeper clearly handled outside the box. The ball ran free for Yakubu to fire into an empty net, only to discover that Mr Knight had disallowed it, having blown for Taylor's indiscretion seconds earlier. Surr-

THE GREAT ESCAPE

Barry Knight failed to please either side in the awarding of a free kick rather than a penalty and sending off Birmingham keeper Maik Taylor. Stefanovic, however, crashed home the free kick.

Lua Lua entertains the crowd with his trademark somersaults after scoring Pompey's second.

ounded by both teams, the referee consulted his assistant before showing Maik Taylor a red card and awarding Pompey a free kick 20 yards out. Reserve keeper Ian Bennett's first touch was to retrieve the ball from the net after Stefanovic had stepped up to belt the free kick, left-footed, past the wall and his belated dive. The incident led to heated post-match debate, Steve Bruce predictably accusing the referee of sticking too pedantically to the rules. In his view

THE GREAT ESCAPE

Taylor should not have been sent off because Yakubu had not been deprived of a scoring chance. Bruce felt Taylor should have stayed and Yakubu's goal should have been allowed to stand. There were no complaints from Pompey, but what if Stefanovic had not scored from the free kick?

Lua-Lua, in a phenomenal burst of speed, eluded Kenny Cunningham on the halfway line for the second goal after 62 minutes, twisting one way and then the other before beating Bennett from ten yards. The goal was greeted with a series of somersaults from the little man so perfect that, had they been performed in front of an Olympic set of judges, he would surely have become Congo's first gymnastics gold medal winner. Stern John, feasting on a surge down the right by Damian Johnson, made it 2-1 and Pompey were, not for the first time, indebted to Hislop's alertness in keeping their lead. A save from Matthew Upson was the highlight. But, just as Birmingham looked as if they might snatch an equaliser, Cunningham handled a centre from Yakubu and Yakubu himself sent Bennett the wrong way with the penalty. End of match, but not end of story. As Bruce raged about his perceived injustice of Taylor's dismissal, Redknapp said: "The keeper had to be sent off. He handled outside the box and that is an automatic sending off offence. I'd rather have had the goal and the keeper stay on if I had the choice. I think the referee blew his whistle a little too quickly. Maybe he should have seen what developed.

Portsmouth (3-4-1-2): Hislop; Primus (Pasanen 50), De Zeeuw, Stefanovic; Stone, Smertin, Faye (Harper 82), Taylor; Berkovic (Quashie 74); Lua-Lua, Yakubu.
Subs Not Used: Wapenaar, Sheringham.
Booked: Quashie.
Goals: Stefanovic 45, LuaLua 62, Yakubu 73 pen.

Birmingham (4-4-2): Maik Taylor; Tebily (Bennett 45), Cunningham, Martin Taylor, Upson; Johnson, Hughes, Savage (Clemence 58), Clapham; Forssell (Morrison 78), John.
Subs Not Used: Motteram, Cisse.
Sent Off: Maik Taylor (45).
Booked: Cunningham, Clemence.
Goals: John 67.

Att: 20,104
Ref: B Knight (Kent).

STATS:
Shots on target: Pompey 5 Birmingham 2
Shots off target: Pompey 6 Birmingham 4
Corners: Pompey 4 Birmingham 4
Fouls: Pompey 18 Birmingham 14
Offside: Pompey 11 Birmingham 1

Redknapp was as concerned about his penalty-taker Yakubu taking over from Sheringham when he would have preferred either Taylor or Stefanovic to have stepped forward instead. "It was Yakubu's decision to take the penalty. I must admit I wasn't so sure. He said before Charlton he wanted to take the penalties but I was hoping someone would take the ball off him. He took penalties for Maccabi Haifa but taking them in the Israeli League is a bit different to the Premiership. But fair play to Yakubu, he tucked it away confidently." None of which interested Bruce, who was still ranting on about Taylor's red card - and the referee. "It was utter chaos. I think 20,000 people were absolutely stunned by the decision. How often are we left talking about the inadequacies of referees? It baffled me why he didn't just give the goal. As the away side, I don't know if we would have got that penalty decision like Portsmouth did. The referee should have kept it at eleven against eleven." Barry Knight was last seen walking unabused out of Fratton Park. His car was not damaged.

Peter Harris, Johnny Gordon and Reg Pickett were the scorers when Pompey last beat Manchester United, 3-0 at Old Trafford on October 19, 1957. Since then Pompey and United had played each other 15 times in the league and on plenty of other occasions in cups and Pompey had never once prevailed. The last time Pompey had beaten United at Fratton Park was December 10, 1955 when the ill-fated Busby Babes were approaching their peak. Tommy Taylor, one of those killed in the Munich air crash, had put United ahead, Jackie Henderson had equalised, only for David Pegg, another Munich victim, to restore United's lead. Jimmy Dickinson, with a rare goal, scored a deflected equaliser and Mark Jones, under pressure from Henderson, gave Pompey victory with an own goal. Since that match took place almost half a century ago, it's fair to assume that the vast majority of the crowd at Fratton Park on April 17 would not have been present that day or would have expected Pompey to end the sorry sequence. Over the intervening years, the two clubs had taken divergent paths and only now were Pompey seemingly on the way back. Sheringham was on the

bench against his old club but United surprisingly went into the match with only Louis Saha up front, although the respective formations provided full-backs Gary Neville and John O'Shea with acres of room down the flanks. Would that prove crucial? Yes and no, as it turned out.

Saturday April 17

PORTSMOUTH (1) 1
MANCHESTER UNITED (0) 0

United enjoyed huge heaps of possession but hardly ever looked like breaking down a disciplined and determined Pompey defence in which De Zeeuw and Primus rose, as expected, to the challenge. Hislop made a superb double save from Solskjaer and Giggs but United looked dull and ponderous and a labouring contrast to their great rivals Arsenal, who had graced Fratton Park with their va-va-voom only a few weeks before. Nine minutes before the break, Lua-Lua raced down the right flank and his low centre was contested by Wes Brown and Stone at the near post. The ball ran free to Neville at the far post who, under pressure from Yakubu, could only prod the ball back to the grateful Stone who lashed it into the top corner from six yards. Fratton Park went wild: one up against United. True champions respond to such setbacks and United tried without ever looking like they could take the game by the scruff of the neck, as they would have done a year or two before. Hislop saved from Saha, Solskjaer and O'Shea but Yakubu missed a

THE GREAT ESCAPE

Clockwise from top left: The evolution of the Steve Stone goal that beat Manchester United, Pompey's first victory over the Reds at Fratton Park for nearly 50 years.

chance for a Pompey second and the half-time whistle was a blessed relief for both sides.

Redknapp decided to sacrifice Berkovic's fitful flair for Quashie's more combative qualities. It worked; United found it far more difficult to build moves although Pompey were still obliged to defend for their lives, even more so once Ronaldo and Darren Fletcher had been sent on by Sir Alex Ferguson. The moment crucial to the outcome was a rejected penalty, a shot from Neville striking Taylor on an upraised arm and, although television replays showed the misdemeanour clearly enough, the referee did not see it - or at least as an offence. In injury time, Ronaldo curled a 20-yard free kick so narrowly wide that hearts skipped a beat among many in the crowd who were convinced it had gone in. At the death, with United committed forlornly to an equaliser, the Yak broke away only to ram a shot against Roy Carroll's legs and soon afterwards a shrill blast on the whistle of referee Neale Barry signalled the start of mass celebrations, the likes of which had not been seen since, well, December 1955. United could point to the fact that van Nistelrooy, Keane, Ferdinand and Phil Neville were all missing but this was Pompey's biggest win in years and, more importantly, opened a five point gap over nearest rivals Leeds, their next opponents coincidentally, with that Arsenal game in hand.

Portsmouth (4-3-1-2): Hislop; Primus, De Zeeuw, Stefanovic, Taylor; Smertin, Faye, Stone; Berkovic (Quashie 45); LuaLua (Sheringham 79), Yakubu.

Subs Not Used: Wapenaar, Curtis, Harper.
Booked: Sheringham, Taylor.
Goals: Stone 36.

Man Utd (4-3-2-1): Carroll; Gary Neville, Brown, Silvestre, O'Shea (Fletcher 74); Scholes, Djemba-Djemba (Ronaldo 58), Butt (Bellion 89); Solskjaer, Giggs; Saha.
Subs Not Used: Howard, Pugh.
Booked: Gary Neville.

Att: 20,140
Ref: N Barry (N Lincolnshire).

STATS:
Shots on target: Pompey 3 Man Utd 6
Shots off target: Pompey 5 Man Utd 6
Corners: Pompey 3 Man Utd 13
Fouls: Pompey 17 Man Utd 8
Offside: Pompey 2 Man Utd 0

Harry Redknapp had never managed a side which had beaten United in the league. "I knocked Manchester United out of the cup a couple of times with Bournemouth and West Ham but not in the league. This is a massive, massive three points and just about my biggest win as a manager. If we had lost to United we would have gone to Leeds with a very slender lead, but we have now taken 13 points out of 15 in a pressure situation." Redknapp labelled all his players heroes but could not resist singling out his back four who had resisted so stoutly and for so long. "The Leeds match is still a big game but we're in great shape. I think one more win will do it. I told the players that if they'd started like this a month ago we'd be in Europe." Sir Alex Ferguson reacted like he'd been given a happy pill. Casting off years of prejudice against referees, he praised Barry for his honesty and Pompey for their hard work. "They worked their socks off and once they had scored I knew it would be difficult. When Matt Taylor handled it was a penalty, but it was a crowded area and I don't blame the referee. I think Neale Barry's integrity is second to none and his judgement is sound." Chief executive Storrie relived the tension in the Directors' box. "This is the biggest result the club has had in years and shows how far we have come. I said to my wife at half-time that if we were 1-0 up at 90 minutes, I bet the referee would add on four minutes, and he did. I thought that if we held on, we'd stay up. It was agony. I had my wife ringing up her dad to check on Sky how many seconds were left. Milan was turning to me and saying 'How long, how long?' so we had a three-way conversation going. The last nine minutes were like 90 and the last four about two hours."

Back behind his desk, Storrie confirmed that Pompey had sold 3,000 tickets for the final two away matches at Leeds and Leicester although the kick-off at Elland Road had been brought forward to 11.30 to accommodate the wishes of the television paymasters. "Our fans have been wonderful home and away but this is another magnificent response, especially when you think other Premiership clubs have been sending back parts of their ticket allocation for Fratton Park. It shows how loyal and great our fans continue to be." How Graham Rix would have liked to have taken a few of them to Oxford where he had just signed a two-year contract as manager while, to the astonishment of many within the game, Paul Merson was appointed caretaker boss at Walsall. As

Pompey's Premiership status grew safer by the day, they were linked with moves for Tomasz Radzinski of Everton and West Ham's Christian Dailly but the main transfer talking point was inevitably Lua-Lua, who had made a huge impact at Pompey, far greater than he had ever done at Newcastle. Sir Bobby Robson had noted Lua-Lua's evident happiness on the south coast and, his own squad heavily depleted before a UEFA Cup game at home to Marseilles, was rumoured to be negotiating to bring him back. Peter Storrie was able to deny this. "We have not had a request from Newcastle but we would not enter any discussion about it anyway."

Sunday April 25

LEEDS UNITED (0) 1
PORTSMOUTH (1) 2

And so to Leeds, a game of quite colossal significance for both sides. Proud Leeds were on the slide, strangled by insuperable financial problems which would have driven other businesses to the wall. But where there was life, there was hope and, all the while they were in the Premiership, there was money. When Pompey travelled to Elland Road, Leeds had not been beaten at home in five matches while Redknapp reckoned a win would be enough, any win would do. By the end of another nervous, draining match it was the Pompey fans who were singing "We are staying up" and it was the Leeds supporters making their disconsolate way home, ready to look up the train times to Plymouth and, as it turned

STAY UP POMPEY!

Lomana Lua Lua had been the catalyst for Pompey's superb finish to the season, scoring again in the win at Leeds. His future as a Pompey player had become a priority for the management.

out, Brighton. Forget Old Trafford, welcome to the Withdean Stadium. Here at Leeds, Pompey were ahead in the ninth minute when Faye sent Stone scuttling down the right, as he had done so willingly and so often over the season, and his perfect centre was turned in by Yakubu. Without the suspended Mark Viduka, Leeds offered nothing and De Zeeuw should have scored again only to shoot over from four yards.

A hip injury kept Dominic Matteo from the second half and Leeds missed his presence when Pompey scored again in the 51st minute. Taylor took a corner on the left, Yakubu's header ballooned off Paul Robinson and Lua-Lua nodded over the line. The somersaults began and so, too, did the celebrations among the 3,200 Pompey fans, many of whom had journeyed through the night. They were in full cry when suddenly they were silenced by a decision from referee Uriah Rennie seven minutes from time. Acting on an assistant's flag, Rennie pointed to the spot after Primus and Michael Duberry had clashed. Ian Harte slotted the spot-kick into the bottom left-hand corner and now it was Pompey who looked nervous. Two minutes later Nicky Barmby, running on to Smertin's inadvertent deflection, saw his shot from four yards brilliantly pushed away by Hislop's outstretched hand. It was enough to ensure the victory Pompey so desperately needed. As Mr Rennie brought proceedings to a close, Pompey had reached the magic safety target of 40 points after a stunning run of 16 points from a possible 18.

Leeds (4-4-2): Robinson; Kelly, Caldwell, Duberry, Harte; Pennant, Matteo (McPhail 45), Radebe (Lennon 71), Milner; Smith, Simon Johnson (Barmby 59).
Subs Not Used: Carson, Kilgallon.
Booked: Caldwell, Kelly.
Goals: Harte 83 pen.

Portsmouth (4-4-2): Hislop; Primus, De Zeeuw, Stefanovic, Taylor; Stone (Harper 80), Smertin, Faye, Quashie; Lua-Lua (Sheringham 74), Yakubu.
Subs Not Used: Wapenaar, Curtis, Berkovic.
Booked: Smertin, De Zeeuw.
Goals: Yakubu 9, Lua-Lua 51.

Att: 39,273
Ref: U Rennie (S Yorkshire)

STATS:
Shots on target: Leeds 4 Pompey 5
Shots off target: Leeds 8 Pompey 2
Corners: Leeds 9 Pompey 2
Fouls: Leeds 9 Pompey 22
Offside: Leeds 0 Pompey 5

Redknapp made no effort to contain his delight and no one expected him to. It may have been mathematically possible for them to go down, but Pompey were safe. "We've been on a great run and it's a season our fans won't forget. At 2-0, I thought we'd be okay but the penalty brought them back into the game. I don't know what the penalty was for, even Eddie Gray said he thought it was our free kick. I can't say I enjoyed the last ten minutes. Waiting for the final whistle is not something you love but we got there. If you are from Portsmouth and love football it has been the best two years of your life. For 12 games we were short of players but otherwise we have done well. It has been terrific." For Mandaric, it was all too much. Choking back the tears of relief, he reflected on a job well done. "I'm a happy chairman. Staying up in your first year in the Premiership is such a pleasing feeling. This confirms the platform I want to build the club on. I didn't want to say it, but if we had gone down we would have had to start again. Now we can add more quality and I will be re-investing on and off the field. I am happy for the whole city of Portsmouth, the players, the management but most of all I'm happy for our loyal supporters. There are no words for them, they're unbelievable."

Mandaric chose the moment of his greatest happiness as Pompey's owner to instruct Peter Storrie to open negotiations aimed at bringing Lua-Lua to Fratton Park on a permanent basis. "Lua-Lua is a talent, the pace he has with Yakubu up front has changed everything." Alexei Smertin had been a big success over the second half of the season and Mandaric wanted to sign him too, but negotiations were never going to be straightforward because of the bizarre way he had slipped into - and out of - Stamford Bridge. Complications set in when Claudio Ranieri was fired and Smertin's concentration was diluted by Russia's involvement in Euro 2004 but, if nothing else, it showed Mandaric's ambition now that he felt Pompey would be staying up. All the while there was reasonable doubt, though, Redknapp was no nearer getting a decent night's sleep. There was still an outside, remote chance of Leeds escaping and, until they were dead and buried, Redknapp was not looking beyond the immediate future. "Nothing is certain yet, " he warned prematurely celebrating fans. "There is nothing to say Leeds can't win their remaining three matches. I have seen it done before when Oldham picked up nine points in the space of a week and stayed up under Joe Royle. We can take nothing for granted." What Redknapp feared for Leeds was a long spell out

of the Premiership while they sorted out their colossal financial problems and, in a roundabout way, he was also making the point that dropping out of the Premiership for any club was the equivalent of falling off the end of the world.

Nigel Quashie, one of the few players to survive from a previous Pompey era, was no nearer earning his first Scottish cap. A calf injury picked up at Leeds prevented him playing against Denmark in Copenhagen though his original

Arjan De Zeeuw was singled out by Redknapp as his man of the season.

selection had boosted his morale. "My mum is having a hard time with cancer so me being picked by Berti Vogts has given her a huge lift." Quashie had done his bit for Pompey but none had surpassed De Zeeuw in Redknapp's eyes. "If I had to put my head on the block, my player of the year would be Arjan De Zeeuw. He's played in almost every game, starting the season at left-back and then switching to centre-half. He's a great guy and a great character, a big, honest defender who gives everything and is a model professional. I didn't think he could play in the Premiership. I didn't think he or Linvoy Primus could handle it. But they have proved me wrong."

What Redknapp did not say was that the whole squad had proved the outside world wrong. Pompey had been firm favourites to go down, precisely because the likes of Primus, De Zeeuw and Quashie and others who had either never played in the Premiership or had played very little. This either said a massive amount for the team spirit engendered by the management and the collective desire to prove a point or it said something about the supposed elite standard of the Premiership. Perhaps it was not as awesome as everyone warned it would be.

The Premiership
BOTTOM 10 AT END OF APRIL 2004

	P	W	D	L	F	A	Pts
Southampton	34	12	9	13	39	35	45
Middlesbrough	35	12	9	14	41	44	45
Blackburn Rovers	35	11	7	17	49	57	40
PORTSMOUTH	**34**	**11**	**7**	**16**	**39**	**48**	**40**
Everton	35	9	12	14	42	48	39
Tottenham Hotspur	35	11	6	18	44	56	39
Manchester City	35	7	14	14	48	51	35
Leeds United	35	8	8	19	36	71	32
Leicester City	35	5	14	16	42	60	29
Wolverhampton Wdrs	35	6	11	18	35	73	29

13.

War and Peace

MAY SHOULD HAVE PRODUCED the great climax to a long and tense season and for other clubs it did. But not Pompey. There were four league fixtures still to play and, in theory, Pompey needed one point to be sure but, in reality, the three clubs at the foot of the table were not now going to overtake them. With Saints struggling for consistency under Paul Sturrock, there was the very real possibility that Pompey's revival might even take them above their Hampshire rivals in the final reckoning. That would have been something to savour but, parochial considerations aside, every place in the table carried with it an incentive of more than £500,000 so there was plenty still to play for. Fulham at home was just the sort of fixture Pompey welcomed at this stage of the season, opponents marooned in mid-table with not much at stake.

Saturday May 1

PORTSMOUTH (0) 1 FULHAM (0) 1

Pompey duly got the point they needed thanks to the Yak's sixth goal in seven matches allowing the fretting Redknapp to relax and reflect on a tough job safely accomplished. Leeds could still overtake them but needed to win their last three matches and there was the small matter of an adverse 26-goal difference, so there was a party atmosphere about Fratton Park on the specially designated 'Linvoy Day' during which the stands were peppered with lookalikes in dreadlock wigs and T-shirts bearing the slogan 'Jesus loves Linvoy'. Richard Duffy got a place on the bench in an unchanged line-up and was in the action after 22 minutes when Primus ruined everyone's day by limping off with a torn hamstring. Duffy kept the dangerous Malbranque quiet and gave an assured debut which suggested a shrewd bit of business had been done. Lua-Lua hit the bar and Yakubu headed over from eight yards but Fulham, after a slow start, responded with greater urgency after the break, Sean Davis hitting the bar from 20 yards. There was an end-of-season feel about the game, a slothfulness which was only shaken off when Pompey took the lead with ten minutes remaining. Steve Stone put Taylor away on the right and, when Edwin van der Sar spilled his shot, the predatory Yakubu was on hand. At last Fulham were spurred into action and, with five minutes left, American substitute Brian McBride beat Hislop with a left-foot shot from the edge of the area. McBride might even have sneaked a stoppage-time winner but fired wide of an open goal.

WAR AND PEACE

The Yak bags his sixth goal in seven games to earn the point that kept Pompey in the Premiership.

Portsmouth (4-4-2): Hislop; Primus (Duffy 22), De Zeeuw, Stefanovic, Taylor; Stone, Smertin, Faye, Quashie; Lua-Lua, Yakubu (Sheringham 90).
Subs Not Used: Wapenaar, Berkovic, Harper.
Booked: Faye.
Goals: Yakubu 80.

Fulham (4-5-1): Van der Sar; Volz, Goma, Pearce, Bocanegra; Sean Davis, Inamoto, Djetou (McBride 77), Malbranque, Legwinski; Boa Morte (John 85).
Subs Not Used: Crossley, Petta, Hudson.
Booked: Legwinski, Bocanegra, Inamoto, Goma.
Goals: McBride 85.

Att: 20,065
Ref: S Dunn (Gloucestershire).

Stats:
Shots on target: Pompey 4 Fulham 3
Shots off target: Pompey 9 Fulham 7
Corners: Pompey 10 Fulham 3
Fouls: Pompey 15 Fulham 17
Offside: Pompey 6 Fulham 1

Redknapp's relief was evident. "I certainly didn't see us being clear with three matches to play. I thought it would go down to the last day with us hanging in there. There have been some tough spells. When we got whacked by Arsenal it could have finished us. But we stuck at it and got our reward. We didn't have enough players but we brought a couple in and when everyone was fit we survived." Redknapp said he had problems only with one player (no prizes for guessing which) and the others had responded to his encouragement and belief in them as a unit. Now, he feared, was the time to start worrying about next season. "We've stayed up this season but the next will be just as difficult. I'll probably have a busy summer." Tellingly, Redknapp

211

added a phrase which had great significance later in the month. "I'll talk with the chairman to see where we are going." Mandaric was just happy to enjoy the occasion and was more optimistic about the future. "This is something we have dreamed of. Now we want to stabilise. We want a team who can go forward. Charlton and Aston Villa have gone forward, why not Portsmouth? I'm here long-term, whatever long-term is. I want the club to be in the premier division, in a new stadium and with respectable facilities. The key thing is this club isn't built around one person, it's built by a team." Just as tellingly, Mandaric also added a key phrase, bearing in mind the ructions to come. "If one of us moves on, the club can still go forward."

Tuesday May 4

PORTSMOUTH (1) 1 ARSENAL (0) 1

Brazilian striker Marcio Amoruso was a surprise visitor to Pompey training, having played for Dortmund in the Champions' League. Hedging his bets, he described the club as "not the best, but not the worst" and watched the Arsenal match next day at Fratton Park with an eye to the future. After the FA Cup debacle in which, for those who need reminding, Pompey were ripped to shreds by Arsenal, the prospect of their visit for the league fixture was met with mixed emotions. Since that fateful day a lot had changed. Arsenal were no longer chasing a treble but had already won the championship and all that remained for them was to go through the entire 38-match programme without losing; they were already tantalisingly close. There had been evidence in recent matches that Arsenal had fallen a little from their high standards while Pompey had put together a seven-match unbeaten run. Perhaps the gap had closed temporarily. Richard Hughes got a chance against his old club in the knowledge that, under the terms of a sell-on agreement which took him from Highbury to Bournemouth, Arsenal profited every time he played up to 40 games. Not enough, admittedly, to pay the drinks bill at the championship celebrations but something like £25,000 over the 40 appearances. Hughes could be pleased with his performance as Arsenal had to settle for a draw. For half an hour there was nothing in it until Kolo Toure failed to deal with a long ball from Taylor and, although Jens Lehmann parried Yakubu's shot, Sol Campbell could not prevent it crossing the line. Jose Antonio Reyes hit the bar, Hislop saved superbly from Henry and Pompey got a standing ovation from their fans at half-time, relieved that Arsenal were not again out of sight. Like true champions, the Gunners stepped up a gear after the break, Hislop deflecting Henry's shot on to the bar and Taylor hacking the rebound from the line. The resulting Henry corner was only partially cleared and Reyes drilled in the equaliser which not even Hislop could reach. Henry might have snatched a winner but so too

WAR AND PEACE

Taylor and Yakubu celebrate their parts in taking the lead against Arsenal.

might Yakubu when played clear by Lua-Lua's flick. In the end, a draw was about right.

Portsmouth (4-4-2): Hislop; Curtis, De Zeeuw, Stefanovic, Taylor; Stone, Faye, Quashie, Hughes; Lua-Lua, Yakubu (Mornar 80).
Subs Not Used: Wapenaar, Duffy, Harper, Sheringham.
Goals: Yakubu 30.

Arsenal (4-4-2): Lehmann; Lauren, Campbell, Toure, Cole; Bentley (Kanu 61), Vieira, Parlour, Ljungberg (Aliadiere 90); Reyes (Keown 90), Henry.
Subs Not Used: Shaaban, Clichy.
Booked: Campbell, Parlour.
Goals: Reyes 50.

Jose Antonio Reyes - equalised for the Gunners.

STAY UP POMPEY!

Att: 20,140
Ref: M Riley (W Yorkshire)

STATS:
Shots on target: Pompey 4 Arsenal 4
Shots off target: Pompey 7 Arsenal 12
Corners: Pompey 5 Arsenal 12
Fouls: Pompey 13 Arsenal 12
Offside: Pompey 1 Arsenal 1

For Redknapp, the result was the equal of wins over Liverpool and Manchester United. "I was pleased at half-time because they hadn't opened us up. I hoped we could keep that up but they came out and got their goal. We hung on and Yakubu had a great chance to win it. Arsenal had a long spell when they were terrific but at 1-1 they could have lost their unbeaten record quite easily. It would have been lovely if we could have ended their run but, now they have drawn with us, I'd love to see them get the record. It's been an incredible turn-around for us, getting results like this. I don't think many clubs have come this far this quickly." Arsene Wenger continued to be amazed by Portsmouth's supporters and Thierry Henry showed his appreciation of them by donning a Pompey shirt. Wenger said: "The fans are absolutely amazing. It was the case at the 5-1 game and it was again in this one. They have a great sense of fair play and they win the league when it comes to supporters." Henry was even more effusive, asking his manager to play in the match though the championship was won because he wanted to sample again being the idol of the Fratton Park crowd. Over the course of a medal-strewn career, Henry has been there, done it and got several different shirts but this was somehow different, as he explained. "They were singing, asking me to sign for Portsmouth. I know I won't be coming here but I just wanted to wear the Portsmouth shirt in their ground, even for a few minutes. This was the only thing I could do to give something back to them." The fans chanted 'Henry for Portsmouth', 'Henry give us a wave' and 'Henry is a Pompey fan' throughout the second half, almost putting the great man off his game. It almost brought a lump to his throat. "I have never experienced anything like it," he added. "I'm speechless. Support like this has much to do with Portsmouth staying up."

Lua-Lua was another player in love with the Pompey fans who had shown him more respect and

Thierry Henry - the Pompey fans' favourite.

appreciation than he had ever received on critical Tyneside. But he was wanted back at Newcastle for the UEFA Cup semi-final in Marseille because of injuries and Pompey felt they were morally bound to let him return with so little left and Newcastle evidently desperate. The decision was left with the player and Lua-Lua, in Newcastle's hour of need, rejected Sir Bobby Robson's pleas. New-castle, without Bellamy, Dyer and others half-fit, duly lost in Marseille as Lua-Lua opted to see out the season at Fratton Park a contented man. Redknapp realised the dilemma: "We said he could go because we don't want to fall out with other clubs. I don't know how Newcastle will react to his decision; they are his employers after all." Courtney

Lua-Lua - like Henry, in love with the Pompey fans.

Pitt, one of the 'stars' of Football Diaries, a series of television documentaries in which he was described as a Premiership winger, did not go down too well at Oxford where Graham Rix had hoped he might re-ignite a fading promotion challenge. According to Oxford chairman Firoz Kassam, who had taken aboard Pitt's high wages, Rix had apologised to him when it became clear Pitt had not worked any Premiership-calibre magic. At the end of the season Pitt was released by Oxford.

Saturday May 8

**LEICESTER CITY (2) 3
PORTSMOUTH (0) 1**

After defeating Saints and Manchester United and drawing with Arsenal, Pompey went to Leicester on the back of an eight-match unbeaten run, confident they could impart a farewell gift to already-relegated Leicester in the shape of another defeat. Leicester had not won at home since November 1 and only twice at the Walkers Stadium all season but, as usual, there is something about Pompey which brings out the best in them. Pompey limped home on the back of a 3-1 defeat with no complaints, beaten by the better side. There was no doubting Leicester would win from the sixth minute when Bent, who attracted Pompey's interest in June before going to Everton, and Dickov combined for Matt Taylor to deflect a shot past wrong-footed Hislop for his second own goal of the season. Izzet struck the bar before Leicester went further in front in the 27th minute when Dickov, who also interested Redknapp, weaved his way into the area, received the ball back from Bent and fired home from 12 yards. Pompey troubled Leicester only rarely but a powerful burst from his own half by Yakubu after 66 minutes set up Quashie to pull a goal back from the edge of the area. Hislop saved brilliantly from Jordan Stewart before James Scowcroft restored the two-goal advantage five minutes after Quashie's only goal of the season. 'Premier League with Harry and Jim' sang the fans at Graham Poll's final whistle but there was no disguising Pompey's poorest performance since the win over Saints that had kick-started the survival process. A match best forgotten.

Leicester (4-4-2): Walker; Sinclair, Dabizas, Heath, Stewart; Scowcroft, McKinlay, Izzet (Nalis 48), Guppy (Ferdinand 74); Dickov, Bent (Benjamin 89).
Subs Not Used: Freund, Gillespie.
Goals: Taylor 6 o.g, Dickov 27, Scowcroft 71.

Portsmouth (4-4-2): Hislop; Curtis, De Zeeuw, Stefanovic, Taylor; Stone (Sheringham 71), Smertin, Faye (Mornar 57), Quashie; Lua-Lua, Yakubu.
Subs Not Used: Wapenaar, Duffy, Hughes.
Booked: Lua-Lua, Hislop.
Goals: Quashie 66.

Att: 31,536
Ref: G Poll (Hertfordshire)

STATS:
Shots on target: Leicester 6 Pompey 4
Shots off target: Leicester 6 Pompey 7
Corners: Leicester 8 Pompey 3
Fouls: Leicester 14 Pompey 16
Offside: Leicester 3 Pompey 3

Nigel Quashie - only goal of the season at Leicester.

Noting Pompey were still above Everton and Manchester City, Redknapp's preoccupations were with next season. "You never know how much longer you'll be managing, you just never know in this game." Sensing the approach of a very welcome summer, tired Redknapp said he was heading home to his garden, to watch the boats go by and play some golf, but nagging at the back of his mind already was the need to be bringing in new players. "We need more quality to survive. I want five, right around the team. But quality costs money and I'm not sure if we've got any. I'll sit down with the chairman." Note that last sentence because, when he did, the meeting sparked a colossal row which threatened to rip the heart out of the entire club.

The six days between Monday, May 10 and Saturday, May 15 will go down as some of the most bizarre in the history of Portsmouth Football Club. Even now it is difficult to piece together what actually happened, there being a big difference between what was said by the chairman and the manager and what transpired - which was nothing. It boiled down to this: The manager met his chairman and asked for money to build a side for next season. The chairman said there wasn't much available and, in any case, he wanted to change the direction of the club. That meant bringing in an experienced, probably foreign, coach, dispensing with the venerated Jim Smith and placing a greater emphasis on the youth set-up in producing the club's own players. He argued that there was a limited future in continually throwing money at older players with a limited footballing lifespan. Redknapp, his sovereignty threatened, threatened to follow Smith and Kevin Bond out of the door and the row rumbled on all week until, to the mystification of all, chairman and manager sat next to each other for the final match of the season, now apparently the best of friends.

An end of season spat between Redknapp and Mandaric over the future of the club, and Jim Smith in particular, threatened to take the gloss off Pompey's progress in the previous two years.

STAY UP POMPEY!

A storm in a Fratton Park plastic tea cup, or two egos colliding head-on? Hard to tell. It went something like this.

MONDAY, MAY 10. Two national newspapers report that Smith and Bond are leaving and that Redknapp is considering his position. Speaking from Belgium, Mandaric accuses the papers of mischief-making by giving out false information. He tried to explain: "The meeting between us was about all areas of the club including training, boardroom and the whole infrastructure of the club. We have survived and now we want to add many things to strengthen internally. This is no time to stand still." This point was further emphasised by Peter Storrie when he said: "Internal improvements are vital and the meeting was the first in a number that will take place about moving on. We are more than surprised and a bit angry at these rumours which have been spread from an unknown source when what we are doing is building a strong and prosperous future for this club." Redknapp, in an interview with The Quay, confirmed that Smith was on his way, but not Bond. "It's very difficult to say what I think, I have to bite my lip. There has been a bad atmosphere since the Fulham game. You'd have thought we had been relegated when I walked into the boardroom. Jim's done nothing wrong, I don't see any reason to change things. It's a very difficult situation. It's the chairman's club and he can do what he wants. It's his decision if Jim leaves as we are only employ-

"I spoke to Harry about what we can do for the future and all of a sudden everyone in the whole country is talking about Jim Smith and Kevin Bond being fired."

ees. Jim and I have been a team, we've worked together and I defy anyone to have done any better." At least Storrie and Mandaric now knew who the mole was who revealed the news of Smith's departure. "I told Jim," admitted Harry.

"He's my mate and has got a right to know." It was all sadly reminiscent of Redknapp's departure from West Ham in May 2001 when he fell out with Hammers chairman Terence Brown over budgets. The day, and the accusations, were not over. Mandaric took another swipe. "I spoke to Harry about what we can do for the future and all of a

"Any coach coming in would have to be of my choice. I don't want a foreign coach and I will not work with one."

sudden everyone in the whole country is talking about Jim Smith and Kevin Bond being fired. I'm sorry, I just don't understand that. I have tremendous respect for Jim but I have to look at what is best, not for me or him, but for the club. I haven't even seen Jim. If we make some changes we will announce them. We don't have any individual in mind. I'm just trying to see it another way. Our youth programme is isolated. What I said to Harry was 'Let's reorganise things, let's do a little more coaching, let's look at youth programmes' and then all of a sudden I hear Jim and Kevin are going. Harry and I had a constructive meeting, nothing unfriendly."

TUESDAY, MAY 11. The nation awakes to discover the affair has now been dubbed Eaglegate and that the two parties are deeply entrenched. Mandaric fired the first shots. "If Harry does not like it maybe he will have to go. No one is bigger than the club, not Harry Redknapp, not Jim Smith, not Milan Mandaric. If Harry wants to stay he should be working with me." There are reports that Mandaric is in Belgium to speak to George Leekens, the 55-year-old former Belgian and Algerian national boss who fitted the description perfectly of an experienced foreign coach. Leekens had just left Mouscron after a row with his chairman. Leekens did nothing to allay the suspicion that he had been lined up by Mandaric. "It must be the ambition of every coach to be involved in the English Premiership. I know Mr Mandaric. He was involved in Belgian football some years ago and I am very pleased Portsmouth are interested in me." Redknapp liked foreign players but the idea of working with a foreign coach did not appeal. He responded: "Any coach coming in would have to be of my choice. I don't want a foreign coach and I will not work with one."

WEDNESDAY, MAY 12. Mandaric, still away, denied having met Leekens, at least not in ten years, and accused 'people' of trying to destroy the club. It is revealed that the infamous meeting between Mandaric, Storrie and Redknapp the previous Saturday had been interrupted at its height by a fire alarm in the team hotel. Redknapp, still training, wanted only to get the Middlesbrough match out of the way as a prelude to any detailed discussions about the future. "I am very disappointed this has come up because it has tarnished the end of the season. I see no super-coaches coming through, I don't know any. If I lose Jim, I'm struggling. We came to Portsmouth together and everyone knows we pulled the club up by its bootstrings."

THURSDAY, MAY 13. It has now emerged from Mandaric that it was Redknapp who had wanted Smith sacked, not himself. This Redknapp refuted strongly. Redknapp said a meeting was planned for the next day on Mandaric's return when Jim Smith would be discussed. He was content for a new coach to come in but he added: "If Jim goes it will be very difficult for me to stay. Jim and I are very disappointed in the way we have been treated after two great

years. It's not been a nice week but I had a feeling things would blow up sooner or later. I've got a two-year contract and I think I deserve another two years but if he wants us gone he will have to sort us out. Milan's record in bringing in coaches is not good. Tony Pulis and Graham Rix were good coaches, but not good enough." It was then that

"Harry told me he did not need Jim Smith... he was worried by what Alex Ferguson or some of his friends might say."

"I wouldn't sack Jim, he is loved and respected by everyone in the game. I love him as a friend and as a workmate."

the chairman delivered the body blow when he said: "Harry told me at Christmas that he wanted to bring in more players when the transfer window opened if we wanted to stay up. I agreed but said certain players felt they were not being coached properly and maybe we should think about bringing in a younger coach. Harry told me he did not need Jim Smith. He pleaded with me not to make any changes there and then because he was worried by what Sir Alex Ferguson or some of his friends might say. Well, what has Ferguson or Harry's friends ever done for Portsmouth Football Club? I agreed to his wishes at the time. I go away and then I read I'm the one who wants to get rid of Jim, which really shocks me. This is not the normal way I communicate with my supporters but I feel they should know the truth. I won't allow the club to be manipulated and I need to sit down with the manager and see if we can still work together." To this Redknapp appeared to give an unequivocal answer when he called the chairman 'a filthy liar'. Surely he could not survive this?

FRIDAY, MAY 14. This is the big day. The media are at the training ground as a gleaming luxury motor comes through the gate and rush to greet the occupant, cameras flashing, questions at the ready. Out steps a surprised Mark Burchill. Redknapp arrived eventually to take training, followed by Smith, attempting to pretend everything is normal and to get the squad ready for the Middlesbrough match. Nothing is normal but Redknapp stopped long enough to state: "Last week at a hotel in Leicester I had a meeting with the chairman. He said to me 'Jim is old, he has had his day, he should walk away now and we should get a younger man.' I told him I would never sack Jim in a million years. Mandaric asked me what part he played but the trouble with Mandaric is that he has a huge ego and doesn't like it when someone else is grabbing the limelight. He is coming out with all this stuff because he knows he will get stick from the fans, so he wants to get off the hook. I have spoken to Jim. He knows what the chairman is up to, he is telling disgusting lies. He wants me to resign but I won't give him the pleasure. He has been on the television this week more than any chairman in history. The whole thing has been a disgrace." Redknapp then spoke of his closeness to old ally Smith. "I wouldn't sack Jim, he is loved and respected by everyone in the game. I love him as a friend and as a workmate." Mandaric stood by his original accusation and told Radio 4: "I tried to protect Harry by not going public. But he said this in an official meeting in front of others, including the chief executive. He told me he could do without him and even said he was useless. I want Harry to stay but he is going to have to tell the truth and apologise." Back to Harry: "Why would I come out and support Jim all week if it meant me probably losing my job? The chairman has been backed into a corner and fought dirty. He's used to dirty tricks, incredible."

STILL FRIDAY, MAY 14. The High Noon meeting is put back an hour so that it becomes High One O'Clock by the time Redknapp and Smith make their way to Fratton Park to meet Mandaric, Storrie and director Terry Brady. They are greeted by around 150 fans who throng Frogmore Road in a baffled state as if queuing for cup tickets. For two and a quarter hours they wait, wondering whose blood will be staining the boardroom carpet, their discomfort eased at last by the sight of media manager Johnny Moore clutching a statement to rival that brandished by Prime Minister Chamberlain after a meet-

Jim Smith was the one person to come out of the affair with his dignity intact.

ing with Hitler in 1938. The message was the same: "Peace in our time". Clearing his throat, Moore said the statement had been signed by all parties. It read: "We believe there has been a lot of unnecessary comment and confusion by us all. For the benefit of our supporters there will be no changes in the current football management team and the dialogue will continue in a positive manner. Everyone in the club is looking forward to the last game of the season and to finishing on a high note." How hands could have been shaken after what had been said through the week will forever defy logic. Did Redknapp really want Smith gone? Was Mandaric protecting his manager? One day we might know the truth but, on that early Spring afternoon, no one was any the wiser. The only man to emerge with any credit from a tawdry affair was Smith, the man at the centre of it all. He kept silent and retained his dignity, which is more than can be said for others.

One man who might have been there that day in Frogmore Road was superfan John Westwood, had he not had other things on his mind. Westwood, that most flamboyant of Portsmouth supporters, had been arrested outside Leicester's ground the previous Saturday and charged with attempting to enter the stadium while drunk. This charge he vehemently denied. If convicted, he faced a ban from all football matches, home and abroad, for three years. For most Pompey fans, for whom he was a talisman in his blue and white wig and bugle, Westwood had become something of a soft tar-

get for police and stewards at away grounds and was being unfairly treated as a hooligan. Westwood is a genuine fan but his extrovert appearance and raucous reputation tended to precede him in the Premiership. On the day of the Fratton Park summit, Westwood was in court attending a three-minute hearing. Granted unconditional bail, the case was adjourned.

As if an internal war was not enough, there were players' futures to be considered. Teddy Sheringham, the job for which he had been signed now completed, was freed and following him out of Fratton Park were Olszar, Burton, Tardif, Hunt, Pettefer, Carl Bradshaw and Terry Parker. Tim Sherwood was given the option of returning, in effect to prove his fitness, on a match-to-match basis. Redknapp, the divisions still not healed, said he wanted to keep Sheringham who, he reckoned, had another couple of years in him but Mandaric saw no point in paying around £15,000 a week for someone to sit on the bench. Redknapp, disappointed in losing such a class act, said: "Teddy could play at the top level until he was 40. He has looked after himself really well and will do a fantastic job wherever he goes as the ultimate professional."

Saturday May 15

PORTSMOUTH (3) 5
MIDDLESBROUGH (1) 1

Bearing in mind what had happened at Fratton Park over the previous five days, the 5-1 win over Middlesbrough was almost beyond

STAY UP POMPEY!

After a week of rumour and counter-rumour, Harry Redknapp was delighted to receive the Barclaycard Manager of the Month award before the game with Middlesbrough.

belief. The big fear was that the players would simply not perform because of the daily upheavals, accusations and counter-claims from the people supposed to be in charge of them, but Redknapp said there was a tremendous spirit in the camp - and he was right. Before taking his place alongside Mandaric in the directors' box, Redknapp received the Barclaycard Manager of the Month award for April yet he must have come perilously close to becoming the first recipient of the award to be unemployed. Arjan De Zeeuw won a handful of player of the year awards and then came the action. Mandaric and Redknapp confided in each other conspiratorially, as if nothing had taken place, and for once the limelight fell on the players, more specifically Yakubu Ayegbeni. The Yak had his detractors, those who said his finishing was not Premiership class, but it is no exaggeration to say he might have hit double figures against Middlesbrough. Taking his total to a highly creditable 19 for the season, the Yak scored four goals and missed many easier chances. Berkovic and Pasanen were recalled and Pompey were ahead in the fourth minute, Berkovic sliding a pass through the defence for Yakubu to race clear. Middlesbrough were on their way to their heaviest away defeat in five years when Danny Mills brought down Yakubu and the Nigerian hammered in the spot-kick. What Mandaric and Redknapp were saying to each other we can only speculate as the team they had so publically squabbled over showed championship-winning form. Bolo Zenden brought a touch of reality to

the occasion by pulling a goal back in the 27th minute but this was Pompey's day and they were soon in control again. Yakubu was in irresistable form and, after 31 minutes, his pace took him away from the lumbering Ugo Ehiogu to complete his first Pompey hat-trick. Middlesbrough wasted plenty of opportunities to narrow the gap before Lua-Lua got an ovation as he left the field and the departing Sheringham got another when he replaced him. Sheringham signed off with a tap-in from Taylor's pass and the rampant Yakubu got his fourth with a right-foot shot. Pompey's fifth goal gave them a total home tally of 35, which was bettered only by Arsenal (40) and Manchester United (37). The fans had a field day chanting "We want Milan with Harry and Jim" and "Stand up if you love Jim Smith". Jim Smith stayed seated.

The Yak's four-goal salvo against Boro gave him 19 goals for the season, just missing out on a £20,000 bonus.

Portsmouth (4-3-1-2): Hislop; Pasanen (Curtis 45), De Zeeuw, Stefanovic, Taylor; Stone, Smertin, Quashie (Hughes 81); Berkovic; Lua-Lua (Sheringham 67), Yakubu.
Subs Not Used: Wapenaar, Mornar.
Goals: Yakubu 4, 14 pen, 31, 83, Sheringham 80.

Middlesbrough (4-4-2): Schwarzer; Mills, Ehiogu, Queudrue, Zenden; Mendieta, Boateng, Greening, Downing (Morrison 62); Nemeth (Ricketts 62), Job.
Subs Not Used: Nash, Wilson, Bates.
Goals: Zenden 27.

Att: 20,134
Ref: M Halsey (Lancashire).

STATS:
Shots on target: Pompey 9 Middlesbrough 2
Shots off target: Pompey 7 Middlesbrough 14
Corners: Pompey 6 Middlesbrough 3
Fouls: Pompey 11 Middlesbrough 10
Offside: Pompey 5 Middlesbrough 2

STAY UP POMPEY!

The traditional lap of honour took place at the final whistle but the football world wanted to know if the row had been resolved. Redknapp attempted to brush it aside, perhaps underestimating the damage done. "Me, Jim and the chairman have managed to sort things out. I did apologise to Milan about certain things. I swore at him and I said sorry for that. My trouble is I've got a quick temper. When I picked up the manager of the month award, the hairs on the back of my neck stood up because of the reception I got from the fans. They don't want any of us to go. Jim is staying but if the chairman wants to bring in a coach, that's fine by me. Deep down I believe he trusts me to do the job." What Redknapp had conveniently forgotten was a pre-season wager with Yakubu. He thought he was safe enough when he promised £20,000 of his own money if Yakubu hit 20 goals. The Yak finished with 19 and was not slow to remind his boss how close he had come. But while Yakubu was a happy man, another striker was plunged into the depths of despair. Svetoslav Todorov, injured in

Redknapp salutes the contribution of Teddy Sheringham, while Sheringham himself salutes the crowd on a lap of honour at Fratton Park.

WAR AND PEACE

An uneasy peace?

August, was told he would require a second major operation in Germany and faced another year on the sidelines. Had Yakubu not filled the void so outstandingly, the news on Todorov would have made headlines but that is the nature of football, heroes quickly replaced.

And so a tumultuous season came to a close. What a staggering year it had been, full of incident on and off the pitch and culminating in the Redknapp-Mandaric saga. But then Portsmouth is that sort of club; nothing ordinary seems to happen to it. The two years of the Redknapp regime have transformed the club in most, if not all, directions. The class of player now on show at Fratton Park is the best for 50 years, arguably the best ever. Yet none of it would be possible without the Mandaric money which gave it all momentum in the first place. Pompey have been lucky to have them both and, in turn, they have been fortunate to have behind them a dynamic and fanatical support. It was a tough year, hard on the nerves, mixing elation with despair in equal measures. The cry was 'Stay up Pompey' and, one way or another, stay up they did. We eagerly await the next fascinating instalment.

FINAL BARCLAYCARD PREMIERSHIP TABLE 2003/04

	P	W	D	L	F	A	W	D	L	F	A	GD	PTS
			Home					**Away**					
1 Arsenal	38	15	4	0	40	14	11	8	0	33	12	47	90
2 Chelsea	38	12	4	3	34	13	12	3	4	33	17	37	79
3 Man Utd	38	12	4	3	37	15	11	2	6	27	20	29	75
4 Liverpool	38	10	4	5	29	15	6	8	5	26	22	18	60
5 Newcastle	38	11	5	3	33	14	2	12	5	19	26	12	56
6 Aston Villa	38	9	6	4	24	19	6	5	8	24	25	4	56
7 Charlton	38	7	6	6	29	29	7	5	7	22	22	0	53
8 Bolton	38	6	8	5	24	21	8	3	8	24	35	-8	53
9 Fulham	38	9	4	6	29	21	5	6	8	23	25	6	52
10 Birmingham	38	8	5	6	26	24	4	9	6	17	24	-5	50
11 Middlesbrough	38	8	4	7	25	23	5	5	9	19	29	-8	48
12 Southampton	38	8	6	5	24	17	4	5	10	20	28	-1	47
13 Portsmouth	**38**	**10**	**4**	**5**	**35**	**19**	**2**	**5**	**12**	**12**	**35**	**-7**	**45**
14 Tottenham	38	9	4	6	33	27	4	2	13	14	30	-10	45
15 Blackburn	38	5	4	10	25	31	7	4	8	26	28	-8	44
16 Man City	38	5	9	5	31	24	4	5	10	24	30	1	41
17 Everton	38	8	5	6	27	20	1	7	11	18	37	-12	39
18 Leicester City	38	3	10	6	19	28	3	5	11	29	37	-17	33
19 Leeds United	38	5	7	7	25	31	3	2	14	15	48	-39	33
20 Wolves	38	7	5	7	23	35	0	7	12	15	42	-39	33

STAY UP POMPEY!

PLAYER STATISTICS - SEASON 2003/04

	Appearances				Goals			
	Lge	FAC	CC	Total	Lge	FAC	CC	Total
Patrik Berger	20	1	1+1	22+ 1	5	0	0	5
Eyal Berkovic	10+ 1	4	0	14+ 1	1	0	0	1
Deon Burton	0+ 1	1	0	1+ 1	0	0	0	0
John Curtis	5+ 1	0	0	5+ 1	0	0	0	0
Arjan De Zeeuw	36	4	2	42	1	0	0	1
Richard Duffy	0+ 1	0	0	0+ 1	0	0	0	0
Amdy Faye	27	2+1	1	30+ 1	0	0	0	0
Hayden Foxe	8+ 2	0	2+1	10+ 3	1	0	0	1
Kevin Harper	0+ 7	2	0	2+ 7	0	0	0	0
Shaka Hislop	30	4	0	34	0	0	0	0
Richard Hughes	8+ 3	2+2	0	10+ 5	0	1	0	1
Lomana Lua-Lua	10+ 5	0	0	10+ 5	4	0	0	4
Ivica Mornar	3+ 5	2	0	5+ 5	1	0	0	1
Gary O'Neil	3	0	1+1	4+ 1	2	0	0	2
Sebastian Olszar	0	0+1	0	0+ 1	0	0	0	0
Petri Pasanen	11+ 1	4	0	15+ 1	0	0	0	0
Vincent Pericard	0+ 6	0	1	1+ 6	0	0	0	0
Linvoy Primus	19+ 2	4	1	24+ 2	0	0	0	0
Nigel Quashie	17+ 4	3	1	21+ 4	1	0	0	1
Jason Roberts	4+ 6	0	2	6+ 6	1	0	3	4
Carl Robinson	0+ 1	0+2	0	0+ 3	0	0	0	0
Sebastien Schemmel	12+ 2	1+1	2	15+ 3	0	1	0	1
Teddy Sheringham	25+ 7	2+1	3	30+ 8	9	1	0	10
Tim Sherwood	7+ 6	0	2+1	9+ 7	0	0	2	2
Alexei Smertin	23+ 3	5	2	30+ 3	0	0	0	0
Pavel Srnicek	3	0	1	4	0	0	0	0
Dejan Stefanovic	32	4	2	38	3	0	0	3
Steve Stone	29+ 3	0+1	2+1	31+ 5	2	0	0	2
Matthew Taylor	18+12	4+1	3	25+13	0	3	1	4
Svetoslav Todorov	1	0	0	1	0	0	0	0
Harald Wapenaar	5	1	2	8	0	0	0	0
Yakubu Ayegbeni	35+ 2	4	1+1	40+ 3	16	1	2	19
Boris Zivkovic	17+ 1	1	1	19+ 1	0	0	0	0

Key: Lge = Barclaycard Premiership, FAC = FA Cup, CC = Carling Cup
Appearances format = Full appearances + substitute appearances

The class of 2003/04

End of term report by Alex Crook

BOARD OF GOVERNORS

Milan Mandaric
(head of governors)

Peter Storrie
(head of school finance)

**Terry Brady
and Fred Dinenage.**

HEADMASTER

Harry Redknapp

Transfer market wizard Harry conjured up a miracle to keep Pompey in the Premiership. The 57-year-old signed 19 players during the course of the season but, ultimately, it was the heroes from the first division championship-winning side, with whom Redknapp kept faith, that found the magic formula to avert an instant return to the Nationwide League without the need for yet another last-day escape.

DEPUTY HEADMASTER

Jim Smith

The true worth of Harry's trusted sidekick to Pompey's most successful boss for 46 years was shown when the manager threatened to stand down after plans to dispose of the Bald Eagle were revealed in the final turbulent week of the season. Smith's insight into the game had proved invaluable as Redknapp led the club into the Premiership and was even more so as he fought to keep them there.

CARETAKER

Kevin Bond

It has gone almost unnoticed among Pompey fans that the man who has quietly helped transform their team plied his trade as a player 20 miles down the coast in the red and white corner of Hampshire. While many ex-Southampton players trying to make the transition were never forgiven for their past sins, Bond was given hero status for his part in the club's rise back into the big time and was even treated to a chorus of 'There's only one Kevin Bond' when his future looked under threat in May.

TEACHERS

Andy Awford
(reserve team coach)

Luther Blissett
(strikers' coach)

Alan Knight MBE
(goalkeeping coach)

Mark O'Connor
(youth team coach)

Shaun North
(youth team coach)

Stuart Morgan
(chief scout)

SCHOOL DOCTOR

Gary Sadler
(physiotherapist)

HEAD BOY

Teddy Sheringham
(striker, Highams Park 2.4.66)

Old master Sheringham showed glimpses of the legendary movement and deft first touch that saw him become a treble winner with Manchester United. The former England striker defied his station as the second oldest player in Premiership history with a flurry of goals at the start of his Fratton Park career and led Pompey to the top of the table for 24 glorious hours with a hat-trick in the 4-0 win over Bolton.

PREFECTS

Shaka Hislop
(goalkeeper, born Hackney 22.2.69)

Ultra-reliable Hislop called upon a Portsmouth seamstress to produce a special four-fingered glove to allow him to play on with a broken finger in the height of the relegation battle. The big Trinidadian could have done with a witch doctor to help him overcome the constant stream of injuries that put his place in doubt even before Pompey had kicked their first ball in the Premiership, but still played a pivotal role in avoiding the dreaded drop.

Arjan De Zeeuw
(defender, Castricum 16.4.70)

De Zeeuw's unrivalled commitment to the Pompey cause was a feature throughout the season. The big-hearted Dutchman's ability to play in the Premiership was questioned even by his own manager but the former medical student responded by leading from the back before eventually succeeding Sheringham as captain when the veteran's age caught up with him in the second half of the season.

Linvoy Primus
(defender, Forest Gate 14.9.73)

The unsung hero of the first division title success continued where he left off when finally given the chance to prove himself in the top-flight to earn the nickname 'Lord Linvoy' from the club's adoring fans. Such was his hero worship from the Fratton faithful that supporters dedicated May's home game with Fulham to the devout Christian, wearing dread-locked wigs and tongue-in-cheek 'Jesus Loves Linvoy' T-shirts to honour their idol.

Steve Stone
(midfielder, Gateshead 20.8.71)

Stone was inspirational in leading Pompey into the Premiership despite being hampered by the long-term hamstring injury that had written off the final year of his Aston Villa career. The ex-England winger put his fitness problems behind him to prove he could still be a thorn in the side of defences at the highest level and missed only six of 38 league games before becoming the deserved recipient of a new one-year contract.

CLASS TRICKSTERS

Lomana Lua-Lua
(striker, Kinshasa, Zaire 28.12.80)

After fleeing war-torn Congo as a schoolboy asylum-seeker, Lua Lua

headed south in search of refuge from his Newcastle nightmare. Made Sir Bobby Robson pay for letting him leave with a goal against his parent club in their 1-1 draw at Fratton Park and, to add insult to injury, snubbed Robson's plea for him to return to St James' Park when injuries wrecked the Toon's bid for UEFA Cup glory.

Yakubu Ayegbeni
(striker, Benin City, Nigeria 22.11.82)

Yakubu's wayward finishing and inability to stay on side in the first half of the season earned the Nigerian the tag of the Premiership's most wasteful striker. But, with a little help from Luther Blissett, the 21-year-old overcame his affinity with the offside flag to become the first Pompey player to score more than 15 goals in a top-flight season since the great Ron Saunders' 21-goal haul 45 years earlier.

CLASS TROUBLEMAKER

Boris (The Terrible) Zivkovic
(defender, Zivinice, Croatia 15.11.75)

Redknapp singled out Zivkovic as a future Pompey captain when he arrived from Bayer Leverkusen in mid-summer. A public row over the manager's love of mobile phones on the training pitch ended with the non-smiling Croat being re-named Boris The Terrible by the man who had worked so hard to lure him to Pompey and was promptly followed by a return to Germany for the centre-back.

NEW BOYS

Patrik Berger
(midfielder, Prague, Czech Republic 10.11.73)

Was kept away from Pompey's training ground while mulling over a move south to make sure the dilapidating facilities did not perturb one of the Premiership's most gifted performers from bringing his undisputed talents to Fratton Park. Berger had barely played in his final season at Liverpool but the Czech midfielder proved an inspired signing in the critical early months of the season before his well-documented injury problems rose to the surface again.

Eyal Berkovic
(midfielder, Haifa, Israel 2.4.72)

A savage attack on 'Big Baby' Kevin Keegan upon his arrival showed Berkovic had not mellowed in his time away from Redknapp under whom he had guided West Ham to the giddy heights of fifth place in the Premiership in 1999. The Israeli hardly kicked a ball in the first half of the season at Manchester City and Redknapp's reluctance to change his 4-4-2 formation to suit the sleight of foot midfielder's unique style limited Berkovic's opportunities to show off his sumptuous skills.

John Curtis
(defender, Nuneaton 3.9.78)

Some supporters questioned Redknapp's judgement when he signed a player unwanted even by relegation rivals Leicester on transfer deadline day. But, while failing to reproduce the form that earned him a Champions' League winners' medal with Manchester United, Curtis's steady performances in the final three games of the season showed horse racing fan Harry was right to take a gamble.

Richard Duffy
(defender, Swansea 30.8.85)

Pompey were accused of using underhand methods to ensure Redknapp's six-week pursuit of Duffy was not in vain. Swansea offered the Welsh youth player a lucrative two-year contract in a bid to keep him but the baby-faced full-back would have walked the 150-

mile journey south to ensure the move went through. An impressive debut performance against Fulham showed the manager's faith in a player with only 18 previous Football League appearances to his name was well-placed.

Amdy Faye
(midfielder, Dakar, Senegal 12.3.77)

Redknapp used his own unparalleled brand of man-management to ensure Faye signed for Pompey by putting him under the guard of his bulldogs when he tried to hold secret talks with Middlesbrough. The tough-tackling Senegal star offered his opponents no escape to quickly endear himself to the Pompey fans who first knew him as 'Andy Henry' after a spoof appearance during the pre-season tour of Scotland.

Ivica Mornar
(striker, Split, Croatia 12.1.74)

Mornar arrived at Fratton Park as famed for his eye for the ladies as he was for his eye for goal, having been married to a former Miss Croatia. Security at the stadium was stepped up as hordes of young girls turned up at reception to declare their undying love for the balding striker who was given plenty of time to work on his chat-up lines from the substitutes' bench on which he spent most of his time.

Dejan Stefanovic
(defender, Nis, Serbia 28.10.74)

Stefanovic used his poor injury record to persuade the Home Office to allow his club record move to go through after having a work permit application turned down because he had not played enough games for his country. The soft-spoken Serb put his fitness problems behind him to become a mainstay in the survival fight and justified his status as the most expensive player in Pompey's history with a string of superb defence displays during the eight-match unbeaten march to safety.

Harald Wapenaar
(goalkeeper, Vlaardingen, Holland 4.10.70)

The Dutchman copied the world's most famous player by having the names of his two young children Jordi and Justin stitched into his boots a la David Beckham in preparation for his Premiership debut against Fulham. But Wapenaar's time between the posts was as short-lived as Posh Spice's solo career as he was displaced by a half-fit Hislop after only five league appearances.

EXCHANGE STUDENTS (IN)

Petri Pasanen
(defender, Lahti, Finland 24.9.80)

Signed on loan from Ajax during the January transfer window to fill the right-back void when Redknapp's feud with Schemmel reached the point of no return, Pasanen was looking to eclipse Sami Hyypia as Finland's top sportsman. But the Dutch club's £1 million pound asking price ensured he would not be given the opportunity to pursue that dream at Fratton Park on a long-term basis.

Jason Roberts
(striker, Park Royal 25.1.78)

After snubbing a move to Fratton Park to join West Brom in 2000, Roberts was belatedly drafted in to add some much-needed fire power to the attack when his relationship with Gary Megson turned sour. The Grenada international added only one goal to Pompey's measly pre-Christmas tally before pitching up at Wigan to renew his partnership with former Bristol Rovers team-mate Nathan Ellington.

Alexei Smertin
(midfielder, Barnaul, Russia 1.5.75)

Smertin was involved in one of the most bizarre transfers in living memory in joining Pompey on loan just 48 hours after arriving at Chelsea in a £3.5 million move from Bordeaux. The Russian captain only met Claudio Ranieri once before becoming part of Pompey's League of Nations, but showed the Italian what he was missing in an impressive debut season devoid only of the goal Blues fans yearned for.

THE REST OF THE PUPILS

Kevin Harper
(midfielder, Oldham 15.1.76)

Harper played a bigger part in Norwich's push for the Premiership during a two-month loan than he did in Pompey's bid to ensure they did not swap places with the Canaries. While his nine league appearances at Carrow Road were not enough to earn another first division championship winners' medal, they brought the Scot more satisfaction than his seven substitute outings in the Premiership.

Richard Hughes
(midfielder, Glasgow 25.6.79)

Was famously compared to Robert Pires by a SKY TV pundit because of his flowing locks after being thrust into the limelight with a high-profile Premiership debut in the derby defeat at Southampton. The Italian-raised Scot relied more on Glaswegian grit than French flair as he put the injury problems that had blighted the previous season behind him to become Pompey's Mr Dependable.

Sebastian Olszar
(striker, Cieszyn, Poland 16.12.81)

Olszar was lucky to escape with his life after a horrific car accident in Austria and signed a short-term contract with Pompey to fulfil the dying wish of his girlfriend, who was killed in the crash, for him to play in the Premiership. The Polish under-21 international was a regular goalscorer in Andy Awford's reserve side but was limited to just 45 minutes of first-team action in the FA Cup draw at Liverpool.

Gary O'Neil
(midfielder, Bromley 18.5.83)

Signalled his arrival in the Premiership with two goals in the 6-1 mauling of Leeds during an explosive top-flight debut. While injuries and international call-ups with the England under-19 squad prevented the 21-year-old from challenging for a regular first-team place, O'Neil did enough in his five fleeting appearances to show he could have a major part to play in establishing Pompey among England's elite.

Nigel Quashie
(midfielder, Peckham 20.7.78)

The one-time England B player's decision to switch his international allegiance to Scotland was the cause of much amusement to his Pompey team-mates. A nagging knee injury forced Quashie to miss a third of the season but his commanding displays when fit prompted a recommendation from the legendary George Best to Scotland coach Berti Vogts, which heralded his unusual change of nationality.

Pavel Srnicek
(goalkeeper, Ostrava, Czech Republic 10.3.68)

Redknapp was famously compared to Dick Turpin for the way he snatched Matt Taylor from Luton in the summer of 2002. The Pompey boss got his bandit's mask out of storage to steal Srnicek away from Wolves, with whom he had already agreed a contract. But the veteran Czech, a former Premiership runner-up with Newcastle, made only three league appearances before moving on again, to West Ham.

Carl Robinson
(midfielder, Llandrindod Wells 13.10.76)

Maverick man Robinson played more games out on loan than he did for Pompey during an unfulfilling two-years at Fratton Park. The Welsh international, who always impressed for his country, was given only a five-minute taster of Premiership life as a late substitute in the December defeat at Chelsea before being offered an escape from his Pompey exile by Sunderland.

Matthew Taylor
(defender, Oxford 27.11.81)

Taylor was forced to wait until the second half of the season to cement a regular place in Pompey's Premiership line-up after almost being forced to quit when a routine heel operation forced his Achilles to shrink. The emerging star of the first division title win had been playing in Division Three for Luton just two seasons earlier but made light work of the step up as Pompey lost only six of the 18 Premiership matches he started.

IN THE SICK BAY

Svetoslav Todorov
(striker, Dobrich, Bulgaria 30.8.78)

Branded a flop after his first stint in the Premiership with West Ham, Todorov was cruelly robbed of the chance to prove his top-flight credentials by a career-threatening knee injury picked up two days before the season's start. His 45-minute appearance at Liverpool apart, the first division's 26-goal leading scorer of the previous season was forced to watch Pompey's survival fight from the stands.

Vincent Pericard
(striker, Efko, Cameroon 3.10.82)

Pericard's sulky French features became legendary with fans and players alike during his loan from Juventus but the gangly striker had plenty of cause to look glum as injury wrecked his bid to become the Premiership's latest star from across the Channel. Showed glimpses of the trickery that prompted Redknapp to pay £400,000 for him in winning the penalty against Bolton that took Pompey top.

Tim Sherwood
(midfielder, St Albans 6.2.69)

A pre-season ear infection delayed Sherwood's season until mid-September and the ex-England player was back on the sidelines after only nine starts because of a campaign-ending broken leg. A typically dogged display to see off former club Tottenham, who had let him go the previous winter, showed Sherwood had lost none of the hunger that had seen him captain Blackburn to the Premiership title.

Hayden Foxe
(defender, Sydney, Australia 23.6.77)

Flame-haired Foxe grew a Robinson Crusoe-style ginger beard in a bid to hide his frustration at seeing his season ended by a fractured foot after an unlucky 13 appearances. The fun-loving Australian, a regular in the centre of defence before the injury, was banned from Pompey's Eastleigh training ground during his recuperation to stop him playing pranks on his team-mates.

STAY UP POMPEY!

Eddie Howe
(defender, Amersham 29.11.77)

Redknapp tipped the ex-England under-21 centre-back to play 200 games for Portsmouth upon his arrival from the manager's former club Bournemouth. The knee injury that had limited Howe to less than an hour in a Pompey shirt kept him on the sidelines for another entire season and even a brief loan spell at Swindon ended prematurely without him playing a game because of an ankle problem.

Deon Burton
(striker, Ashford 25.10.76)

Jamaican international Burton returned to Pompey midway through the first division championship-winning campaign desperate to play in the Premiership for the club that launched his career. A knee injury restricted the ex-Derby striker to only 17 minutes of league football and wrecked his hopes of repeating the form shown during an earlier loan spell that initially persuaded Redknapp to sign him.

IN DETENTION

Sebastien Schemmel
(defender, Nancy, France 2.6.75)

The Frenchman became the latest West Ham reject to follow Redknapp to the south coast after being caught abusing Glenn Roeder in his native tongue during a TV interview. The full back was dubbed the 'Tasmanian Devil' by fans in light of his infamous training ground tantrums and fell foul of the management by asking for time off to care for his sick mother in law in France.

Mark Burchill
(striker, Broxburn 18.8.80)

Stripped of his squad number in pre-season as his Premiership career was humiliatingly ended before it had even begun. Redknapp promoted two pie-eating youth teamers to the bench for the FA Cup tie with Blackpool rather than recall Burchill and even Sheffield Wednesday, still in freefall after their relegation from Division One, could find no place for the Scot during one of many failed loan spells.

EXCHANGE STUDENTS (OUT)

Neil Barrett
(midfielder, Tooting 24.12.81)
Joined Dundee on four-month loan in January.

Lewis Buxton
(defender, Isle of Wight 10.12.83)
Spent seven months on loan at Bournemouth.

Rowan Vine
(striker, Basingstoke 21.9.82)
Spent most of the season on loan at Colchester.

EXPELLED

Lee Bradbury
(striker, Isle of Wight 3.7.75)
Joined Walsall on a free transfer
before the March lower division
transfer deadline.

Craig Bradshaw
(goalkeeper, Chertsey 31.7.84)
Released in June.

Mark Casey
(midfielder, Glasgow 9.10.82)
Moved to St Patrick's Athletic on a
free transfer in March.

Warren Hunt
(striker, Portsmouth 2.3.84)
Released at end of the season.

Yoshikatsu Kawaguchi
(goalkeeper Shizuoka, Japan
15.8.75)
Sold to Danish side FC
Nordsjaelland for £200,000 in
September 2003.

Terry Parker
(defender, Southampton 20.12.83)
Snapped up by Oxford after being
released in June.

Carl Pettefer
(midfielder, Taplow 22.3.81)
Released in June and joined
Southend.

Courtney Pitt
(midfielder, London 17.12.81)
Had final three months of his contract taken over by Oxford in
March.

Chris Tardif
(goalkeeper, Guernsey 10.9.79)
Signed a two-year contract at
Oxford after being released in
June.

Jamie Vincent
(defender, London 18.6.75)
Moved to Derby on a free transfer
in January.

INCOMING PUPILS

Chris Clark
(midfielder, Shoreham 9.6.84)

Shaun Cooper
(defender, Isle of Wight 5.10.83)

Anthony Pulis
(midfielder, Bristol 21.7.84)

Gary Silk
(defender, Isle of Wight 13.9.84)